D-DAY

D-DAY

Intelligence and Deception

JOCK HASWELL

Times
BOOKS

Published by TIMES BOOKS, a division of Quadrangle/The
New York Times Book Co., Inc., Three Park Avenue, New
York, N.Y. 10016

Published simultaneously in Canada by Fitzhenry & White-
side, Ltd., Toronto.

Library of Congress Cataloging in Publication Data

Haswell, Chetwynd John Drake,
  1919–D-Day: intelligence and deception.

  Bibliography: p. 195
  Includes index.
  1. World War, 1939–1945—Campaigns—France—
Normandy. 2. World War, 1939–1945—Secret service. 3.
Normandy—History. I. Title.
D756.5.N6H37 1980   940.54'85   79–19273
ISBN 0–8129–0877–5

Contents

The Illustrations

Between pages 96 and 97

For
James and Angela

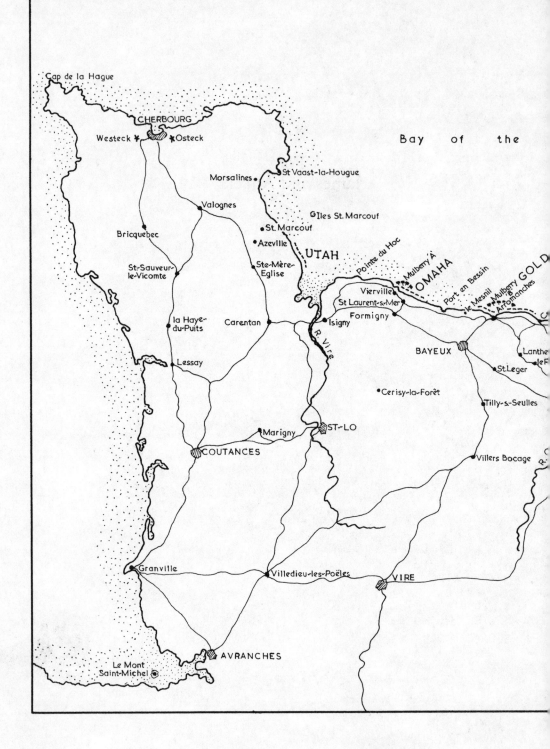

Cap de la Hague

CHERBOURG

Westeck ✶ ✶ Osteck

Morsalines ● St Vaast-la-Hougue

Valognes ●

● Iles St Marcouf

Bricquebec ● St Marcouf
● Azeville

St-Sauveur-
le-Vicomte ● Ste-Mère-
Eglise UTAH

Pointe du Hoc

Mulbery A OMAHA Port en Bessin
Vierville ● le Mesnil Mulbery B GOLD
St Laurent-s-Mer Arromanches
la Haye-
du-Puits Carentan Formigny
R. Vire Isigny
BAYEUX
Lessay ● Lanthe
St.Leger le F

● Cerisy-la-Forêt
Tilly-s-Seulles

Marigny ● ST-LO
Villers Bocage
COUTANCES

Granville ● Villedieu-les-Poëles VIRE

AVRANCHES

Le Mont
Saint-Michel ◉

Bay   of   the

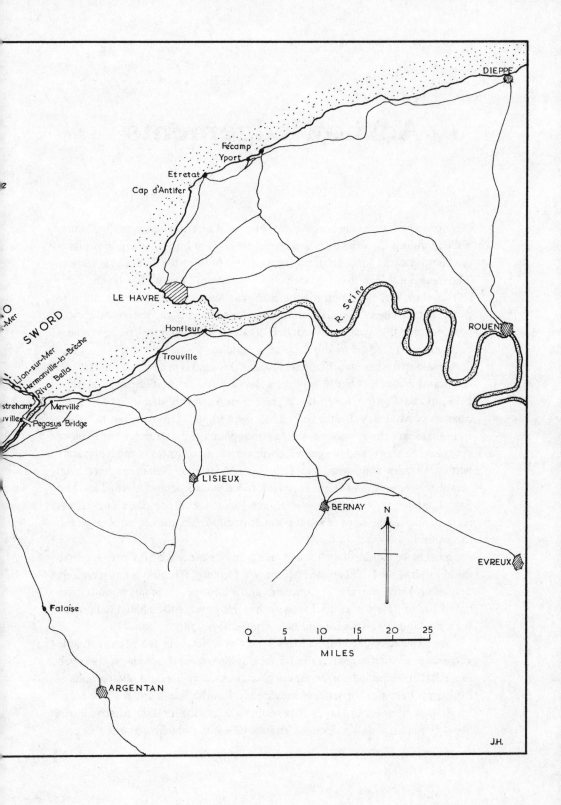

DIEPPE

Fécamp
Yport

Etretat

Cap d'Antifer

R. Seine

ROUEN

LE HAVRE

Honfleur

O

SWORD

-Mer

Lion-sur-Mer
Hermanville-la-Brèche
Riva Bella

streham
Merville
uville
Pegasus Bridge

Trouville

LISIEUX

BERNAY

N

EVREUX

Falaise

0   5   10   15   20   25

MILES

ARGENTAN

J.H.

Acknowledgements

With my wife I went slowly along the Atlantic Wall, from Calais to Cherbourg, walking quite a lot of the way. Sometimes we had our lunch in the grassy pits of old bomb craters round the many fortifications built by the Todt Organization. The guns are still in the emplacements at le Mesnil, and graffiti on the rusty shields show little affection for the men who once manned them. I talked to people in the villages, especially those close to the beaches and the coastal battery positions, and they gave me a great deal of information, supplementing what has been written already. For this I am very grateful.

It is said that when the clouds are low and the wind is in a certain quarter you can hear the sounds of battle on Omaha Beach; but many battlefields, Waterloo, Edgehill and Towton, for instance, have their legends of haunting. The great caissons of Mulberry 'B' still lie in a half circle round Arromanches, but apart from them and the massive concrete strongpoints and casemates either on or very near the shore, and the graves, there are not many traces of the Normandy battles. Villages and towns like Tilly-sur-Seulles and Vimoutiers have been completely rebuilt, and there are many more houses behind Gold, Juno and Sword beaches today than there were on 6 June 1944. Yet despite all the efforts made to remove the signs of war it is not difficult to trace the course of events on the ground.

I must make it clear that although, as a member of the RUSI, I have access to the libraries of the RUSI and the Ministry of Defence, this book is based entirely upon sources freely available to anyone, and at no time and in no circumstances have I had any form of official sponsorship. However, I have benefited greatly from the kindness, patience and help of several people.

I am extremely grateful to Miss Jane Sayle not only for her invaluable suggestions about sources but also for various discoveries she made on my behalf in the RUSI—especially of the album of engineer drawings and photographs of Mulberry. I am also particularly indebted to Hamish Eaton and his wife Mary for all their kindness and hospitality while I was looking for illustrations for this book. Hamish not only helped me enormously with photographs but also gave me a copy of his fascinating *APIS, Soldiers with Stereo. An Account of Army Photographic Interpretation,* published by the Intelligence Corps Museum, on which the 'PI' history in this book is based.

In my search for information about pigeons I learned that Mr Leonard Bunn, a noted pigeon fancier and the Sub-Postmaster in our village whom I have known for more than twenty years, was in the Pigeon Service during the war and was in fact the recipient of the first pigeon message sent back by the first assault wave on D-Day. I am most grateful to him, and also to Miss Stephanie Glover of the Ministry of Defence Central Library. Mr Richard Walker has again photographed old photographs with results that are better than the originals.

J. H.
Lyminge
1979

1
Background

Until the attack on Dieppe in August 1942 the landing of an armed force on the shores of enemy-held country had been generally regarded, in military circles, as a hazardous operation of war but not a particularly difficult one. An attacker always has the initiative, and therefore has certain major advantages. He can choose the time, place and strength of his attack, and if he pays proper attention to the Principles of War he has good reason to expect success. But 'attack' is one thing; 'invasion' is quite another.

The heroic attack on St Nazaire on 27 March 1942 achieved spectacular results in destroying the great dock which was the only one along the whole Atlantic coast of France capable of accommodating the *Tirpitz* if she were damaged, but this was the limited objective of a specific operation. Commander Ryder of the Royal Navy was able, somewhat miraculously, to bring the survivors of the attacking force safely home; and this is the essential difference between attack and invasion. It is nearly always possible to disembark and re-embark troops on a hostile shore. The real problem is to keep them there.

The St Nazaire operation was a text-book example of a small-scale raid. Five months later, the landing at Dieppe — a far greater effort involving in the original plan some 10,000 men as opposed to the 250 commandos at St Nazaire—revealed all the problems and difficulties likely to arise when a seaborne attack is lifted out of the 'raid' category and becomes a major operation.

The Dieppe disaster—in terms of casualties it was a disaster—has since been justified by many authorities. Winston Churchill himself wrote that 'tactically, it was a mine of experience', but it was also a classic example of what can happen when all the Principles of War have not been applied. There was no 'Surprise' and very little 'Security.'

The 'Principles', which existed long before commanders in the field were made consciously aware of them, largely by von Clausewitz's analysis in his *Vom Kriege,* are by definition immutable. They relate to all forms of warfare, at sea, on land and in the air, and the commander who does not base his operational plans on them is asking for trouble. Since they are of such vital importance there is perhaps something to be gained by listing them.

Being more or less equal in value they are not necessarily in any set order, but a logical sequence begins with 'Selection and Maintenance of the Aim'. The purpose of every operation must be exactly defined in terms of the task to be done. 'Maintenance of Morale' echoes Napoleon's dictum that the moral is to the physical as three is to one, and Field Marshal Montgomery wrote that 'morale is probably the most important single factor in war, without high morale no success can be achieved, however good may be the strategic or tactical plan, or anything else'.

'Offensive Action' needs little qualification; battles can be won by defenders, but not wars. If the enemy is to be defeated, sooner or later he must be attacked. 'Surprise', catching the enemy unawares when he is least expecting trouble, can be conclusive, and so can the 'Concentration of Force'; making the best use of available assets to strike a decisive blow.

'Security' can have two meanings; tactical security, in that it is no bad thing to choose positions, routes and so on which the enemy cannot exploit to his own advantage; and secondly, the state or condition in which information can be protected against espionage, *matériel* against sabotage and personnel against subversion. 'Economy of Effort' is linked with 'Concentration of Force'; although the blow with the right strength in the right place at the right time can be decisive, there is no need, and indeed it can be dangerous, metaphorically speaking, to use a pile-driver to hammer in a carpet tack. The need for 'Flexibility' applies to the disposition of forces, operational and administrative plans, and especially to the minds of commanders.

'Co-operation', as a principle, is so obvious that it is often overlooked. The British Army has a long history of the lack of it, particularly between cavalry and infantry, ever since the days of Prince Rupert of the Rhine. The wild charges of the Royalist Horse were a matter of personal honour and glory and seldom of much help to the infantry in the Civil War that began in 1642. In modern war there must be complete co-operation not only between all the units of a Service but between all Services, so that all the elements of a mixed force are welded into a team which has only one aim. Finally, without adequate 'Administration' no force can fight any battle anywhere.

Although Field Marshal Montgomery stressed the importance of morale, an exactly similar remark could be made about Intelligence, and it is curious that this vital Principle of War is not listed with the others in military manuals, despite the advice of such authorities as Sun Tzu, Vegetius, Frederick the Great and Jomini. Frederick the Great expressed the principle in one brief sentence: 'One should *know* one's enemies'.

Unless a commander knows where the enemy is and what his capabilities and intentions are, he cannot apply any of the Principles of War. He cannot act with any confidence. He can only react. He cannot take offensive action without unacceptable risks and he cannot achieve surprise; the concentration of force and economy of effort are beyond him. He has no security, he must rely on intuition and luck, and thereby court disaster.

'How can any man say what he should do himself if he knows not what his enemy is about?' wrote Jomini in 1830. In other words, accurate and reliable intelligence is the essential basis for any operational plan.

The reason why a landing on an enemy coast had not, before the Dieppe raid, been regarded as especially difficult was that it had been done so often with reasonable success. Indeed it is not surprising that a small island race which in its history acquired dominion over nearly a quarter of the earth's surface should have had considerable experience of putting troops ashore in areas where they were not particularly welcome. What perhaps is remarkable is that so many of these operations were successful even though the commander had little or no idea of the nature of the country or the opposition, and in many cases the enemy were ready and waiting for him.

Great commanders such as Marlborough, Amherst and Wellington all 'knew' their enemy. Marlborough laid it down that 'no war can be conducted successfully without early and good intelligence', and none of these three were ever defeated. They were exceptional.

At the beginning of the campaign which ended with the victory at Crécy and the capture of Calais, Edward III landed in the little bay on the Cotentin peninsula protected by the castle of St Vaast la Hogue without apparently giving much thought to possible hostility or resistance; perhaps because he possessed a new and devastating weapon, the longbow of Gwent. In fact, all the raids on the coast of France in the so-called Hundred Years' War seem to have been made in the belief that an offensive spirit, stimulated by the promise of loot, was all that was needed to get the soldiers ashore and put the enemy to flight. It was a tradition that died hard because these raids had the advantage of surprise. It was impossible to defend the whole coastline of France; the attacking forces were small and could pick their targets at random. If the opposition was too determined, the raiders returned to their ships and tried again somewhere else.

Another tradition grew up, that of co-operation between the navy and the army, although there were notable cases where there was none, or virtually none: for example, the expedition to Hispaniola and Jamaica led by Admiral

Penn and General Venables in 1658. The sailors were so disgusted by the performance of the soldiers at Santo Domingo that when the fleet reached Jamaica the Admiral announced that since he could not trust the army he would lead the assault landing himself — which he did.

On the other hand, General James Wolfe's operation against Quebec in 1759 owed everything to Admirals Saunders, Holmes and Durell, and was a model of its kind. Many of the seaborne operations of the Seven Years' War, the French Revolutionary War and the Napoleonic War appear to have been influenced by the supposition that since surprise was the factor of paramount importance, which might be prejudiced by the gathering of intelligence, it was better to land and see what happened rather than try to find out beforehand what was likely to happen.

The Helder campaign of 1799 was a typical example. The object of the expedition was to capture the Dutch town of Helder and with it the Nieuwe Diep, the passage into the Zuyder Zee, from whence operations could be launched against the French who had overrun Holland and most of Europe. It was an invasion, not a hit-and-run raid.

On the morning of 27 August the troops were rowed ashore from the transports in flat-bottomed boats. They disembarked on a gently sloping beach with 100 naval guns thundering behind them, formed up and advanced towards the enemy in the sandhills barely 100 yards away. The 2nd, 27th, 29th and 85th Foot made their attack under heavy fire from the front and flanks, and by the end of the day had secured a beach-head. During the night the French withdrew from Helder and all seemed to be going reasonably well. It may seem remarkable that the 2nd Foot (The Queen's Royal Regiment), having endured what one officer in the regiment described as 'exceeding hot fire' for most of the day, lost only one sergeant and two privates killed, and one officer and 21 men wounded and missing. The range and accuracy of the muskets used on both sides were greatly affected by 'windage', most of the explosive force of the charge going round instead of behind the lead bullet as it rattled down the barrel.

Despite this initial success the campaign was a miserable failure because those responsible for planning it had failed to appreciate the difference between attack and invasion. The commander, Sir Ralph Abercrombie, had not been provided with adequate logistic support. His men were defeated by starvation, disease and exposure, not by the French.

The enthusiasm of Henry Dundas, the Secretary for War at that time, for ill-conceived and unco-ordinated operations remained unaffected by the failure of similar expeditions to Quiberon Bay, Ferrol, Vigo and Cadiz, and so

Abercrombie naturally had misgivings when ordered to collect a force from the garrisons in the Mediterranean, invade Egypt and evict the French army of occupation abandoned there by Napoleon in August 1800—after Nelson had destroyed the French fleet in the Battle of the Nile. Abercrombie's force arrived off Aboukir on 1 March 1801, in full view of the French. The invasion began at nine o'clock in the morning of 8 March and, according to the military historian Richard Cannon, 'the clear silence of the morning, broken by the deep murmur of thousands of oars urging forward the flower of a brave army, whose polished arms glittered in the morning sun, produced an interesting scene'.

Climbing out of the boats, the British troops advanced across the beach in carefully aligned ranks to attack the French waiting in the sand dunes. Subjected to a storm of musketry from the front and raked by enfilade fire from French cannon mounted in Aboukir Castle on their right flank, the attackers suffered 750 casualties as they drove the French out of their positions in an engagement lasting two hours. Fortescue, in his *History of the British Army*, describes it as 'perhaps the most skilful and daring operation of its kind that was ever attempted'. There was no great skill in it. Everything depended on the discipline and courage of the British troops. Admittedly, the French soldiers, first under Kléber and then Menou, had a morale problem. Napoleon had made it clear he was not interested in what happened to them and without ships they had little hope of ever getting safely back to France. No doubt this affected their determination to resist the invaders, and in due course General Menou did capitulate, but not until 2 September and on condition that he and his men were taken back to France in British ships. Abercrombie had been killed in battle on 21 March, but his troops conquered Egypt and the 'invincible French Army of the East' ceased to exist.

Yet the logistic backing for this success depended very largely on improvisation, a certain amount of luck and the requisitioning of local supplies to supplement what the navy could provide. There was still far too great a tendency to make a very sketchy operational plan and put it into effect without giving much thought to the overriding problem of maintaining an invasion force in a hostile country.

Sir Arthur Wellesley, later Lord Wellington, made sure he was in a better position when he landed his army of 30,000 men at the mouth of the Mondego River in Portugal in July 1808—in response to the Spaniards' appeal for help after Napoleon had kidnapped their king, Charles VI, and put his own brother Joseph Bonaparte on the throne. Wellesley had sent a 'military mission', consisting of intelligence officers, on ahead. When he arrived he was told where

General Junot was, and given details of the strength and morale of his army. Within four weeks the French army had been defeated twice, at Roliça and Vimiero. Like General Jeffery (Lord) Amherst in Canada, Wellesley was reluctant to land 'blind' in enemy-occupied territory, and he took pains to see that his supply system was effective and adequate.

The example set by Wellington was not followed by those who came after him. The expedition to America in August 1814 was a strange muddle of divided command and divided aims, and it was just as well that the landing of the British force at the little town of Benedict, on the Patuxent River in Maryland, was unopposed.

Ten years later, on 11 May 1824, one of the veterans of the Peninsular War, Major-General Sir Archibald Campbell, led an army of 10,000 men into the unknown reaches of the Rangoon River, took the port of Rangoon and advanced up the Irrawaddy to capture the capital city of Ava in the First Burmese War, without having any maps or any reliable information about the nature of the country, its people or its resources. He was merely obeying the orders of the Governor General of the Honourable East India Company, Lord Amherst, nephew of the conqueror of Canada, who had told him to go and deal with the Burmese and put an end to the continual trouble they were making in the border provinces of Chittagong and Assam.

In 1854, two years after Wellington's death, when Lord Raglan was given command of the British expeditionary force being sent to the Crimea, he complained that 'the Crimea was as completely an unknown country to the Chiefs of the Allied Armies as it had been to Jason and his Argonauts when they journeyed to the same place'. He knew it contained a harbour and that the harbour was fortified, but he would not even have had that information had not a certain retired officer named Major Thomas Jervis accidentally come across a secret Russian map while browsing in a bookshop in Belgium. Raglan should have known better. As Lord Fitzroy Somerset, he had been one of Wellington's senior staff officers in the Peninsula and he knew how much importance had been attached to what Wellington called 'finding out what was on the other side of the hill'.

In its long history the British Army has gained a great deal of experience in assault landings, and the oft-repeated drill seemed to be simple enough. The navy carried the army to what appeared to be a suitable beach, and the sailors rowed the soldiers ashore in the ships' boats. The soldiers, often soaked to the skin and thoroughly unhappy because of seasickness, formed up on the beach in their parade-ground order, carrying 60 or more pounds of equipment and trying to drill in soft sand. They then marched forward until the enemy was within the range of their muskets and fired volleys under the orders of their officers until the enemy had had enough and withdrew. Soldiers were trained to ignore the enemy's fire completely and gaps made by it in their ranks were filled immediately by men stepping forward automatically from the rear. This is how infantry battles were fought. If charged by cavalry the battalions formed square, with the officers in the centre, and continued to fire volleys as ordered. They could usually count on the initial support of naval artillery but this could not fire when the assault force moved forward into contact.

Infantry tactics were based, logically enough, on the capabilities of the infantry weapons, the musket, the bayonet and the sword carried by officers. The best known of the flintlock muskets was Brown Bess, first issued in 1700 and still in service more than 150 years later, in the Crimean War. The accuracy of it can be judged from the anti-invasion instructions issued by the government at the time when Napoleon's Army of the Coasts of the Ocean was waiting for a favourable opportunity to cross the Channel: 'any degree of precision with a common musket is not to be reckoned on at a greater distance than from 50 to 60 paces'. According to the *Short History of Small Arms,* published by the Small Arms Wing of the School of Infantry, round targets, 8 feet in diameter, at distances of 30 and 50 yards were used for recruit training, and few trained soldiers could even hit a house at 100 yards. A musket had no sights except a small knob near the muzzle to give the general direction.

The lack of any repeating weapon of reasonable range and effectiveness — such as, for instance, the longbow which had been the decisive factor in the great battles of Crécy, Poitiers, Agincourt and Verneuil — was another reason why assault landings did not appear to present any major problem. Even cannon were really only effective against large targets, and there was very little to prevent the landing of a force which, at the time of greatest vulnerability while approaching the shore, presented only small targets in the form of ships' boats. The difficulties associated with invasion were logistic, not tactical. It was the invention of the repeating, breech-loading rifle with its tight-fitting bullet, long range and accuracy, the introduction of the machine gun, and finally the development of smokeless powder which did not give away the position of the firer, which altered the whole pattern of this type of operation, and indeed of warfare.

Even so, the slaughter at Gallipoli in 1915 indicated that the fundamental changes had not really been appreciated. Few of the vital lessons had been learned. This was the first major amphibious operation to be fought under new rules — the Principles remained unaltered — and thousands of courageous men died because their commanders had failed to work out what those rules were. Rifled artillery, which had first proved its devastating effect when used against General Robert E. Lee's infantry at Gettysburg, fired projectiles very different from the cannon-balls whose flight could be seen. New forms of artillery and small arms, and Turkish riflemen and machine gunners who shot straight, made it perfectly clear that the daylight landing across open beaches against an alert and well-entrenched enemy was no longer a feasible operation of war unless special precautions were taken.

One of those precautions was security, in the sense of concealing intentions, because the critical factor is surprise. Troops en route to the Dardanelles were asked by street urchins in Alexandria and Suez whether they were going to Gallipoli, and everyone seemed to know they were. There was no secrecy, no security and no surprise. The Turks were given time to make their preparations and when the time came they were ready.

Between 1916 and 1939 a great deal was written about the gallant failure of the Gallipoli operation, and the main point made to young officer cadets at the Royal Military College, Sandhurst, and to students at the Staff College, was that if you want to land an invasion force on an enemy's shores you really must make sure he is not eagerly awaiting your arrival. If he is, you may not get ashore at all, and if you do, it is unlikely that you will be able to stay there because he can probably call up reinforcements to counter-attack your beach-head more quickly than you can bring yours ashore to expand the area you hold. Furthermore, you are dependent upon supplies brought by sea and which may be delayed by bad weather. The enemy's supplies come up by road and rail and can be managed much more easily.

In fact, an alert and determined enemy, in good defensive positions and armed with modern weapons, presents what may well be an insuperable problem, especially if he has adequate air support. Secrecy and surprise are essential; without them it is better to call the whole thing off.

Bearing this standard teaching in mind, the Dieppe raid in August 1942 becomes almost incomprehensible.

2
The Operational Problem

One of the snags in trying to apply historical precedents to current operational plans is that no two operations are ever exactly similar. One cannot, therefore, study for example the mistakes of Methuen and Redvers Buller in South Africa in December 1899, and the achievements of Allenby in Palestine in 1917, and relate the actual tactical lessons to a possible future conflict in north-west Europe. All one can do is interpret the tactical lessons in terms of axioms, such as 'do not launch a night attack over ground you have not reconnoitred', as Methuen did at Magersfontein, and use them to supplement the Principles of War.

The St Nazaire operation, like many other lightning commando raids in the Second World War, was an excellent example of the principle of surprise, gained by careful planning and a very high standard of security. Shock tactics bring their own reward because there is nearly always a time-lag while the enemy is recovering from the initial surprise and organizing himself to retaliate, and this brief but crucial period can be exploited. At St Nazaire the old American destroyer *Campbeltown* was jammed into the lock gates before the Germans had time to work out what was happening. This was the first surprise.

The second came on the following day when a large party of German officers and technicians were inspecting the damage and the wreck and wondering how they were going to cope with it. They had not discovered that the *Campbeltown* had 3 tons of explosives in her bows and something had gone wrong with the fuse. Without any warning at all the ship suddenly blew up with appalling force, killing hundreds of Germans and putting the lock out of action for the rest of the war, thus providing an illustration of the relationship between surprise and deception. The Germans apparently deceived themselves into thinking that because the *Campbeltown* had not exploded during the raid—as had been the original intention—she would not explode at all. There can be no other explanation for their lack of precautions before crowding into her.

It was abundantly clear that this success against a target which the Germans knew was a potential commando objective and therefore were ready to defend, was the result of security, surprise and speed, but the lessons to be learned from it were not applied to the Dieppe operation.

Planning for this began in April 1942, only a matter of days after the raid on St Nazaire, and on 13 May an outline plan for what was to be known as Operation Rutter was approved by the Chiefs of Staff Committee as a basis for the detailed plans to be drawn up by the Force Commanders. It was to be the largest attack launched so far against Occupied France, and what made the idea especially attractive was an intelligence report that the German garrison was only one battalion of 'low-category' troops, with supporting units, making a total of not more than 1,400 men.

On 3 July the troops who were to take part, mostly Canadians, embarked at ports and harbours in the Isle of Wight, but because of bad weather the attack planned for 4 July had to be postponed for four days. Meanwhile a few German aircraft attacked the concentration of shipping. The weather did not improve, it was decided to cancel everything and the soldiers disembarked. General Montgomery, then Commander-in-Chief, South-Eastern Command, felt very strongly that the operation should not be remounted because by now the Germans probably had a good idea of what was in the wind. He was quite sure that security had been compromised and therefore surprise could not be attained.

However, Churchill himself wrote that he thought it 'most important that a large-scale operation should take place this summer', and he added that until such an operation had been undertaken, no responsible commander would accept the task of planning for the main invasion. Thus Dieppe was to take its place in history as the test and rehearsal for what has since become known as D-Day, although in the middle of July 1942 it was by no means certain that the experiment would be held at Dieppe.

Churchill discussed the question of a large-scale operation with Lord Louis Mountbatten, in charge of Combined Operations, and was told there was not enough time to mount and carry out an entirely new scheme that summer. On the other hand, the original Dieppe plan could be put into effect within a month, 'provided extraordinary steps were taken to ensure secrecy'.

Operation Rutter thus became Operation Jubilee, with no substantial change in design except that Rutter had envisaged a force of 10,000 men whereas only half that number embarked for Jubilee.

There is no evidence that the Germans received any direct information about the timing and strength of the attack, but they had made careful assessments of the threat to the Channel coast and it required no stretching of the imagination to come to reasonably accurate conclusions. They knew, from air reconnaissance and the interception of radio traffic, that an amphibious operation was being mounted, and they had attacked the shipping assembled for it. Dieppe was an obvious landing-place in a threatened sector and so they moved up considerable reinforcements and made special efforts to defend it. It was easy enough to calculate the danger periods in relation to tides and the moon, and orders were issued that at these times all coastal-defence units were to be placed on special alert. One such period was between 10 and 19 August. So, when the attack went in on 17 August it was met by an alerted division at full strength.

It has been said that if the raid be regarded as a reconnaissance in force it was a success because it achieved all its aims. Radar was still in its infancy; a valuable German installation was destroyed and much information gained from it, but more important, certain lessons written out in Canadian blood were, as Churchill wrote, taken to heart, and it may well be that because of this the immensely high proportion of casualties — four-fifths of the force, in one form or another — was not a sacrifice in vain.

The principal lessons were that the British suffered from dangerous short-comings not only in the whole planning concept of a seaborne landing in strength but also in types of landing craft and military equipment. They had not fully appreciated the need for the close support of heavy naval guns and fighter-bombers. A high standard of training, determination and courage in units and individuals could not compensate for the lack of formations specially organized and trained for amphibious operations. Moreoever, and above all, as the lessons of Gallipoli and the teaching at Sandhurst and the Staff College between the wars had stressed, without secrecy and surprise the risks in such· operations are unacceptable.

Thus the Dieppe raid put the problem of invasion in its right perspective. It was now apparent that preparations for the invasion of Occupied Europe would take a long time, and against an enemy as efficient, effective and resolute as the Wehrmacht, there was no guarantee it would succeed. The only hope lay in the proper application of the Principles of Security, Surprise and Concentration of Force.

The attack on Dieppe also had its lessons for the Germans. It underlined the important fact that the people of Britain and the Commonwealth had not abandoned Europe to Hitler and Nazism. The British were resolved to do more than merely mind their own business and defend themselves in what Shakespeare described as 'this little world, this precious stone set in the silver sea'. Sooner or later they and their allies would cross the Channel with the object of liberating all the countries conquered in the *Blitzkrieg* and utterly destroying the Third Reich. The Germans knew well enough they had to make preparations against the offensive action that would be taken, possibly on a scale never even contemplated before, and initially it would come in the form that Marshal Brune had seen at the Helder, and General Menou had watched from the battlements of Aboukir Castle—armed men coming out of the sea.

German strategy and tactics were therefore based on one straightforward operational aim, to annihilate the invaders on the beaches. This was Hitler's personal decision, his own policy, and he would not deviate from it.

Just before the war a columnist in the *Daily Sketch* wrote a scathing little article on Adolf Hitler's qualifications for the supreme command of the armed forces of Germany. 'Picture to yourselves,' he said, 'this amazing soldier who in the four years of the 1914-18 war rose to the rank of lance corporal.'

Hitler himself claimed to have a unique intuitive skill in high command, and many of his senior commanders and staff officers who despised him as a political upstart had to admit that at the beginning of the war he was remarkably successful. One of the exceptions was Field Marshal Gerd von Rundstedt who, in selected company, never referred to him as anything but 'the Bohemian corporal', but such men as Keitel, von Brauchitsch, Model, von Kluge and Rommel were much affected by Hitler's strangely hypnotic and personal magnetism, greatly strengthened by his military achievements.

Yet Hitler's early triumphs were facile enough. When he became Chancellor of Germany in 1933, memories of the First World War were still fresh in the minds of many people. The British and French governments, in particular, wanted no repetition of the horrors of Verdun and Passchendaele, whereas the defeated Germans dreamed of *'der Tag'* and revenge. Hitler created a massive army—massive in comparison with British and French resources in 1939—with its tactics modelled on the mobile war extolled by British military writers such as J. F. C. Fuller and Liddell Hart, and took every advantage of the appeasers and their fear of war. The bully in the school playground relies on intimidation and the threat of violence against those who do not want to fight. He gets what he wants because his victims know he is ready and willing to be extremely unpleasant.

From 1938 to 1941 Hitler, as the aggressor, held the initiative and decided who, when, where and in what strength he would attack, knowing that psychologically as well as militarily the British and French were not in a fit state to counter force with force. In these circumstances it is not difficult to be a successful commander-in-chief. The real test of ability comes when enemies unite in crushing force; one example being Napoleon's brilliant defensive campaign after his defeat at Leipzig and his tactical use of the valleys of the Marne and Seine in February 1814.

It is a tactical axiom that one does not defend an obstacle by sitting on top of it in a 'thin red line', because once that line is broken, all is lost. If the obstacle is the sea, the defence of the shore must be based on a system of initial resistance which forces the enemy to concentrate in order to break through, and what the French call the 'mass of manoeuvre' in the form of strong, mobile counter-attack forces to deal with the breakthrough.

Hitler's insistence that an invasion force must be destroyed on the shoreline was therefore tactically unsound. As both von Rundstedt and Rommel pointed out to him, the decisive factor would be the availability of sufficient mobile reserves to fight on ground of their own choosing when it became clear what the enemy's main thrust lines were. They were able to persuade him that some form of counter-attack force, located well back from the beaches, was essential; at least, he assured them that adequate reserves would be allocated to them. But they could not make him see that determined invaders, with naval and air support, would get ashore, and once they did, the coastal-defence units must be withdrawn to fight the second, and decisive, battle inland, probably on the line of a suitable river obstacle.

Thus, right at the beginning, Hitler's concept of an impregnable Atlantic Wall from which defenders could drive invaders back into the sea was based on a false premise. With a proper concentration of force, using all the resources of modern weapons and equipment, part of the Wall would be broken down and would become a sluice gate through which the tide of war would flow. The only way to cope with it would be to let it flow and disperse so that it could be mopped up effectively some distance from the breach.

Thus, on both sides of the Channel, the operational aims were unclouded. The Allies intended to liberate Europe. The Germans intended to prevent any invasion of their conquered territories. The allies appreciated that the prelude to liberation would have to be the defeat of the German forces in Occupied Europe, and made their plans accordingly.

Edward Gibbon defined history as 'little more than the register of the crimes, follies and misfortunes of mankind', and the history of the invasion of Normandy certainly contains a number of misfortunes which were, as they so often are in war, largely a matter of bad luck, bad weather and a lack of vital intelligence. On the question of follies, opinions differ, and since it has been alleged that two particular follies had a profound influence on the whole course of the war in north-west Europe, it might be as well to deal with them now.

One was the Allies' policy of insisting on unconditional surrender which, so it has been said, in removing from the Germans all hope of being able to salvage anything by treating for peace, compelled them to fight on to the end in desperation, bitterness and despair. The other was the failure to exploit the potential of the *Schwarze Kapelle,* The Black Orchestra, the name given to the German conspirators who tried, without success, to assassinate Hitler on 20 July 1944. (*Kapelle*/orchestra was the slang term used by German Intelligence for a ring of spies or plotters.)

The two are related, in that the declaration of the policy might have had a disturbing effect on the conspirators, and in the light of hindsight which has apparently revealed them as follies, they have given rise to several questions. Was the armed assault on Hitler's Fortress Europe really necessary? In other words, if the Allies had played their cards right, would it not have been possible for them simply to have walked ashore, welcomed by all the senior German army commanders and staff officers who, in the interests of Germany and the German people, had decided that Hitler had to go?

Was D-Day in fact a political blunder of incalculable magnitude?

The declaration of insistence upon unconditional surrender was made by President Roosevelt, who had a strong sense of history and remembered the words of General Ulysses S. Grant in the Civil War, at a press conference called by him and Winston Churchill at the end of the Casablanca Conference in January 1943. He stated that he and the British Prime Minister had resolved to accept nothing less than the unconditional surrender of Germany, Italy and Japan – the alliance known as the Axis. He took Churchill by surprise, and Churchill said later that the words were not ones he would have used himself, although once stated he was prepared to defend them.

Several Allied service chiefs such as General Dwight D. Eisenhower and Marshal of the Royal Air Force Sir John Slessor announced their disapproval unequivocally. The head of MI6, General Sir Stewart Menzies, known as 'C', warned Churchill that the effect would be to make the Germans 'fight like cornered rats'.

In Germany, opinion was divided. The flow of German victories had been reversed at Alamein and Stalingrad, and the seeds of doubt about Hitler's infallibility as the greatest commander and strategist since Frederick the Great were beginning to germinate in the minds of even his most ardent supporters among the General Staff. There was, apparently, a taint of revolution in the wind. The fervent Nazis were delighted by the declaration because it would stiffen the sinews and summon up the blood of all the faint-hearted, uniting all Germans in determination to defend the Fatherland to the last round and the last man. On the other hand, Admiral Wilhelm Franz Canaris, head of the intelligence and counter-intelligence service of the General Staff, Abwehr, and an anti-Nazi deeply involved in the *Schwarze Kapelle* from its inception, said he believed the Allies had now removed from the conspirators the last weapon with which they could have brought the war to an end.

On 30 January 1943 Dr Josef Goebbels, the Reich Minister of Propaganda, made a counter-declaration of 'total war', telling the German people their enemies had sworn to enslave them and so the war had now become a fight for survival in which no sacrifice was too great. Many believed him, and there was a considerable, if somewhat paradoxical, upward surge of morale.

It has been claimed that the declaration by Roosevelt, which he later admitted had been made on the spur of the moment, was expensive in terms of human life. But was it, in fact? Do people really believe the portentious remarks of professional politicans made spontaneously at press conferences? Admittedly, in the mess of government since the Second World War politicians have managed to discredit themselves to a point approaching total disbelief, but they still had some credibility during the war. The real point is that in general, people only believe what they want to believe, and it is probable that the Germans, especially the senior officers involved in the plot against Hitler, felt that when the time came it would be possible to persuade the British and Americans not to be too beastly to them. General Hans Speidel, Rommel's Chief of Staff in Normandy, certainly felt this.

Furthermore, the soldier on the battlefield is not interested in surrender policies, conditional or otherwise, concocted at the highest government level; he is far more concerned with the more simple issues of *esprit de corps* and survival. While there is still any semblance of morale, the men of a good regiment, proud of its great traditions, tend to fight to the end. An exhausted, hungry man with his boots full of water and a heart empty of hope will surrender so as to put an end to his own personal hell.

It is impossible to calculate the cost of Roosevelt's declaration because at the lower levels surrender is not related to the future of one's country, and it must be remembered that during the last phase of the war, after the crossing of the Rhine, many German soldiers who wanted to surrender were compelled to fight on because they knew they would be hanged for cowardice on a nearby tree—as many were—if they did not. Moreover, personal fear of retribution for horrible crimes committed in occupied countries was, in many cases, a far stronger motive for fighting on than defence of Nazism and the Third Reich.

The story of the *Schwarze Kapelle* is well known and there are plenty of details of the plot, its failure and the dreadful aftermath of murder and suicide when Hitler and the grotesque little Nazi oligarchy, none of whom, except possibly Heydrich, even remotely resembled the splendid Aryan type they had pledged themselves to perpetuate, took their revenge. But the assassination attempt was made six weeks after D-Day and therefore this narrative is concerned with the conspiracy only as part of the general background to the situation in northern France in the spring and early summer of 1944, and with its effect on the morale and loyalty of some of the senior German officers.

The more junior officers of the Wehrmacht — the German Armed Forces — and the Schutzstaffel (SS) — the political/military organization of the Nazi Party — knew nothing about it. This is not surprising. In the atmosphere of terror, torture and death created by the Gestapo — the *Geheime Staatspolizei,* the secret state police controlled by the SS under Heinrich Himmler — the removal of Hitler either by violence or political means was not a subject to be discussed outside a small coterie of trusted friends.

It is of course easy enough to say now, more than 30 years after all these events, that the Allies should have grasped the opportunity apparently offered to them by the *Schwarze Kapelle,* and that they should have negotiated with such men as Marshals Model and von Kluge when they tried to get in touch. It is equally easy to claim that the D-Day landings were a terrible political mistake, but to do so is to fall into the common error of judging events out of their immediate context. In forming any opinion of anyone's decisions or actions, due consideration must be given to the intelligence available *at the time* and on which the decisions were based. Hindsight provides a very much clearer picture, much of which may well have been obscured then.

Although the full horrors of the Belsen, Buchenwald, Auschwitz and other extermination camps were not known at that time, by the fifth year of the war the Allies no longer had any doubt about the aims of the Nazis nor about the support given to them, whether willingly or not, by the mass of the German people. Hitler and his gang may well have been regarded as the personification of evil, but they were not the only evil Germans. It would be quite wrong to imagine that the war was fought against only a handful of National Socialist thugs holding a largely innocent people in thrall.

By any standard the Wehrmacht was a magnificent fighting machine and its task, undertaken knowingly and with enthusiasm, was Hitler's objective — nothing less than world domination. The Germans were to be the Master Race and Germany was to be the unchallenged superpower, by right of conquest.

Bearing this in mind, and relating it to the dictum of Josef Goebbels that a lie repeated often enough becomes truth, it is not surprising that Allied leaders were sceptical enough to distrust what they heard about plots to kill Hitler. It was of course quite possible that a number of senior German officers had come to the conclusion they could not win the war and all that Germany could look forward to was an unpleasant and painful form of *Götterdämmerung*; but this was their affair. Hitler had always had his enemies, especially in the ranks of the German General Staff. The 'framing' of General Baron Werner von Fritsch, the able and respected Commander-in-Chief of the German Army before the war, on a disgraceful charge of homosexuality, had alienated from Hitler all the associates of an officer generally liked and admired and whose character was regarded as stainless. But disapproval among the German High Command of the methods Hitler used for removing those who opposed him, or of the way in which he was running the war, did not necessarily mean that his staff would resort to open treachery, to the extent of overthrowing him, or murdering him, and suing for peace.

Not only were the eyes of the Gestapo ever-watchful, but the code under which the officer corps lived, and the *Fahneneid*, the oath of allegiance, made quite unthinkable any possibility of challenging the Supreme Commander of the armed forces. Obedience was instinctive, 'authority' was omnipotent and never to be questioned. Indeed, it is not easy for people with British or American ideas about war and democracy to understand the psychological element that was so potent a factor in the Wehrmacht. From the time of Bismarck the whole German nation had been imbued — one might perhaps say indoctrinated — with an intense patriotism, an unshakeable belief in the splendour and magnificence of their country's destiny, and this was expressed in a tremendous pride in their army and its invincibility; hence the aura of infallibility surrounding the leader, whether he be a Kaiser or a dictator. The fact that in due course Hitler's conduct of the war was severely criticized and condemned by so many of his commanders and staff officers is a direct reflection of his incompetence; but outside Germany, where the discipline and obedience of the officer corps were known, there was good reason to believe that the *Schwarze Kapelle* might be part of a deception plan.

The secret war is a dirty business. Ends justify means and methods are judged by results. Treachery, whether genuine or feigned, is all part of it, and there was no German in a position of real authority who could have been trusted by the Allies in clandestine dealings designed to remove his own Head of State. A possible exception was Marshal Erwin Rommel, who had gained a reputation for chivalry in the later campaigns in North Africa, but even so, in the climate of hatred and distrust deliberately fostered by Goebbels' Ministry, it is difficult to believe that an approach by Rommel would have achieved anything. The Allies knew he owed his rapid promotion to Marshal entirely to Hitler, who trusted him. It was also known that he admired Hitler as the man who had built and established the new Germany from the ruins of the Kaiser's legacy. If Rommel were suddenly to turn his coat the natural deduction would be that it was a lure and deception.

Admiral Canaris was equally suspect. Some writers since the war have gone so far as to suggest that Canaris was an agent of MI6 and that as a dedicated anti-Nazi he was working for the Allies. Much of this stems from the horrifying story of what happened to him at the hands of the Gestapo butchers in Flossenburg Prison; the argument being that he would not have been arrested, beaten, tortured and finally dragged naked from his cell and hanged if he had been a loyal German.

He was a loyal German. He loved his country and had the interests of the Fatherland very much at heart. He foresaw clearly enough the utter ruin and degradation of Germany as a result not only of the Nazi regime but of Hitler's obvious intention that all Germany should emulate his own squalid extinction. One must not lose sight of the fact that Canaris, whatever else he was, was also a very professional intelligence officer, thoroughly well acquainted with all the subterfuge and tricks of the secret war. He knew the value of well-organized deception. He was an expert in what is now called 'disinformation' and the apparently genuine ingeniousness which has a far deeper design. All this was known to the Allies.

To understand the attitude to the *Schwarze Kapelle* in London and Washington one only has to consider what the probable German reaction would have been to an approach by a senior British or American commander with a plot to assassinate Churchill or Roosevelt. The analogy is by no means exact because the circumstances were so different, but the point is that no one trusts a traitor. There is much irony in the fate of Marshal Pétain and the politician Pierre Laval. They brought the war in France to an end in 1940, undoubtedly saving many thousands of French lives but making no allowances for the honour of France. When the war was over, both were tried as traitors and collaborationists, and condemned to death. Laval was tied to a chair and shot in the back of the head. Pétain died in captivity on the Île de Yeu in 1951.

It must also be remembered that in the crucial period just before D-Day, when earnest efforts by the German Command in France to negotiate for a peaceful landing might have aroused interest, no approach was made by any member of the *Schwarze Kapelle*. Indeed none could have been made because the generals in the plot had no idea how their subordinate commanders and troops would respond to a suggestion that it might be a good idea to get rid of Hitler. One possible and immediate outcome could have been civil war between SS units and the Wehrmacht. Furthermore, there was no acceptable representative of non-Nazi Germany.

There has been a lot of discussion about Rommel's part in the plot, and General Speidel has stressed that although Rommel knew all about it, he was insistent that Hitler must be removed by political and not by violent means. He was thus outside the little ring that planned the unsuccessful assassination attempt. These plans and counter-proposals were all seething in a very small pot at the time when the Allies landed, and as so often happens, events overtook those who were trying to control them.

Thus, from the historical point of view, the influence of the *Schwarze Kapelle* on the invasion of Normandy should be discounted; and so, for that matter, should the policy of unconditional surrender.

Broad-minded, intelligent people can of course sit now in impartial judgement on these great events and say, with all the advantages of hindsight and the lapse of more than 30 years, that this or that was an appalling blunder or, like the bombing of Dresden or the destruction of Hamburg, totally unjustified and indefensible by any humane standard. They can say now, as some said then, that insistence on unconditional surrender was a mistake but, at the time, the vast majority of people on the Allied side would not have settled for anything else; and this seems to have been forgotten.

The utter ruthlessness of the Nazis, their bombing of open cities, their murderous reprisals so often against women and children, and their complete disregard for human life, filled Europe with fear. Fear generates hatred. It became very clear to most people that if ever peace, order and justice were to be restored again, the Nazis would have to be exterminated so that the rest of the world could live; and at that time few made any distinction between Nazis and other Germans. They were all the enemy, and however frightful it may seem now, the news of thousands of the enemy dying in Allied air raids and the holocaust following the high explosive, aroused no pity, only satisfaction if not delight. War is not humane, it is all-consuming. People are not humane in war, especially when they have lost those they love, though they may well look back with horror on the way they felt while it was still to be endured.

Thus any scholarly analysis of decisions and events in war is a waste of time unless a deliberate effort is made to recall or reconstruct the background of fear and hatred and urgency against which they must be judged.

In the spring of 1944 neither the Allies nor the Axis had any illusions about the operational issues. The Allies knew that the time for offensive action was fast approaching, and there was no alternative. Hitler and the German armies, on the defensive since the failure of Operation Citadel in July 1943—the attack on Kursk which was to enable the Germans to regain the initiative on the eastern front—knew they were entering the last phase of the war.

3
Objectives

'War,' wrote General James Wolfe, 'is in its nature hazardous and an option of difficulties.' This was an eighteenth-century understatement. Although great strategic or operational issues can usually be reduced to a brief sentence, in itself an aim, it is when the aim is being converted into definite plans and effective action that the difficult problems arise.

Hitler's answer to the Allied threat of invasion was the Atlantic Wall. He would repeat Wellington's successful design to prevent Massena and Ney from pushing him into the sea: the Lines of Tores Vedras. But the Atlantic Wall would be an inversion of this; it would prevent the Allies — the Anglo-Saxons, as Hitler called them — from pushing the German armies inland. The invasion would be stopped and broken on the beaches. If the Allies could not get ashore, they could not invade. The logic was irrefutable; and one only had to look at the map to see where the invasion was bound to come.

The pre-requisites for successful seaborne invasion are wide, gently shelving beaches with reasonably open hinterland beyond for the deployment of infantry, armour and artillery; adequate air cover and at least one major port. The port is essential for handling the immense amount of bulk supplies needed to maintain the initial assault force and the reinforcing formations coming in over the beaches. The English Channel is notoriously the most unpredictable stretch of water in the world, and therefore it was extremely unlikely that the British and Americans would make their main effort anywhere except across the shortest possible distance — the Pas de Calais, also known as the Straits of Dover, some 22 miles.

In this area are the three large harbours of Dunkirk, Calais and Boulogne, and there are miles of open beach between Cap Blanc Nez, six miles west of Calais, and Dunkirk. Round the corner, south of Cap Griz Nez, there are reasonable beaches at Ambleteuse and Wimereux although the high ground behind them is easy to defend. South of Boulogne, right down as far as le Crotoy at the mouth of the Somme, are half-a-dozen suitable beaches with good roads leading from them inland to the lateral Route Nationale 1. No doubt there would be diversionary attacks, perhaps as far away as the coasts of Norway and Brittany, but the area of the major threat and high risk was certainly the Pas de Calais. Hitler made up his mind that the Allied invasion would come somewhere between Dunkirk and the mouth of the Somme.

All this was equally obvious to the Allies. They also knew that no matter what claims of impregnability Goebbels might make, the Atlantic Wall was not in fact a feasible proposition. There are about 3,000 miles of coastline between the Norwegian Nordkapp (North Cape) and the port of Brest in Brittany and it was not possible to build a continuous line of defences along so great a distance. The Germans would undoubtedly place mines and mined obstacles on the more vulnerable beaches, cover them with fire from strongpoints, and put coastal artillery on high ground further back, but from the point of view of invasion the problem would not be the immediate coastal defences so much as the enemy's resources for counter-attack.

It was assumed that Hitler would concentrate on the defences of the Pas de Calais coast and this simplified the invasion strategy. He must be given every encouragement to focus on that area and the actual invasion must be made somewhere else. He must also be made to think that the invasion in the other place was only a diversion which had the object of making him disperse his resources, and that the main effort would still be on the coast closest to south-eastern England. Not much imagination was needed to work out this strategy, but it was immediately apparent that the success of it would depend primarily on deception and intelligence.

Deception in war goes a great deal deeper than mere ruses such as the carefully arranged tree trunks that gave the appearance of batteries of artillery at the first Battle of Bull Run in the American Civil War. This was tactical deception; making the enemy think you are strong where you are weak, and vice versa. Sometimes it affects the battle, sometimes it does not. For example, Rommel does not appear to have been unduly influenced by the dummy infantry brigade and minefields in the Qaret el Himeimat, the southern sector of the el Alamein front. Strategic deception is infinitely more complicated.

As a military art, deception has two facets; persuading the enemy to do something which you can exploit; and providing him with the information he has been expecting while in reality you do something quite different. Deception must never seem incongruous, and it must be conveyed in such a way that the enemy thinks he is being remarkably astute in fitting the story together. This indeed is the essence of deception, that the enemy should be made to work out what you are trying to make him believe, and therefore think he is several jumps ahead of you. Above all, deception must be logical and preferably based on the principle of the Apparently Unintentional Mistake.

The story of the bloodstained haversack dropped by Colonel Richard Meinertzhagen, Allenby's intelligence officer, in front of a Turkish patrol in Palestine in 1917 is well known, and it certainly had a great influence on the subsequent battle of Gaza because the Turks altered their defensive positions in accordance with the false information which came into their possession apparently by accident. The same sort of trick, but on much more elaborate lines, was just as successful when it was tried again in April 1943. The story was that of 'Major William Martin,' Royal Marines—'The Man Who Never Was'—the body and briefcase washed ashore near Huelva in the Gulf of Cadiz. The papers in the briefcase revealed that the awaited Allied invasion of southern Europe would not be in Sicily, as the Germans expected, but in Sardinia, with diversionary attacks in Greece. Being sympathetic to Hitler, the Chief of the Spanish Naval Staff allowed a German agent to examine and reseal the documents before the briefcase was handed over, apparently intact and unopened, to the British Ambassador. In both cases, in Palestine and in Spain, the documents and the circumstances in which they came into enemy hands were excellent examples of practical deception, but the final touch which seems to have convinced the Turks and the Germans—even so experienced an intelligence officer as Canaris—was the interception and deciphering of an exchange of anxious signals between Allied headquarters. One of the signals relating to Meinertzhagen's ruse was a demand that he be court-martialled for his negligence. In the case of 'Major Martin' the messages passing between London and North Africa made it clear that no one knew what had happened to him or his briefcase, which contained highly classified material.

Intelligence and deception must go hand in hand because only the intelligence officer, with his detailed knowledge acquired from a study of the enemy, is in a position to deceive the enemy and to spot the enemy's deception; and deception must always be based on first-class intelligence and up-to-date knowledge of the enemy. One tiny thread of fact which is the wrong colour can ruin the whole carefully woven fabric and perhaps focus attention on the one place where it is least welcome. If the disaster at Dieppe were not to be repeated on a far greater scale and with far more momentous effects, the deception plan for the invasion of Fortress Europe would have to rank as equal in importance with operations and logistics.

The objectives of the intelligence staff were also clearly defined, and this was somewhat of an innovation. For a long time in military history it had been the practice to give as little thought as possible to Intelligence until a war actually started. Then it was realized that some sort of system for acquiring information about the enemy might be an advantage, and so an 'Intelligence Corps' of a sort was hurriedly formed and immediately regarded with suspicion, if not contempt, by most of the army. Since many intelligence officers recruited in these circumstances were civilians with considerable intellectual powers, they had little in common with the professional 'Horse, Foot and Guns', many of whom considered that intelligence as an organization was a refuge for military misfits. The tasks of these 'misfits' were not made easier by a lack of proper direction. Many commanders merely told them they were to find out, and report, everything about the enemy, but the fault lay primarily with the succession of pamphlets on Military Intelligence issued from 1912 onwards. They stated that 'It is the responsibility of the Intelligence Officer to provide his commander with all available information about the enemy', and the unfortunate intelligence officer was often discredited because he could not perform this impossible task and therefore could not answer questions he had not anticipated.

The intelligence staff cannot be expected to rely on intuition and inspired guesses to divine the intentions and intelligence requirements of the commander. He must tell them exactly what he wants to know so that they can make the best and most economic use of their resources.

In the planning and preparation before D-Day there were two principal categories of intelligence requirements; those of the operations and logistics staffs in connection with the actual invasion, and those directly related to the deception plan. The list was a long one. Intelligence had to keep a close watch on everything that was happening in the Pas de Calais, especially the construction of defences and the locations, communications, strength, roles, combat efficiency and morale of all enemy units deployed within reach of them, as well as collect detailed information on the invasion beaches and what lay beyond them, as soon as it had been decided where the landings would take place.

There were, initially, several possibilities; on the Mediterranean and Atlantic coasts of France, in Brittany and Normandy, and the final decision depended, among many other things, on currents, tides and prevailing winds, the distance from ports in the United Kingdom, the range of fighter-bomber air cover, the gradients, width and load-bearing capacity of beaches, and the exact nature of the enemy's defences. The planning team that had to make this decision consisted of General Dwight D. Eisenhower, General Sir Bernard Montgomery, Admiral Sir Bertram Ramsay, Air Chief Marshals Sir Arthur Tedder and Sir Trafford Leigh-Mallory, and Lieutenant Generals Omar Bradley and Walter Smith.

In brief, the operational plan decided upon by this team was that the 21st

Army Group, commanded by General Montgomery and consisting of the 1st United States Army under General Bradley and the 2nd British Army led by General Dempsey, would land on the Normandy coast on a line running from the south-east corner of the Cotentin peninsula eastwards to the mouth of the river Orne. This line would be divided into separate beaches, each given a codeword whose initial letter was that of each supporting naval task force. The American 7 Corps and 5 Corps, in the west, would land on Utah and Omaha beaches respectively; the British 30 Corps would land on Gold beach and the British 1st Corps on Juno and Sword. The seaborne assault would be preceded by airborne landings. In the west the 81 and 101 US Airborne Divisions would land in the area of Sainte-Mère-Église, and in the east, units and formations of the British 6 Airborne Division were to capture bridges over the Orne and destroy those over the river Dives. While these airborne landings were being made, a force of approximately 1,100 heavy bombers would attack the enemy coastal defences and gun positions. The seaborne assault would have the close support of naval artillery. It was hoped that by D + 1, 24 hours after the landings, a beach-head would have been established on a line running east and west just to the south of Bayeux and Caen.

In a lecture to the Staff College after the war, Field Marshal Montgomery said that the making of war resolves itself into very simple issues, the simplest being: what is possible and what is not possible? The historian S. G. P. Ward, in his book *Wellington's Headquarters*, takes this a stage further by saying that a commander has to choose between the possible and the impossible as he conceives it from his information. Thus information is the factor which weights the balance between success and failure.

The plan for the D-Day landings, Operation Overlord, was not drawn up in a matter of hours, in discussion round a table. It was the result of assessing all the available information, taking into consideration a multitude of facts, factors, capabilities and imponderables and arriving at what was possible. Though Intelligence played a vital part in this, a great deal depended on the availability of manpower, shipping and aircraft, and on solving a stupendous supply and maintenance problem. The Overlord plan involved conveying the largest force in the history of combined operations across a hundred miles of sea, and maintaining it in a country where every yard was likely to be disputed by some of the most tenacious and courageous troops in the world. It was an ambitious project, and the planners were always conscious of the 'spectre of Dieppe' and the possibility of failure, if only because so much would depend on things like wind and weather, sea and cloud cover which cannot be controlled.

Yet, assuming that the proposition was feasible and that the logistic problems could be solved, the success of Overlord depended primarily on achieving tactical surprise. If the Germans were ready and waiting, as they had been at Dieppe, the consequences could be disastrous.

In the second act of *King Henry V* Shakespeare put into the mouth of the Dauphin the remark: 'In matters of defence 'tis best to weigh the enemy more mighty than he seems'. The German commanders in the West had no illusions about the problems facing them. They knew that when the invasion came it would be in massive strength supported by all the resources of the American continent. They did not underestimate the threat, and they also knew they had a virtually insuperable security problem.

The Wehrmacht and the SS, with its various offshoots, was an army of occupation in a country controlled by force, most of whose inhabitants prayed for liberation. The defences of the Atlantic Wall had to be built by these people and by imported slave labour from conquered countries just as hostile to the conquerors. All the details of the defences and of the troops who were to man them would become common knowledge. The whole labour force and indeed the populations of France, Belgium, Holland and Norway, were potential sources of the information the Allies wanted. It would be impossible to keep preparations secret.

Yet perhaps the greatest disadvantage with which the German commanders had to contend was Hitler himself. The operational directive he gave to von Rundstedt, the Commander-in-Chief of Western Command, contained three main points:

1 The decisive action was to be fought on the Atlantic Wall itself.
2 The defence must be concentrated on the coast as the main line of battle, and this line was to be held at all costs.
3 All attempts of the enemy to land were to be broken up before and during beaching, and any local lodgements of enemy forces were to be destroyed immediately by instantaneous counter-attacks.

This removed all freedom of action from the commanders on the ground, and also they were expressly forbidden, in their operational planning, even to consider either the possibility of fighting inland or what the enemy might do if he succeeded in breaking through. (Both von Rundstedt and Rommel ignored this part of the directive and held staff studies to examine all possibilities.) The instruction also foreshadowed what the German commanders feared most, that Hitler, probably trying to direct the battle from his *Führerhauptquartier* many miles away on the other side of Bavaria, would keep all reserves under his own control and so, if committed at all, they would probably be too late. The main lesson that German commanders and staffs had learned from the campaigns in Russia and North Africa was that the commander on the spot must be able to fight the battle in his own way, making his own immediate decisions, and not be hamstrung by the tactical intuition of the Fuehrer.

When reading German accounts of the invasion, written only a few years after the war, allowances must be made for human nature, for in the aftermath of total defeat it is only natural for the defeated to look for scapegoats — preferably ones that are dead and therefore silent — and to justify mistakes and make excuses. Even so, and bearing this in mind, there is no doubt that especially in Co-operation as a Principle of War, the Allies had certain advantages over the Germans defending what General Eisenhower used to call the Far Shore.

Hitler, like every dictator before and since Pompey the Great, was always afraid that disparate groups in the forces he had created might one day unite against him, and therefore his whole administration was based on the principle of *divide et impera*. Nowhere is this better illustrated than in the defence of Occupied France, and the whole staff system was so chaotic that it is surprising that anything worked at all.

The ground forces in the West were organized in two Army Groups. Army Group B, under Rommel's command, was in the geographical sector stretching from Holland to the Loire. Army Group G, under Colonel-General Blaskowitz, covered the area from the Loire to the Spanish frontier and included the Mediterranean coast and the Alps. Both were under von Rundstedt's command. In addition there was a General of Armoured Forces in the West, General Baron von Schweppenburg, who commanded all the Panzer formations and units from his headquarters in Paris. Although in operational matters von Schweppenburg was subordinate to von Rundstedt, he was also directly responsible to Colonel-General Guderian, the Inspector General of Armoured Forces, for organization and training.

The German Naval Staff exercised direct control over the Western Naval Command under Admiral Krancke, whose headquarters were also in Paris. The 3rd Air Fleet under Marshal Sperrle, received its orders from *Reichsmarschall* Göering, and no one else. The Army Commander-in-Chief took his orders from the *Oberkommando der Wehrmacht* (OKW), the German Supreme Command.

Von Rundstedt and his Army Group commanders had no authority to co-ordinate the three Services of the Army, the Kriegsmarine (Navy) or the Luftwaffe (Air Force) in any local area, and in practice there was very little contact between them. Each of them seldom knew what the others were doing, or proposed to do, and if any such information did come it was usually out of date. Co-operation could, of course, be asked for, formally and through the proper channels to the appropriate high command, but this took a long time and since such matters were normally referred to Hitler for a decision, it was unlikely that anything would happen.

As if to make von Rundstedt's task more difficult, there was also a collection of Military Governors—General Karl Heinrich von Stülpnagel, in charge of one part of France; General Alexander von Falkenhausen, responsible for Northern France, and Air General Christiansen, who was the Military Governor of the Netherlands—and although they were supposed to be under von Rundstedt's command for all military matters, they were in fact directly responsible to OKW for administration and anything concerned with developing or exploiting local resources for the war effort.

Yet, in effect, the SS and the Gestapo held the real executive power and had done, ever since 1942. Their orders came straight from Heinrich Himmler and they made sure the Military Governors knew nothing about them. And so, especially in Civil Affairs, von Rundstedt as the Commander-in-Chief never knew what was really going on in his area of responsibility and usually heard about such things as executions, reprisals and the deporting of slave labour by chance and from sources which had little to do with them. He was well aware that SS and Gestapo agents were everywhere and that one of their tasks was to keep an eye on him and his troops.

To add to the confusion, if this were possible, the building organization run by the engineer Fritz Todt, which was responsible for the defences of the Atlantic Wall, worked to a system of 'Führer Directives' issued by Albert Speer, Reichsminister for Arms and Munitions, and OKW. Thus when Rommel took over command of Army Group B and became responsible for defending the coast in the area of the main threat, he could give no orders about the construction of field works or defensive positions; he could only indicate, tactfully, what he would like—through the proper channels to Western Command, OKW and the Ministry of Arms and Munitions.

Since local commanders had no control, and instructions came from a remote office guided only by a map and Hitler's intuition, the over-organized and over-manned Todt Organization had little knowledge of urgent military needs and, since 1942, often enough had been building merely for the sake of building.

Anyone who goes today to the little seaside town of Etretat, beloved by the School of Impressionists in the nineteenth century, will see large defence works protecting an area where no one in their senses would ever try to invade and where there were no targets to justify a commando raid. There are miles of unscalable cliffs on either side of a steep shingle beach, blocked by the town wedged into a narrow death-trap of a valley completely overlooked by abrupt hills crowned with hedges and thickets. There are similar defences in the even smaller town of Yport to the north east, where the rocky coast and dangerous reefs are protection enough and only one narrow street leads to the shore.

A final garnish to this administrative mess was the existence in Paris of a German Embassy under Ambassador Abetz—although there was no state of peace between Germany and France. Abetz was the representative of Ribbentrop, the Foreign Minister, and he was meant to work with the Vichy Government, nominally presided over by Marshal Pétain, but Hitler and Himmler disowned Abetz whenever it suited them. So, no doubt as a matter of deliberate policy, in the political world no one really knew who was responsible for what.

The practical effect of all this was that during the period of maximum tension before the invasion there was virtually no inter-Service co-operation. Men like Rommel and Sperrle knew what ought to be done and had many discussions, but they could take no action. When the crisis came, some of the concrete strongpoints on the invasion beaches had not been completed and naval and airforce units in the operational area were moved, in some cases back to Germany, without any reference to von Rundstedt.

Rommel had foreseen all this and had told Hitler that all land, naval and air forces, and the Todt Organization in the area for which he was responsible, must be placed under his command. Hitler rejected his proposal out of hand. He had a reason. Rommel, the 'Desert Fox', was a national hero, extremely popular and with great influence. Hitler was determined that he should be given no opportunity to acquire more power than was absolutely necessary, and so it can be said that vital operational needs were sacrificed to political suspicions.

Thus, although faced with the threat of invasion on an unprecedented scale, the German command structure was in a permanent and contrived state of chaos. The Allies worked as a team, and although the members had their disagreements and differences of opinion, they were united by a common aim and sought to achieve it by the most practical and efficient means. The Germans were split into factions deliberately encouraged by Hitler to squabble with one another and question the authority of each other. In the end his policy of divide and rule destroyed the Third Reich.

In March 1944, in conference with von Rundstedt, Krancke and Sperrle, Hitler announced that everything depended upon victory in the West. Defeat of the invasion would have so profound an effect upon the Anglo-Saxons that it would be a long time before they could recover and re-mount such an operation. This delay would give him time to transfer to the Russian front all the divisions now tied down in north-west Europe so that the critical situation in the East could be completely reversed. As soon as the Russians had been defeated and were out of the war, Germany's full strength could again be concentrated in the West.

Hitler went on to say that this assessment might well have to be amended in the light of the probable effect of the secret weapons now approaching the last stages of development: the V-1 pilotless aircraft and the V-2 rockets. These, in combination with the new jet fighters coming into service with the Luftwaffe and the submarines equipped with the *schnorkel* breathing device for operating over long distances under water, would force Britain to sue for peace. In which case the Americans would have to withdraw from Europe and would no doubt revert to their previous isolationist policy. The Service Chiefs, knowing that secret weapons had now become another of Hitler's obsessions, did not share his faith in them, but they did agree that the war and the fate of the Third Reich would be decided in the West.

Like many of the strategic concepts Hitler outlined to his commanders, this one was based on a myth, because the Atlantic Wall was very far from being the impregnable barrier on which his plans were based; and since it was so important to him it is strange that he never bothered to go and look at it. Von Rundstedt described the Wall as a mere showpiece with nothing in front of it and nothing behind. He thought it might perhaps hold the Allies up for about 24 hours, but they were bound to burst through it. Thereafter all the defences could be cleaned out from the landward side because everything pointed either out to sea or along the shore. The defenders, surrounded and forced to fight in the open, had no hope of survival.

In reality, this gloomy attitude was not justified, because of the weight and power of German armour. In the spring of 1944 there were ten armoured divisions in the West, among them the Panzer Lehr and the 12th SS Hitler-jugend, the strongest in the German Army. The Tiger tank had 7 in. steel-plating protecting it from frontal attack and its main armament was an 88 mm gun. The Panther tanks were armed with 75 mm guns and their frontal armour could withstand the fire of any Allied tank, even the American Shermans. Both types of tank were vulnerable to flank attack but their guns could stop any armoured vehicles the Allies sent against them. Furthermore, although the combat efficiency of some of the Wehrmacht infantry units might not be entirely satisfactory, the Panzer units had all fought in Russia and most of the

SS troops were fanatical Nazis led by such men as the notorious General Kurt Meyer who commanded the 12th SS Panzer Division.

On the debit side, at least 23 of the infantry battalions in the Normandy area might prove to be unreliable because they contained a high proportion of Russian prisoners of war, offered service in the Wehrmacht as the alternative to starvation. General Speidel says that 70 Division 'consisted of men with stomach ailments, but it fought well for all that'.

Nevertheless, the German Panzer units in the West could, if concentrated as an immediately available reserve and then deployed in the right place at the right time, break up and destroy the Allied invasion. Von Rundstedt was aware of this and so were the Allies. Both were also aware that deployment of the armour was indeed the critical factor. Therefore the intelligence task facing the Germans was to discover when and where the landings would be. If they had this information there was a reasonable chance that Hitler's strategic plan could be put into effect, and he would be able to extricate himself from the very difficult position of having to fight a war on two fronts against numerically superior enemies — the one situation that the military writers Karl von Clausewitz, Helmuth von Moltke and Alfred von Schlieffen had all said must be avoided.

The Allies, on the other hand, had a threefold task: to learn all they could about the defences of the Atlantic Wall, to convince the Germans they were going to land in an area where they had no intention of landing, and to keep the vital secret of the real place and time. The Germans needed intelligence; the Allies had to achieve a perfect blend of intelligence, deception and security.

4
German Intelligence

One of the fundamental principles of intelligence is that any system must be centralized, preferably under one man who is the undisputed head or director, or at least under a single committee in which all interests are represented. Ideally, all information from all sources is processed and filtered at each level in the intelligence structure as it flows along a single channel to the man or committee at the top who can see the whole picture. There are two main reasons for this: centralized control is as good a way as any of making sure that the organization is reasonably efficient and economic, and it prevents the growth of independent systems which can be penetrated and exploited by the enemy.

In recent times, one of the problems in Vietnam was the proliferation of unco-ordinated intelligence agencies. There were similar difficulties in Aden in 1964 and at least one resourceful Arab benefited financially from them. He was a benign old gentleman of no particular political persuasion who cycled round to the various intelligence agencies and sold to each of them the same spurious pieces of information. Since the agencies were working for different departments and were reluctant to disclose their sources, the fact that several of them had the same information appeared to confirm its accuracy and reliability. It was some time before the old man's profitable little scheme came to light, and it underlines the dangers inherent in the rivalry and competition which are likely to feature in a system that is not centralized.

Possibly because knowing something that other people do not know tends to impart a feeling of satisfaction and superiority, Intelligence can easily become a breeding ground of rivalry, jealousy and one-upmanship, and it is rare that complete co-operation is achieved between agencies that do not share a common allegiance. In one respect this is understandable because of another intelligence principle — the need to protect sources — but any element of competition can affect the efficiency of the whole organization. There will always be problems but many of them can be solved in integrating all resources in one organization which has a common purpose and makes allowances for the proper protection of sources.

Though not as chaotic as the command structure, the intelligence system in Germany suffered acutely from rivalries and, at least until the beginning of 1944, a lack of centralization which made it vulnerable to the deception schemes of the Allies. Military intelligence was run efficiently enough, especially on the eastern front, although in the past there had been a prejudice against it similar to the feeling in the British Army.

In the days of Frederick the Great, who ran his own organization, intelligence was well planned and effective. Frederick thoroughly understood the importance of it and stressed this in his *Instructions for His Generals,* written in 1747. His crushing victory at Rossbach over the Prince de Soubise and the Prince of Saxe-Hildburghausen on 5 November 1757 was largely the result of his ability to see an operational situation from the enemy's point of view—the essence of the military intelligence function. Yet to enable him to do this he had to have reliable information, and as he said himself, 'Marshal de Soubise is always followed by a hundred cooks; I am always preceded by a hundred spies...the proportion of spies to cooks in my army is twenty to one'.

Thus it is curious that the Prussian General Staff which Frederick created should have developed, after his death, so strong a prejudice against intelligence—especially that obtained by espionage.

The aristocratic members of the Prussian officer class regarded espionage as being a despicable business, they considered that any commander in the field who wanted information about the enemy should send out a cavalry patrol to collect it. This was overt and honourable; spies were not.

In his book *The German Secret Service* Colonel Walther Nicolai, head of German Intelligence in the First World War, gives an account of the pre-war training of intelligence officers for the secret service and illustrates the prejudice that existed. Any officer who did particularly well on the course was allowed, as a reward for his hard work, to return to regimental duty and not be associated with the collection of information. Intelligence did not feature in staff studies or training, and army commanders held the view that it was not a practical proposition in mobile operations. During the advance through Belgium at the beginning of the war, one army commander, describing his intelligence officer as 'needless ballast', left him behind at Liège.

Nicolai succeeded in building up an intelligence organization but its record was not particularly good. In the early hours of 5 August 1914 all the agents planted in England before the war were collected by the police, acting on information provided by the recently formed British counter-intelligence service known as MI5 and all the spies sent over subsequently were arrested because they soon gave themselves away. The exception was Jules Silber, often described as the perfect spy, who worked undetected in the Directorate of Postal Censorship, but he was not sent over; he was a volunteer who had not been trained either in Germany or in the notorious School for Spies run by Elspeth Schragmüller in Antwerp.

After the defeat of Germany in 1918 Colonel Nicolai's intelligence and counter-intelligence organization continued to exist, largely on paper, as a department of the General Staff, and it was not until Rear Admiral Canaris became the Director of Abwehr—literally, 'defence'—on 1 January 1934 that it began to grow into a service employing some 3,000 men and women.

Its function was to provide Hitler, the OKW and the General Staff with military, political, technical, diplomatic and economic intelligence, and at the same time maintain their security. Since it was still a department of the General Staff its allegiance was primarily to the Supreme Command of the Wehrmacht.

Like all dictators, Hitler trusted no one, least of all his senior generals who opposed his plans for world conquest. He arranged for three of them, Ludwig Beck, Kurt von Schleicher and Kurt von Bredow, to be murdered during the Night of the Long Knives—30 June 1934—and even before he came to power he took steps to see that he had his own Nazi intelligence service which was quite separate from anything organized by the Army. In the summer of 1931, when Heinrich Himmler was planning the formation of the *Schutzstaffel* (SS) which was to be to Hitler what the Imperial Guard had been to Napoleon, a young man named Reinhard Heydrich was introduced to him as a man who might be of value to the Nazis when they came into power and built the new Germany. Of the little gang of paranoiacs and psycopaths who surrounded Hitler, Heydrich was perhaps the most intrinsically evil. It is said that he had an ungovernable sexual appetite but this accusation seems to be based on an incident which terminated his extremely promising naval career in April 1931, and his appetite may not have been any more ungovernable than that of most young men who follow the advice of Kipling's soldier and 'take their love where they find it'. He refused to marry a girl he had made pregnant and was cashiered from the German Navy on the grounds of 'impropriety'. He was retrieved from what would have been social and financial ruin by another girl, Fraulein Mathilde von Osten, whom he subsequently married. She was an enthusiastic member of the Nazi Party and she introduced him to Himmler.

Himmler invited him to create an intelligence and security service for the Nazis, the *Sicherheitsdienst* (SD), entirely separate from Abwehr, and on 5 October 1931 Heydrich was given the rank of *Sturmführer SS* on the staff of *Reichsführer SS* Himmler. Heydrich was a man without morals, scruples or humanity, ruthlessly ambitious and coldly, impersonally cruel who moved in an extraordinary aura of fear. Even much older and more experienced men like Canaris were genuinely frightened of him. His merciless persecution of Jewish people is made even more horrible by the fact that he had a Jewish grandmother, and it is perhaps ironical that she, after her death, played a considerable part in the extinction of the Nazis.

It is not surprising that the SD, controlled by a fanatical Nazi, soon came into direct conflict with Abwehr, led by a patriotic German who regarded Hitler's *coup d'état* in October 1931 as a national disaster. What is surprising is the ability of Admiral Canaris to remain in charge of Abwehr even after Hitler had, by murder, dismissal and disgrace, removed from the higher echelons of the Wehrmacht all those who did not actively support him. General von Blomberg, the Minister for War, and 16 other generals were dismissed soon after Baron von Fritsch had been forced to retire. Von Fritsch and von Blomberg were replaced by Keitel and Brauchitsch who were prepared to obey Hitler's orders, and Canaris was subordinate to them.

Heydrich understood the dangers inherent in rival intelligence and security services and, because of his influence in the Nazi Party, it would seem that all he had to do was recommend to Himmler that the SD should absorb Abwehr in a single centralized system. Himmler would then arrange for a 'Führer's Directive' and Canaris would disappear; but this did not happen because Canaris not only knew about the Jewish grandmother but could prove it, and he had arranged for friends in Switzerland to keep the written evidence on his behalf in case it might one day be needed. Also there is little doubt that the same friends were looking after equally useful secret information about Himmler, because neither Heydrich nor Himmler ever moved overtly against him. It was Walther Schellenberg, one of Heydrich's deputies and a *Brigadeführer SS* in charge of the foreign intelligence section of the SD, who finally achieved the downfall of Canaris, but it took him a long time. Painstakingly Schellenberg collected evidence of Canaris's anti-Nazi activities and laid it in front of Himmler, but nothing was done. When Heydrich, directly responsible for the slaughter of six million Jews, and having earned the title of the Butcher of Prague, was assassinated in Prague his place as head of the SD was taken by the uncouth Ernst Kaltenbrunner, but Schellenberg, officially a subordinate, was given direct access to Himmler and for all practical purposes was in control.

Heydrich's Jewish grandmother ceased to be a factor in the politics of German Intelligence when he died of gangrene from bomb wounds on 4 June 1942, but for eight years her existence had prevented the amalgamation of intelligence resources, and by that time the rivalry and antagonism between Abwehr and the SD had reached such a pitch that peaceful amalgamation and co-operation were out of the question. Schellenberg, by now aware that Canaris must have some hold over Himmler, knew there could be no centralized control until Canaris had been removed, and this was not within his personal power.

Unwittingly, the grandmother had achieved a great deal.

The German Intelligence Service was profoundly affected by Heydrich's death, and it also may well have had an effect on Overlord. He had been determined to eliminate Canaris, and so ruthless a murderer might have been successful. He was on his way to Paris at the time when he was killed, to become the head of the SS in France. In this appointment, and with Canaris out of the way, the story of Overlord might have been very different, if only because he belonged to Hitler's select inner circle and might have persuaded him to listen to the soldiers who had to fight the battle.

Heydrich and Schellenberg had not been the only powerful Nazis to campaign for a centralized intelligence system. Disregarding any personal motives he might have had for wanting to get rid of Canaris, Himmler himself had long felt that Hitler's policy of divide and rule should not apply to intelligence, and that it was dangerous for any intelligence and security system with its own agencies to be outside Party control. But he had to be careful. Any attack on Canaris would have to come from elsewhere, and his dismissal could be ordered only by Hitler. It was not until January 1944, only a few months before D-Day, that his chance came.

The principal Abwehr agent in Istanbul was Dr Erich Vermehren. He was also a friend of a certain Frau Hanna Solf who held tea parties at her house in Berlin where there was unwisely frank discussion of Hitler and his regime. One of Frau Solf's guests was Otto Kiep, who had been a diplomat in New York. Schellenberg learned of these tea-table conversations and informed Himmler. Himmler ordered the arrest of Kiep, and fearing that under Gestapo interrogation Kiep would implicate him, Dr Vermehren and his wife, Countess Elizabeth von Plettenberg, asked MI6 for protection and were immediately whisked away from Istanbul to safety in Egypt.

For obvious reasons the British gave wide publicity to this defection, implying that Vermehren had brought with him the German diplomatic cipher and a great deal of valuable secret information about Abwehr and German intentions in Turkey. Hitler ordered a thorough investigation which, in the absence of Vermehren himself, did not reveal very much, but it gave Himmler the opportunity to suggest that the time had now come to bring all intelligence agencies under the control of really trustworthy members of the Nazi Party —

such as Kaltenbrunner and Schellenberg. He said nothing about Canaris. Hitler agreed.

Field Marshal Keitel and General Jodl called on Canaris, told him he was to be decorated for his great services to the Reich, and invited him to take over the sinecure of Head of Economic Warfare. Canaris slid silently into virtual retirement. His execution, on 9 April 1945, was the result of his association with the *Schwarze Kapelle* and one of many following the abortive attempt to kill Hitler. Even so, it was long delayed because Himmler was afraid to kill him in case his friends abroad released the secret information which had been his shield for so long. Hitler personally ordered his execution.

With Canaris in retirement, Schellenberg at once began a major reorganization of intelligence and security, but the General Staff insisted that Military Intelligence must remain under their control. Schellenberg therefore formed a special section which he called Amt Mil, and placed it under the command of Colonel Georg Hansen who, unknown to the SS, the SD or the Gestapo, was a loyal follower of Admiral Canaris and an active member of the *Schwarze Kapelle*. Thus Himmler and Schellenberg had not achieved very much by at last getting rid of Canaris, and by now it was much too late even to hope that the defunct Abwehr might be of any use to Schellenberg.

Canaris is a strange figure in Intelligence history. There is no doubt that his genuine abhorrence of the Nazis and their methods, and his attempts to protect Germany from the effects of them, made him a traitor to the regime, but the men who had been under his command remained loyal even to his memory. In contrast to the Nazi leaders he was an intellectual, an idealist, a man with high moral scruples who seems to have had a profound hatred of violence. When he saw the ruins of Belgrade, systematically destroyed by the Luftwaffe in April 1941 in three days of constant attacks which killed some 17,000 civilians, he had a nervous breakdown from which he never really recovered. Even so, he was shrewd and cunning, and his pale-blue eyes had a look of innocence which gave no clue to his real character.

His staff were horrified by his removal. They were not Nazis, they would not have been on his staff if they were, and they had no intention of being compulsorily transferred to the SS, with its reputation for fanaticism and cruelty. The Abwehr agents in France formed themselves into a unit and sought protection by attaching themselves to the Wehrmacht.

But if Canaris was a traitor, so was Schellenberg, who was by no means as reliable as Hitler and Himmler thought he was. He could not persuade himself that Hitler would win the war and so he took steps to prepare an escape route. Though he disliked and distrusted the British he had his contacts with the

Americans, mainly through Allen Dulles who was running the Berne detachment of the Office of Strategic Services (OSS).

In theory, all the information collected by the German Intelligence Service — which consisted of Abwehr, the SD and the separate intelligence departments of the Army, the Navy and the Air Force — was sent to OKW, the Supreme Command, at its headquarters at Zossen, about half an hour by train from Hitler's Chancellery in Berlin. In practice, however, when the SD had technically absorbed Abwehr, Schellenberg exercised his discretion about the material provided for the Supreme Command by his SD/Abwehr, but he insisted that all intelligence would pass through his office on its way from OKW to Hitler. Ostensibly, this was to ensure it was accurate and up to date, but in reality it was all part of the rivalry, competition and antipathy in the various intelligence departments. Schellenberg had no intention of allowing Hitler to see anything which might contradict SD opinion, nor was he going to let any department bring off an intelligence 'scoop' behind his back. This insistence on checking and filtering all reports and assessments finally led to an extraordinary situation of great benefit to the Allies.

The processing of all military information — the collation, evaluation, integration and interpretation which converts information into intelligence — was done by two separate intelligence departments of OKW: *Fremde Heere Ost* (FHO) and *Fremde Heere West* (FHW). General Reinhard Gehlen took over FHO on 1 April 1942 and developed an extremely efficient service covering the whole of the eastern front. From February 1943, FHW was run by Colonel Alexis Baron von Roenne, a Prussian officer of 'the old school'. He had served in FHW before, having been posted to the department in 1939, but in the summer of 1941 he volunteered for active service when the Wehrmacht invaded Russia. He was so badly wounded that he had to spend nearly a year in hospital, but when he had recovered sufficiently he was asked by Hitler to return as head of the department in which he had served.

Hitler had good reasons for this promotion. At the time when he had been planning the attack on Poland, von Roenne had been responsible for assessing the intentions and capabilities of France. He had advised Hitler that according to his calculations Britain and France would not attack Germany while the Polish campaign was going on. Had they done so they would have found that the Wehrmacht had only 23 divisions, below strength in manpower and equipment, in western Germany. France and Britain had a combined mobilization strength of 110 divisions, and so von Roenne's assessment was of some importance. Later, during the *Blitzkrieg* against France in 1940, von Roenne told Hitler that a powerful armoured thrust in the Sedan sector would bring about the collapse of the French army, and again he had been right.

Initially, the role of FHW and FHO had been the dual one of providing the Supreme Command with the intelligence needed for making decisions and penetrating enemy deception, but as every intelligence officer soon learns, information does not flow in automatically, especially during a battle, because soldiers in contact with the enemy are far too busy coping with what is happening and have no time to give the intelligence staff the information they need for assessing what is going to happen. Thus, using the communications centre at Zossen which provided contact with any unit anywhere in Occupied Europe in a matter of seconds, both FHO and FHW undertook the careful tasking of all military sources and agencies. The interception of enemy signals traffic was one of the more important sources, and the agencies collecting this type of information and processing it into intelligence were special units of what was known as the Y Service. All the information obtained from military sources and agencies was used to supplement the reports from Abwehr and SD.

Both von Roenne and Gehlen formed a close association with Canaris when he was the Director of Abwehr. Von Roenne became involved in the *Schwarze Kapelle* and, like so many other senior officers, was killed after the failure to kill Hitler. It may well be that one of the reasons why Schellenberg kept so close an eye on the intelligence products of FHO and FHW was that he suspected treachery in all friends of Canaris. However, the strange situation brought about by the SD checking system was very largely the fault of Schellenberg himself, and it arose when *Fremde Heere West* was given the task of producing an accurate Allied Order of Battle in the months just before D-Day.

At the end of 1943 Colonel Staubwasser, who had been in charge of the FHW desk known as Group England, was posted to Rommel's headquarters as his intelligence officer. He was replaced by Lieutenant Colonel Roger Michel. A few weeks later, in January 1944, Michel reported to von Roenne that on its way to Hitler his estimate of the number of Allied divisions in England was being halved by Schellenberg, simply because he wished to demonstrate to Hitler that information from SD was the most accurate and reliable.

Von Roenne said that Schellenberg was too powerful and too close to Hitler to be contradicted, but two months later, in March, less than three months before D-Day, he realized that something would have to be done because Hitler, not realizing that the FHW figures were being altered, and trusting von Roenne implicitly, decided to reinforce the eastern front with divisions from the West at a time when von Roenne was advocating the exact opposite. But by now Abwehr had virtually ceased to exist; Schellenberg was in charge of the recently centralized intelligence service and was more powerful than ever.

Michel suggested that if FHW doubled their estimate, and this was then halved by Schellenberg, the figure that reached Hitler would be reasonably accurate. Von Roenne, brought up under the strict code and jealous of his personal honour and integrity, was at first shocked by such an idea. He was also well aware of the danger of falsifying such figures because if by any chance Schellenberg did not halve them, and if Hitler based his strategy on a deliberate and gross overestimate and subsequently learned the truth, Michel and he would probably lose their heads, literally. Beheading was the normal fate of traitors and foreign agents in Germany.

Nevertheless, after much deliberation, von Roenne *did* double the figures and to support them he reported as true what he felt were false reports and radio transmissions put out by the Allies as part of their deception plans.

For no apparent reason Schellenberg *did not* halve the inflated estimate, and thus it was that Hitler and the OKW believed the Allies had between 85 and 90 divisions available for the invasion of Fortress Europe whereas the true figure was only 35. In May 1944 von Roenne's false figure was accepted and entered on the enemy Order of Battle charts in all German formation headquarters in the West. There is a touch of irony in the fact that when the Allies stepped up their deception and flooded German Intelligence with evidence of very large resources—such as the imaginary First United States Army Group (FUSAG) and the equally mythical 4th British Army—von Roenne and Michel both began to feel they had miscalculated and their doubled estimate was probably the correct one.

Thus, during the period between the raid on Dieppe and the first week of June 1944, when knowledge of when and where the invasion would come was vital to OKW planning and the defence of northern France, there was no co-ordinated and centralized intelligence system in Germany and there was bitter rivalry in the services that did exist. At the beginning of the war Abwehr had been told by Canaris that it must do nothing to further Hitler's aims, and was therefore fundamentally disloyal to the Nazi regime. The SD was more interested in counter-espionage, Nazi security and opposing Abwehr than in acquiring the information on which the existence of the Third Reich depended.

Himmler knew that Germany was losing the secret war. In the speech he made beside Heydrich's coffin he implied that the British Secret Service was far superior to anything run by Heydrich or Canaris, though he was careful to mention no names.

In running *Fremde Heere Ost,* Gehlen's task was very different from that of von Roenne because most of his sources were in actual contact with the enemy on the ground. Von Roenne's difficulty was that he had to rely on three indirect sources of information, all of which could be used to deceive him: aerial reconnaissance, radio interception and espionage.

The Germans never achieved air superiority over the British Isles and therefore it can be said that after the Battle of Britain their air reconnaissance was somewhat dependent upon permission from the Royal Air Force. False messages as a means of deceiving the enemy are a ruse as old as warfare itself, and from their performance in both World Wars it can be said that the Germans are not very good at espionage. They never really appreciated the problems or mastered the techniques of placing, maintaining and communicating with agents ferried to or dropped over an island. In every way their management of espionage showed an extraordinary naivety. Lord Jowitt, who became Lord Chancellor in 1945, has said that of the number of spies he prosecuted only one could speak English reasonably fluently, and practically all the ones caught in Great Britain had little or no knowledge of local conditions, customs or even geography.

Only a very brave, self-confident man, or a very stupid one with no imagination, sets out on an espionage mission in a strange country of which he knows nothing and cannot speak the language. There is no excuse for sending untrained spies into enemy territory, but the Germans may perhaps have been taking a calculated risk. During the war, Britain was full of refugees from the rest of Europe; men and women of many different nationalities who spoke no language but their own and knew no country but the one from which they had fled in escaping from Nazi persecution. All sorts of different uniforms could be seen on the streets of London and very few people made any effort to identify them. It was an unpleasant shock to the security services when, as an experiment not long before D-Day, a British officer correctly dressed in Luftwaffe uniform walked about the West End of London for some hours in the middle of the day without being challenged by anyone.

It was not, therefore, unreasonable for the Germans to assume that a Belgian, or a Dutchman, or a Frenchman, who was also one of their agents, could claim to be a refugee in need of protection and, under this cover, do what he had been sent to do. It appeared that he did not have to know the language or the country or its customs; in fact, the risks he ran might be increased if he did. But this was a false assumption because all refugees were carefully screened by MI5. Any arriving in circumstances that were at all doubtful immediately attracted closer attention, especially if they behaved as anything other than refugees. A spy sent to discover the place and date of the invasion had to get out and about. He had to find out where military units were concentrating; he had to make contact with service personnel who might know what he wanted to know, and in doing so would certainly arouse the liveliest suspicion. Furthermore, the idea that a refugee from the Nazis could acquire the closely guarded secrets of another country without causing comment reveals an unusual degree of optimism.

German spymasters might perhaps have had better results from espionage if they had made a closer study of the areas where their spies were to operate, and if they had 'known their enemy', as Frederick the Great had advised. But, by apparently assuming that British and American counter-espionage was as naïve as they were, they made it difficult for agents who were either loyal or of no use to enemy Intelligence to avoid the scaffold and the hangman. The sad case of Joseph Jan Vanhove is an example.

Claiming to be a leading figure in the Belgian Resistance, in March 1944 he went to the British Embassy in Stockholm, having arrived in neutral Sweden in a cargo ship from neutral Spain. He said he had been running the financial affairs of several Resistance groups and had only just succeeded in escaping from Belgium after the Gestapo had put a price on his head and threatened to execute anyone who might be foolish enough to assist him. To prove his story he produced newspaper clippings from the German-controlled Belgian press which had published photographs of him.

He was sent to England on the weekly flight from Stockholm to Scotland, interrogated on arrival and then allowed to go free. MI5 wanted to see whether he would lead them to any contacts, and when it became clear he was working on his own he was arrested. A few notes on shipping movements and bomb damage were found on him and he was sentenced to death at the Old Bailey on 26 May 1944. While in the condemned cell he may well have wondered what had gone wrong and what mistake had led to his arrest. It would probably have surprised him to learn that the MI5 interrogator had known what he was as soon as he produced the newspaper clippings. A genuine member of the Resistance would never have dared to travel right across France, through German-occupied territory, carrying in his pocket-book pieces of paper that were the equivalent of his own death warrant.

5
German Espionage

Within a few hours of the declaration of war in 1914 the whole German espionage organization in Britain ceased to exist because courteous police officers called at the addresses of all the German spies, planted in some cases years before, and asked them to come to the local police station. The result was that the German Supreme Command knew nothing of the mobilization and move across the Channel of the British Expeditionary Force until the leading elements of von Kluck's 1st German Army ran into its accurate and rapid fire near Mons.

The Kaiser lost his temper and shouted at his staff, 'Am I surrounded by dolts? Why have I not been told that we have no spies in England?'

He probably knew the answer; but the information which enabled the British police to round up all his agents had been supplied indirectly and unwittingly four years previously, by a Captain of the Imperial German Navy who was the acting head of German Naval Intelligence. He had been a member of the Kaiser's retinue at the funeral of King Edward VII in 1910, and his movements had been watched unobtrusively by a security department known as Military Operations 5 (MO5), subsequently MI5, founded in 1909 by Captain (later Major-General Sir Vernon) Kell of the South Staffordshire Regiment.

During his brief visit, the German naval officer hired a cab which took him to a barber's shop in the Caledonian Road, run for the past 16 years by a man named Karl Gustav Ernst, born in England and therefore a British subject. This visit to Ernst's seedy little establishment seemed odd, but it transpired that Ernst was a 'letter box'. German Intelligence sent him packages containing a number of letters already stamped and addressed to their agents. His task was to forward the letters individually, for which he was paid £1 a month. By keeping a check on Ernst's outgoing mail it was easy enough to make a list of all the German spies in Britain.

Admiral Canaris, responsible for a similar network in the period before the Second World War, did not make such elementary mistakes. He built up two systems. One consisted of minor, unimportant agents, many of them women, whose cover story—often true—was that they had Jewish blood and had had to flee from Germany and Austria. (Canaris saved a large number of Jews from the Nazis.) They were encouraged to become domestic servants and report anything they saw or heard which might be of intelligence interest. These were the screen to keep MI5 and Special Branch of Scotland Yard fully occupied and distract attention from the second network of professional spies trained at the Abwehr school for secret agents in Hamburg. The scheme was sound enough because it presented the British security services with the difficult problem of numbers. There were more than 73,000 aliens in Britain, and the screen might have been very effective had it not been for one of the instructors in the Hamburg School.

He had been up at Oxford and his function in Hamburg was to train the student agents to behave in every way exactly like Englishmen. He pointed out that there was nothing to be gained by trying to avoid the police in Britain, and it was far better to get in touch with them as soon as possible in a way which would establish the respectability of the individual spy. He said that in Britain, respectability and the integrity of a citizen were judged by the size of the citizen's bank balance. Therefore, when a graduate spy arrived in England he should place in the Post Office Savings Bank all the Abwehr funds supplied to him, and the Post Office would give him a savings book. After a while, the spy should go to the police and report the loss of this book and say how much was in it. The figure would be enough to convince the police that the spy was a very respectable person.

When war was declared on 3 September 1939 the police had a list of practically all the agents in the second network, because the Abwehr instructor was a member of MI6.

In a combined operation, MI5, Special Branch and all the police forces in the United Kingdom checked all aliens, arrested 1,000 and put restrictions on the movements of another 6,000. This virtually destroyed both networks in the first weeks of the war, but the Germans claimed that a few agents managed to escape the security sweep and remained in radio contact. One of them had the codename Snow.

Snow was a Canadian, an electrical engineer, who first drew attention to himself in 1936 when he approached British Naval Intelligence, and then MI6, offering to become a professional spy. Since neither showed any interest he became an agent for Abwehr, a fact which very soon became known to MI5. He was arrested by Special Branch on the day after war was declared, and it was suggested to him that he might care to become a double agent. Since it was obvious that refusal would lead to a trial and the unpleasant feeling of a rope being placed round his neck, he accepted the offer. He maintained communication with Abwehr in Hamburg, using the wireless transmitter they had provided, and it was because of the instructions and information sent to him from time-to-time by his German handler that many German agents were picked up soon after arriving in England. Even so, quite a number of them were so untrained and so lacking in common sense and a reasonable interest in self-preservation that they gave themselves away and were brought in without any help from Snow.

After the first big security operation Canaris had to start all over again, and he followed a principle that had been laid down centuries before, by Genghis Khan, that a spy should have the same appearance, background and language as the people in the country where he is to operate. The British might be more easily deceived by spies who were not Germans but came from occupied countries and, as unfortunates driven into exile by the Germans, might attract some sympathy. Moreover, they could mingle easily with genuine expatriates who had sought refuge in Britain.

What German Intelligence did not apparently appreciate was that the war had wrought great changes in England, and the effect of the threat of German invasion—Operation Sealion—was profound. Apart from the fact that a well-trained member of the security services is innately suspicious and sceptical, the British were becoming extremely spy-conscious. Everyone was alert to the possibility of spies coming in by parachute or submarine on a dark night. Although a man with very little knowledge of English, or who had a very guttural accent, might be accepted in a local community provided he wore uniform and lived in a camp with others like himself, any stranger in plain clothes who had those disadvantages had no chance of passing unnoticed.

Two Dutchmen, Carl Meier and Sjord Pons, another Dutch national called Charles van der Kieboom whose oriental features had been inherited from his Japanese mother, and a German, Rudolf Waldberg—the only one of the four who could speak English—were all brought across from Le Touquet and landed in St Mary's Bay, between Dungeness and Dymchurch, at first light on 3 September 1940. Pons and Meier were arrested almost at once by a beach patrol of The Somerset Light Infantry which found them sitting in the lee of a sand-dune breakfasting off *Wurst*.

Waldberg walked across the open, flat marshland to Lydd and, being thirsty and knowing nothing of local licensing laws, knocked on the door of a pub and asked for a bottle of cider—at nine o'clock in the morning. He was arrested. Kieboom, whose appearance was somewhat against him, lasted a little longer— nearly 24 hours. At their trial, Pons, who had been a medical orderly in the

Dutch Army, was able to persuade the jury that his reason for joining Abwehr had been to get to England and serve under Prince Bernhard of the Netherlands. The other three were hanged in December 1940.

Just before dawn on 30 September 1940, Werner Waelti, a Swiss, Karl Drueke, a German, and a girl whose parents were Russian emigrés, came ashore in the Moray Firth from a submarine and walked the short distance to one of the little railway halts on the branch line that runs from Inverness along the coast to Fraserburgh. Drueke roused the stationmaster and asked for tickets to London. On the pretext of having to find out the price for so long a journey, the stationmaster closed the booking hatch and telephoned to the police. Drueke and Waelti were hanged, but it is not quite clear what happened to the girl. There is reason to believe she was a British agent who had infiltrated Abwehr and came over here with considerable Abwehr funds. A few years ago a woman remarkably like her was living in reasonably comfortable circumstances in England.

Four more spies landed in England during that September and all were caught. Two were 'turned' and became double agents, supplying their German handlers with information given to them by British Intelligence as part of the deception plan known as Fortitude. The others, in company with all spies who for one reason or another were of no value after they had been captured, were hanged.

This intelligence 'attack' by Canaris was the first part of an operation with the codename Lobster, the prelude to Sealion, and it was a complete failure. In fact it was so mismanaged and the agents were so incompetent that when one bears in mind the efficiency with which Canaris conducted his intelligence operations elsewhere, it looks very much as though there was a deliberate lack of real effort against England—as if he had no enthusiasm for the task of providing the Wehrmacht with the intelligence needed for the invasion and subsequent occupation of England.

In his memoirs, General Gehlen writes of the valuable, accurate information supplied to him by Abwehr agents in Moscow—one of them had even succeeded in penetrating an Allied Military Mission—and if Canaris could achieve that in Russia, it is difficult to understand why so capable and professional a spymaster should have failed completely against England. Perhaps he regarded England as the last bastion against Nazism which must therefore be preserved for that reason alone.

The agents he recruited in England, or sent there after the round-up in September 1939, were all well below the normal Abwehr standard. An example, not untypical, was Pamela O'Grady whose name alone could suggest a reason why she should work against England. She kept a boarding-house in the Isle of Wight and sent information, written in the crudest of invisible inks, to a handler in Portugal. Motivated by greed and hatred, and entirely untrained, she was not in a position to provide anything of much value. She was caught, sentenced to death and reprieved.

Throughout the war the standard did not really improve. In May 1942 a Czech named Karel or Karl Richter parachuted into the St Albans area. He landed in the dark and hid in a wood until the following night. Venturing out, he walked along a road and was stopped by a lorry driver who had lost his way. Richter's accent aroused the driver's suspicions, he drove on, contacted the police, and Richter was picked up and taken to the nearest police station. While being searched he was unable to explain why he had been walking along a country road on a warm May night wearing three sets of underclothing and two pairs of socks.

One spy aroused suspicion that proved fatal to him when he offered food coupons to a waitress in a restaurant (coupons were only needed for buying food in shops). Another, told by a railway booking clerk that his ticket would cost ten and six, handed over ten pounds and six shillings. Without the knowledge to enable them to avoid such elementary mistakes, espionage agents have very little chance of survival, and although this sort of ignorance was dangerous enough, the risks were made even greater because they apparently knew nothing of routine security procedures in England.

For example, a Belgian named Alphonse Timmermans did not know that all new arrivals in England were screened by MI5 at an interrogation centre in Battersea which had the rather misleading title of The Royal Victoria Patriotic Asylum for the Orphan Daughters of Soldiers and Sailors Killed in the Crimean War. If he had known, before his arrival in April 1942, he probably would not have carried in his wallet the materials for making invisible ink which he could have bought later, easily enough, at any chemist's shop. His cover story was the by now familiar one of a wanted member of the Resistance, but security officers had learned what genuine *Résistants* were like. They also knew how such men reacted after being on the run from the Gestapo and living under the fear of capture, torture and death. In the case of Timmermans his calmness prompted the detailed search which revealed the little packet of powder, the cotton wool and the thin wooden sticks, like cocktail sticks.

When Pierre Neukermann, another Belgian, arrived just over a year later with the same Resistance story, he did not know that by this time — July 1943 — MI6 had good radio contact with the Belgian Resistance who confirmed the suspicion that he was in fact a notorious collaborator.

Jan Dronkers, a Dutchman, was a little more intelligent. With two compatriots he came across the Channel in a fishing boat, and when interrogated at Battersea by a Dutch intelligence officer, Colonel Pinto, his story sounded convincing. He said the two men with him had come to join the Dutch military units in England—which was true—and he went on to say he was not quite in the same category as they were. With disarming frankness he admitted he had escaped from the German police who wanted him because of highly disreputable black-market activities. He described them. Although finding nothing very attractive about the man he was questioning, Colonel Pinto nevertheless felt he did at least have the moral courage to confess what he had been doing. A few more routine questions were asked, about the trip across the Channel and the fishing boat. Dronkers was hanged a few months later because he said he had bought the boat in Rotterdam, a city very well known to Pinto, from a fisherman he met in a café. He named the café, and Pinto happened to know that the chances of meeting a fisherman in that particular place were so remote as to be negligible.

In the duel between the spy and the counter-espionage expert, only a very exceptional spy can recover and survive after one bad mistake, because the interrogator has been given the opportunity and the advantage he has been looking for. In the motley crowd of men and women who floated down or came ashore to discover where and when the Allies would attack Hitler's Fortress Europe, there was only one man, Hans Sorensen, who was known to be a spy and interrogated at great length but made no mistakes. He provided no evidence which would convince a jury and so spent the rest of the war in an internment camp.

Canaris had considerable problems in his intelligence attack against Britain. In Europe, a spy could slip across a frontier at night; it was not so easy to slip across the Channel, especially while Britain controlled the sea and sky. Even so, the infiltration of agents was not beyond the resources and skill of a man like Canaris and an organization like his Abwehr. Yet, even when a spy is 'in place' and protected by thoroughly plausible cover, his or her troubles are only just beginning. The real problem is always communication. It is sometimes quite easy to get hold of wanted information—it may be only a matter of sitting on a hillside and counting the number of ships in a harbour. The difficulties arise when it has to be conveyed to those who want it, in time for it to be of use to them, without being detected.

In the Second World War urgent information had to be sent out of England across the Channel by radio, and there were no techniques such as 'burst transmission'—passing a message on tape through a transmitter at very high speed so that actual despatch takes only a fraction of a second — and Direction Finding (DF) stations made it possible to locate an agent's radio very rapidly. Agents and their radio sets had to be very mobile.

The failure of Abwehr to place any agents in the United Kingdom had the effect of creating an intelligence void so far as OKW were concerned, yet no one in Germany knew that the void existed. They had good reason to believe they had agents in place, ones that provided valuable information and were entirely satisfactory. They were not aware that all of them were under the strict control of British Intelligence.

The efficiency of the security and secret services, and the 'spy-consciousness' of the people of Britain, created the right conditions for the vast and complex deception schemes formulated under the codenames of Jael, Bodyguard and Fortitude. The German Intelligence void would indeed be filled, and it would be filled with deception. Therein lay the real hope for the success of Overlord, the Allied invasion of France, and in particular, Neptune, the assault phase of Overlord.

All through the war there was a marked difference between the standards of Service Intelligence on the German eastern and western fronts. In *Fremde Heere Ost,* General Gehlen worked in close harmony with Admiral Canaris until the Admiral was retired, and the system devised for the collection of information and the dissemination of the intelligence Gehlen and his staff produced from the raw material, was very effective. His assessments of Russian capabilities and intentions were accurate and timely, but like many other competent intelligence officers he found that only too often his labours were in vain because Hitler, the self-styled military genius, not only refused to believe bad news but would not even listen to it. Even so, Gehlen supplied OKW and formation commanders with accurate and up-to-date facts and figures in his daily intelligence briefings, and everyone knew what was going on. According to General Speidel, Intelligence was not so well organized in the West.

He says that as Rommel's Chief of Staff he had great difficulty in making any assessments of the enemy potential because his headquarters in the Château de la Roche Guyon, on the north bank of the Seine not far from Mantes, received intelligence reports from several different sources. These included OKW, the Supreme Command of the Armed Forces, OKH, the *Oberkommando des Heeres,* the High Command of the Army, and von Roenne's *Fremde Heere West.* The agencies supplying the information from which the summaries were compiled were Abwehr, the SD and the intelligence departments of the Army, Navy and Air Force, who sometimes issued their own reports which contained conflicting opinions.

By the time intelligence reached Speidel it was all third- or fourth-hand, and there was no way of checking it because von Rundstedt had given orders that formations under his command were not to bypass his headquarters and deal direct with the Intelligence Services. Any specific question or requirement had to be sent to OKW. The gaps in military intelligence were large, mainly because it was not only divided into separate compartments for each theatre of war but was also divorced from 'civil' intelligence — what was going on in occupied countries. Thus, although by the winter of 1943/44 Schellenberg's SD was devoting time and energy to the Resistance in France, the military commanders in the field were given no information on its scope or activities, or on the assistance it might give to the Allies during the invasion. Commanders in one theatre of war were not told what was happening in any other; for example Rommel in France was given no information about events in Russia or Italy and, as Speidel says, it was only because Rommel had good friends and connections that he was able to collect a certain amount of military and political intelligence by stealth. 'The telephone', wrote Speidel, 'and other means of contact had to be used with the greatest caution.'

No written technical information on the development of new weapons, jet engines for aircraft or the *schnorkel* for submarines was ever distributed by the Supreme Command, and the only intimation of such things came from Hitler himself who was wont to assure commanders anxious about the Allied threat and the inadequacy of measures to meet it, that Germany's secret weapons would win the war.

The rivalry between intelligence agencies, and the atmosphere of distrust and antipathy, did not change when Schellenberg at last managed to get rid of Canaris and, on paper, merge his SD with Abwehr. It was too late. The traditions and loyalties had taken root and could not be removed overnight by a signature on a departmental instruction, and it does seem that the Germans never really understood the intelligence problems posed by Resistance movements in occupied countries. The SD and the Gestapo were politically motivated. In their opinion the Resistance had to be crushed because it opposed the rule of the Nazis in conquered territory. Its members were rebels who had to be hunted down and shot simply because they were rebels. There was no room for dissidents or Jews in the new German empire, and the evidence for this political attitude lies in the complete lack of any liaison between the Gestapo and the Military Governors who were subordinate to the Commander-in-Chief in the West.

The indications are that the intelligence and security departments of the SS did not really appreciate the military potential of the French Resistance in terms of the sabotage, disruption and guerrilla activity of which they were capable after the battle for France had begun. Possibly they had no great opinion of the courage and determination of Frenchmen who in 1940 had surrendered their country after a campaign of only 42 days; or perhaps any Germans who did see the sabotage threat in perspective may have felt it was too big to tackle. In any event, although they were compassed about with so great a cloud of witnesses that it was virtually impossible to maintain security, they failed to exploit this cloud for purposes of military intelligence. They do not seem to have anticipated that even small bands of Frenchmen cutting telephone cables and railway lines, and blowing up bridges, could create chaos for the Wehrmacht at the moment when success or failure on the battlefield depended on the rapid movement of reserves and reinforcements. Even so, they did appreciate that the Allies would probably make use of the Resistance, although its operational potential was underestimated, and they also realized that if the invasion, the avoidance of very large numbers of French civilian casualties, and the activities of the Resistance were all to be co-ordinated, the Allies would have to tell *les résistants* something of their plans.

Schellenberg and the Gestapo did concentrate on penetrating the Resistance, but in order to eliminate it and not primarily for military intelligence purposes. They did in fact gain vital information on the date of the invasion, but by that time everything was so enveloped in the fog of Allied deception that no use was made of it.

Although the Channel prevented any of the normal operational contacts between enemies facing each other on the ground, the Germans could still collect information from the three main sources of espionage, air reconnaissance and radio interception. So far as military intelligence is concerned, all three are complementary; the information supplied by one can usually be checked by the others, and this is of some importance when trying to cope with enemy deception.

OKW's principal intelligence requirement was the time and place of the invasion, and the answer to this question was likely to be found only in England. The exact time and place were, obviously, secrets known to a very few and difficult to obtain, but there would undoubtedly be 'indicators' from which conclusions could be drawn. For example, the concentration areas of invasion forces would be a clue to the place to be invaded, because a force destined to attack the Pas de Calais would not assemble in Devon and Dorset, and an army that was going to land in Normandy or Brittany would not collect in Kent. An indication of time would be the loading of stores and the embarkation of troops in the vessels of the invasion fleet.

Information of this nature could be obtained by the comparatively simple method of a spy on a bicycle, and what he saw could be checked against air photographs, and vice versa. A spy can see columns of vehicles moving into a port, and he can tell the difference between dummy assembly areas of empty huts and tents and tanks made of rubber or plywood, and ones that are full of troops. A pilot—and his cameras—cannot always make such distinctions, especially if forced to fly very high and harried by anti-aircraft guns and enemy aircraft. The evidence of air photographs and the reports of the pilot and the spy can both be checked against the intelligence obtained from listening to enemy signal traffic.

A skilled intercept analyst can build up an enemy Order of Battle from call-signs and the volume of traffic, since the number of messages put out over a given period by, for instance, an army or corps headquarters differs markedly from that of a brigade or battalion. Using standard direction-finding techniques —the bearings from two or three different DF stations, spaced well apart, will cross at the point where the target is broadcasting—the area, pattern and strength of enemy deployment can be plotted accurately, provided the enemy is not practising deception.

The German Y Service was highly trained and very competent. Their analysis of radio traffic was painstaking and exact and they were alert to all the little nuances that may indicate deception. For example, it is rare that operators can pass a long message without a single request for a group or groups to be repeated. So, when an analyst hears such messages being put out at speed and without a single check, he has good reason to suspect they may be for his benefit. Often it is immaterial whether he can read the signals or not. He soon develops a feel for what is genuine and what is not, although he might not always be able to describe how he can tell the difference.

There is always some danger in contrived breaches of security which are part of a deception plan, because it is a great mistake to underestimate the enemy's analysts who can become expert at spotting deliberate mistakes. Skilled analysts dealing mostly with enciphered messages they cannot read tend to concentrate on the 'handwriting' of enemy operators until they become instantly recognizable. Every operator has an individual and distinctive touch on the Morse key. The analyst who spends much of his time listening to the flicker of Morse in his headset soon associates 'handwriting' with call signs and is likely to detect what is happening at once if an operator tries to simulate several different stations as part of a design for radio deception.

The Germans were reasonably confident that their agents in England, in whom they placed great trust, their Y Service and their reconnaissance pilots would, between them, discover the D-Day information, and even if they failed, there were still two other possible sources: a breach of security and the French Resistance.

Breaches of security can happen at any time, through carelessness, a momentary lapse which is the result of fatigue or overwork, or just bad luck, and the ever-present possibility is a constant nightmare to security staffs. The Resistance was a source because of the instructions which had to be given to its leaders by coded radio messages which the Germans would intercept. If by penetrating the Resistance groups they discovered the code, they would have time to alert the coastal-defence units on the Atlantic Wall, and the Panzer units behind it, whose intervention in the early stages might be decisive. They did discover the code and identified the final alert warning. Von Rundstedt refused to believe that Eisenhower would announce on the radio that he was coming.

Deception, if it is to be convincing, must be conveyed by many different means working in concert but, human nature being what it is, intelligence officers are more likely to believe the reports of spies they regard as thoroughly trustworthy than evidence from air photographs or radio interceptions, both of which can be suspect. For this reason the double agents operating in Britain were of crucial importance to the success of Neptune and Overlord.

6
British Intelligence

British Intelligence has, for centuries, been regarded by continental nations as uncomfortably efficient. Philip II complained bitterly that his most secret instructions to his naval and military commanders engaged in assembling and equipping the Armada were read by Sir Francis Walsingham and Queen Elizabeth I, and then leaked to his own courtiers who discussed them before he had time to issue them himself. The first Duke of Marlborough remarked that a diplomat could not sneeze in Vienna without word of it reaching him. When the de Witt brothers were ruling Holland in the seventeenth century, British agents run by Sir George Downing were wont to take the brothers' keys from their pockets while they slept, extract and copy documents in their safes, and pass Dutch secrets to England for the benefit of Charles II—who seldom showed much interest. One of the greatest tributes to British Intelligence and Security was paid by Sagredo, the Venetian Ambassador at the time when John Thurloe was in charge of Oliver Cromwell's intelligence organization. 'There is no government on earth,' he wrote, 'which divulges its affairs less than England, or is more punctually informed of those of the others.'

Sir Francis Walsingham, who died in 1590, was the true founder of the counter-intelligence and security organization that was to become MI5 and it was also he who put on a proper footing the overseas espionage service that became MI6. The fortunes of both passed through good and bad times in the succeeding centuries but no one really doubted the need for them—in some form or another. It is therefore perhaps a little surprising that the general standard of Military Intelligence should have been so very different from its 'civilian' counterparts.

Many British commanders in the past shared the view of officers of the Prussian General Staff, that there is something unchivalrous about intelligence and despicable about espionage. Though some sort of intelligence system has had to be set up in every war, there has always been a rush to get rid of it as soon as the last shot was fired. The result has been that most of the knowledge and expertise gained on active service were lost. This certainly happened after the Crimean, Boer and First World Wars. Between the First and Second World Wars, Military Intelligence was reduced to a small department in the War Office which consisted of a few officers and clerks, none of whom had any formal intelligence training because there was no school which provided it. Had it not been for the foresight and energy of Major Templer (later Field Marshall Sir Gerald) in the War Office, and his personal efforts in the few months between the Munich Crisis of 1938 and the outbreak of war in September 1939, there would have been virtually no military intelligence organization in the British Army at the time when Hitler sent the Wehrmacht into Poland.

A military intelligence staff must have a sound and detailed background knowledge of the armed forces of the enemy, his capabilities, intentions, tactics, organization, strength, vulnerabilities, and so on, because their principal function is to forecast what the enemy is going to do, and where, when, how and in what strength he will do it. As Colonel Furse wrote in his book *Information in War* as long ago as 1895, the ability to do this cannot be acquired overnight. The setting-up of an effective intelligence service is a long, difficult and delicate process, and fortunately this is a point that has always been appreciated by the Foreign Office.

The theories and practices of the great spymasters such as Walsingham, Cardinal Richelieu, Thurloe, and Fouché have not been forgotten, even though they may not always be acknowledged, and despite the financial stringency between the wars, which affected MI5 and MI6 just as much as the armed services, the intelligence and counter-intelligence organization remained in being.

A considerable intelligence asset, common to all nations and exploited by most of them in varying degrees, is the Diplomatic Corps, for one of its functions is to keep the home government informed on events and developments in the countries to which embassies and legations are accredited. Service attachés in particular were long ago described as 'accredited spies', and diplomatic representation, in general, has always provided cover and offered scope for clandestine espionage activities. The Russians have acquired a reputation for taking advantage of this. In the first decade of the twentieth century Colonel Zantiewitz had to leave Vienna at short notice, and Colonel Michelsen and Bazarov were escorted to the German frontier from Berlin. Since then, the list of Russian diplomats declared *persona non grata* has become a long one. They were not the only ones to make use of opportunities. While serving as an attaché in Turkey, Major (later Lord) Kitchener secretly made maps of Palestine which were of great value to Allenby in his campaign of 1917, 30 years later. Colonel Baron Stoffel was the French military attaché in Berlin from 1866 to 1870, and in 1871 he published his *Rapports Militaires, Ecrits de Berlin* which show that he was an extraordinarily efficient and industrious spy. It is sad that so little heed was paid to his warnings.

Diplomatic means of access make it possible for any nation to establish espionage networks in a foreign country, and when war or some other upheaval causes the severance of diplomatic relations, it does not necessarily mean that all covert connections are cut. There may well be problems, especially over communications, but if the network has been carefully arranged, well-placed sources can continue to provide useful information.

When war was declared in 1939, Britain had considerable advantages over the Germans in espionage, notably after the fall of France. Inside Germany there were Germans who, like Canaris, were loyal to the Fatherland but not to Hitler. They were the secret force opposing Nazism in the hope of saving Germany. With a few exceptions—William Joyce was one—the British, and the Americans who came to Britain, had only one motive—to win the war. Even Joyce was not a spy. Of Irish parentage and born in Brooklyn, he went to Germany before the war began and from September 1939 until 1945 broadcast from Radio Hamburg the propaganda put out by Goebbels. He was tried, convicted and executed for treason after the war.

Apart from the fact that British and American secret services were far better organized than those of the Germans, the training was meticulous and comprehensive, but the greatest advantage of all was the considerable field for recruitment among the people of occupied countries who had no love for the Germans. The feeling against them was strongest in France where the capitulation of 1940 piled fuel on the embers albeit widely scattered but still glowing after the German invasions of 1870 and 1914.

Thus, although at the beginning of the war there was a certain amateurishness about the British military organization, this was not of great importance. Lack of an experienced intelligence staff with the field formations of the British Expeditionary Force undoubtedly had an adverse effect on operations when the *Blitzkrieg* began in May 1940, but in the light of German superiority in ground and air forces, and the collapse of allies, it had no real influence on the outcome. When the British military forces had to leave the continent, many sources of information remained behind, so there was never any concern about the future of espionage.

Of the two other principal sources, air reconnaissance and radio interception, air reconnaissance presented no serious problems after the defeat of Goering's

Luftwaffe in the Battle of Britain, and the exploitation of enemy signal traffic had a profound effect on the planning and conduct of Allied operations throughout the war.

There is nothing new about collecting information from enemy communications. It goes back to the very beginning of warfare, to the waylaying of the runner or rider carrying a message. One of the first practitioners of electronic-signal intelligence was a young man named J. O. Kerbey, in the American Civil War. He was a supporter of the Union cause who tapped the Confederate telegraph lines in Richmond, Virginia, and sent information by letter to Federal headquarters in Washington through a secret system devised by the famous spy, Elizabeth van Lew.

The use of codes and ciphers added problems to line-tapping, but there was nothing new about them, either. Alexander the Great used a code for all messages that had to be sent through hostile territory, but it was not until the First World War, and the use of radio in all ships and all formation headquarters of ground forces, that ciphers became so important. The affair of the Zimmerman Telegram taught the Germans a sharp lesson about the need for ones that were unbreakable. (The ability of Admiral 'Blinker' Hall, Head of Naval Intelligence, to read the Telegram and so discover Germany's intentions towards the United States, was instrumental in bringing America into the war against Germany.) Thus, when he came to power, it was only natural that Hitler, who had no illusions about the need for secrecy and security, should take a careful look at German diplomatic and military ciphers—which the British had been decrypting for years. In 1934, MI6 learned that all these ciphers were being replaced by an entirely new system, and the discovery of what it was became a priority espionage target.

The story of the Enigma Machine, the Turing 'Bomb'—the computer used for decoding messages transmitted on the Enigma Machine—and Ultra, the codename given to the signal intelligence derived from Enigma-enciphered radio transmissions, has been told in great detail and need not be repeated here. However, the ability of Station X at Bletchley Park to read messages in a cipher made infinitely variable by mechanical means, and therefore, in the opinion of the Germans, outside the scope of even the most expert cryptologists, underlines the intelligence principle that sources must be protected—which becomes vitally important when great reliance has to be placed on one special source. For obvious reasons this is dangerous and wherever possible is avoided in intelligence practice. If the source is suddenly compromised or disappears, the intelligence service is left in darkness, and a comparable source may be very difficult to find.

In the case of Ultra, all this was realized by General Sir Stewart Menzies who, on the death of Admiral Sir Hugh Sinclair, became the temporary head of MI6 in November 1939. He fully appreciated the basic facts about signal intelligence. First, that ability to read enemy communications provides knowledge not only of what the enemy intends to do but what he is actually going to do, *before* he does it. Secondly, that this source of information will continue to exist only while the enemy has no reason to suspect that his cipher has been broken. Accordingly, Menzies set up a security system of Special Liaison Units (SLUs) manned by MI6 personnel who handled all Ultra material, and under the control of Wing Commander F. W. Winterbotham, security was so effective that despite several alarums and excursions the Germans never knew that their 'unbreakable' mechanical cipher had been penetrated.

Inevitably there were disadvantages in maintaining so high a degree of security. For instance, before the German attack on Crete—Operation Mercury—in 1941, British and Commonwealth commanders on the spot were told by London what was going to happen, but they were not given the source of the information. Not surprisingly, they were sceptical, seeing no reason why London, so far from the theatre of operations, should have better information than theirs. In military history there are countless illustrations of how difficult it is to persuade senior commanders in the field to believe a report which contradicts or conflicts with their own considered opinion.

Operation Mercury was successful, although the toll taken of German airborne forces was so great that they never again operated effectively as such. Churchill ordered an inquiry, and as a result the rules governing Ultra material were modified so that in future the authenticity of it would not be questioned.

MI6, the secret service responsible among other things for the control of espionage on the continent now overrun by the Germans, was now also in charge of the security of radio interception, one of the most fruitful sources of intelligence throughout the war, and because of the 30-year rule governing the release of highly classified material, the part it played in winning the war is only just becoming known.

MI6 came into being in 1911, under the control of Captain Mansfield Smith-Cumming, the original 'C', a sailor who had lost a leg and had the disconcerting habit of digging a paper-knife into the cork replacement to emphasize points in conversation. He was followed by Admiral Sinclair, and Menzies was confirmed in his appointment as Sinclair's successor at the end of 1939. Government neglect of the intelligence services after the First World War had considerably reduced the strength and capabilities of MI6 although some financial transfusions were made at the time of the investigation of Enigma and the building of Alan Turing's decrypting machine between 1936 and 1939, but it was not until the Second World War was imminent that Admiral Sinclair, though dying of cancer, was able to revive and reorganize his department. Menzies built it into a large, complex and efficient secret espionage system.

The centre of the crest of the modern Joint School of Photographic Interpretation is a dove on the wing with a sprig of olive in its beak, thus acknowledging that Noah was the pioneer of air reconnaissance. During the First World War its potential was developed by men like Lieutenant Moore-Brabazon (later Lord Brabazon of Tara) who took photographs of enemy positions with a hand-held camera while rifle and machine-gun bullets from the ground ripped through canvas wings and fuselage.

The great advantage of the camera is that it stops time. The print made from exposed film reveals what has been 'seen' by the lens at a particular moment, and the picture can be enlarged and examined meticulously in three dimensions through a stereoscope. Things that the pilot may not have seen, for example, the faint track made by men moving in and out of a camouflaged position, the marks of wheels or tank tracks on the edge of a wood, or signs of recent digging, show up clearly; but they created a need for a new skill—Photographic Interpretation (PI).

The first successful experiments in aerial photography were made by an ingenious and enterprising Royal Engineer officer named Major Elsdale, when he was serving in Canada in 1883. He attached cameras, fitted with clockwork mechanisms to operate the shutters at predetermined times, to tethered balloons, and according to Captain Hamish Eaton who has written the history of Army Photographic Interpretation, his vertical photograph of Halifax Citadel, taken at 1,450 feet, is still preserved. In May 1908, another Sapper officer, Lieutenant Vyvyan Thomson, developed stereoscopic photography to the point of being able to give an illustrated lecture on the subject to the Royal Geographical Society; but apparently no one appreciated the military applications of his ideas.

In 1909 air photography was lifted out of the balloon age by a Frenchman, M. Meurisse, who took pictures of Mourmelon airfield from the cockpit of an Antoinette aeroplane, and two years later, the French Army made good use of airborne cameras during operations in Morocco. In England, the pilots of No. 3 Squadron, Royal Flying Corps, were the first to develop aerial photographic reconnaissance, in 1912, the year in which a photographic section was established as part of No. 1 Airship Squadron, Royal Flying Corps, at Farnborough. The 3 Squadron pilots bought their own cameras and devised a system of processing the film while in the air. With great enthusiasm they took the results of their work to the War Office early in 1914, and were told that the pictures they had taken—of the defences of the Isle of Wight and Solent—were quite interesting but of little value because all the information was shown rather more clearly on the ordinary Ordnance maps.

However, when war began in August 1914, one of the functions of the Photographic Section at Farnborough was to train Photographic Officers for the Royal Flying Corps, and the Section became a School when the Royal Air Force was formed in 1918. The techniques of air photography improved a great deal during the First World War, and when the initial prejudice against the unsporting practice of photographing the enemy's back yard had been overcome, the demand for photographic reconnaissance increased to such an extent that considerable problems arose over interpreting the prints. It became apparent that the pilot who took the photographs was not necessarily able to assess the significance of what was in his pictures, but it was not until 1924 that an Army officer was posted to the School to teach the Army aspect of PI within the Royal Air Force. However, in December 1916 Major General (later Lord) Trenchard's proposal that each formation of the Royal Flying Corps should have its own intelligence section was approved and came into effect soon afterwards.

By 1924 the School of Photography was running nine-month courses for RAF photographic officers who flew their own reconnaissance sorties and still developed and printed their films themselves, but the first Manual of Photographic Interpretation, written by Captain Churchill MC of the Manchester Regiment, was not published until 1939.

Between the wars the PI skill gained in the First World War might have been lost had not a few enthusiasts kept it alive in remote corners of the Empire, such as Miranshah and Peshawar on the North-West Frontier of India. The Germans understood the importance of aerial photography and interpretation. In 1938 General von Fritsch said that 'the military organization with the most efficient photographic reconnaissance will win the next war', but no doubt his beliefs were discredited when he himself was disgraced, because in the Wehrmacht, photographic interpretation was regarded as a menial task suitable only for NCOs. Furthermore, German photographic interpreters were not issued with stereoscopic equipment. They had to work with an ordinary magnifying glass, and without a three-dimensional view they had great difficulty in estimating height or the shape of ground. Moreover, there was no properly organized or centralized photographic interpretation system and the work was limited mainly to the immediately tactical needs of ground forces.

In England the Photographic Interpretation Unit was formed at Wembley early in 1940, and this had a training section which ran two-week courses for PIs, but as the result of a German air raid at the beginning of 1941 the PI Unit moved to Medmenham, where it became the Central Interpretation Unit. The training section went first to Harrow, then back to its parent unit at Medmenham and finally, because of the shortage of accommodation, to Nuneham Park near Oxford where, as the School of Photographic Interpretation, it remained until the end of the war.

Medmenham became the centre of air photographic intelligence, and in March 1942 a new department known as R Section, operating under strict security cover, was formed to give photographic intelligence support to the new Combined Operations organization. The Section's first task was a study of St Nazaire, for the raid in March 1942, and the operation was planned on a detailed model. All the information required for making it was obtained from air photographs. The Dieppe raid was also planned from a model, and those built for Neptune showed the exact shape of the ground, fields, hedges, buildings, trees, all German fortifications and strong points, the landing beaches and the drop zones for the airborne forces. They were used for briefing the assault troops just before D-Day.

This form of briefing added considerably to the photographic interpreter's responsibilities. For instance, when Lieutenant MacBride of the Intelligence Corps said he could not be certain whether a German battery position on the coast of Holland was occupied or not, because details in the photograph were somewhat obscured by thin cloud, the Dutch insisted on dropping an agent by parachute to make sure.

'This,' said Lieutenant MacBride, 'taught me a sharp lesson about my responsibilities.'

Early in 1943 a special 'B2' Section was added to the Central Interpretation Unit at Medmenham, and its task was to pin-point the launching sites of German secret weapons. Very little was known about them, but it was believed they would take the form of a missile of some sort, fired from large tubes or barrels located perhaps in disused mineshafts. Certain works were seen near Calais, but these did not fit the imprecise specifications, reported by agents, of the so-called *Vergeltung* (retaliation, reprisal) weapon that would be able to bombard London from the other side of the Channel. A very careful watch was kept on all activity of this sort.

By the beginning of June 1944, 1,093,500 prints of air photographs had been used in the preparation for Neptune, and special maps at a scale of 1:25,000 overprinted with complete details of the Atlantic Wall defence system, were issued to all assault units.

The enormous importance of the part played by the Unit at Medmenham, the School at Nuneham Park, and the Air Photograph Interpretation Sections (APIS) in all theatres of war has not always been realized or acknowledged, but, for good reasons, air photographic reconnaissance by manned aircraft is largely a complementary and confirmatory source. It is impossible to maintain regular photographic surveillance over a vast area of enemy territory in the hope that from literally millions of prints the PIs will be able to extract new and valuable information. Aircraft are vulnerable and the wastage of men and machines would be unacceptable. Because of this, air photography should normally be a check on information received from another source, and thereafter a means of watching developments. In relation to the Atlantic Wall it was ideal for confirming the reports of agents on the ground and watching the progress made by the Todt Building Organization.

Even so, it had its limitations, not only because a pilot and his cameras can be deceived by good camouflage but also because air reconnaissance cannot supply certain details which may be of great importance; for example, the underwater gradient and load-bearing capacity of a beach, the composition of beach obstacles, the thickness of concrete forming the roof of a gun emplacement, or the range of coastal artillery. Information of this sort can only be obtained by someone in much closer contact with the 'intelligence targets'.

In espionage, radio interception and air reconnaissance the organization and resources of the Allies were far superior to, and more fruitful than, those of the Germans, largely because very soon after Churchill assumed responsibility for running the war—on 10 May 1940—he resuscitated the Joint Intelligence Committee (JIC). This was the controlling body of a centralized intelligence system; something that Schellenberg and Himmler knew was essential but failed to achieve.

When Churchill first came to power he gave instructions that all intelligence reports were to be shown to him; perhaps he wished to emulate his famous ancestor who had run his own political and military intelligence systems. But Marlborough's communications operated at the speed of the horse. Winston Churchill soon found that he could not cope with the mass of material and it was far better to delegate such matters to the JIC.

No matter how good Intelligence may be, it cannot by itself win a battle or a war. It is only a service to commanders, to assist them in making decisions, and the Intelligence tail must never be allowed to wag the Operations dog. Its function is to provide the commander and his operations staff with the answers to their questions—in connection with the enemy, not with our own troops.

When making preparations for Overlord the Joint Planning Staff told the Joint Intelligence Committee what intelligence they needed, and when it had been provided, the planners had to decide what use they would make of it, and the degree to which it would influence the making of their plans. They did not, naturally, ignore intelligence estimates based on entirely reliable sources such as Ultra. Hitler lost the war because, as the supreme planning authority in Germany, he ignored the advice of his intelligence staff—he finally dismissed General Reinhard Gehlen for telling the unpalatable truth.

At the beginning of 1944 Hitler and Goering, who had once boasted that his invincible Luftwaffe would not allow a single bomb to fall on German soil, were both living mainly in a world of fantasy. Hitler refused to listen to reason and became transfigured by demoniacal rage if contradicted or opposed, and it is said that Goering spent much of his time in his country mansion of Karinhall, his corpulence swathed in the toga of a Roman senator, out of touch with what was going on outside and refusing requests by army commanders for help or co-operation from the Luftwaffe. Himmler too, lived in his own little world, convinced that he was the reincarnation of Heinrich I, one of the Germanic tribal 'kings' of the eleventh century, and Goebbels had reached the stage of believing his own lies. Germany was in the hands of very peculiar people who knew but would not admit that the Third Reich, which was to have lasted for a thousand years, was about to perish. Guilty of the most appalling crimes against humanity, conscious that the tide of victory had turned, they tried to believe that insoluble problems, if ignored, will solve themselves.

The Allied cause was in the hands of realists who could see clearly what had to be done, whose misgivings were based primarily on the cost, in blood, and in their calculations, intelligence and deception were the only means of reducing it. High on their list of intelligence targets was the Atlantic Wall, and it first appeared on this list in March 1942, when Hitler issued Directive No. 40. This gave orders for the building of a continuous line of fortifications, from the North Cape in the Arctic Circle to Hendaye, where the Bidassoa river, flowing down through the Pyrenees, falls into the Gulf of Gascony.

Just over a year later, in May 1943, Colonel Rémy of the French Resistance Group Confrérie Notre-Dame arranged for intelligence officers in London to be presented with a map, drawn by the Todt Organization, of the coastal area between Cherbourg and le Havre. It was a blueprint of the Wall in the area where the Allies were to land.

The large-scale map showed in great detail all the machine-gun posts, trench systems, gun emplacements and battery positions that were to be constructed. It gave all the technical specifications such as ranges and fields of fire, the

layout of communications and command posts, and the location of ammunition and supply dumps. The immediate reaction in London was to congratulate
the Colonel on a remarkable espionage feat and privately to regret that such a
magnificent achievement would be of no practical value. There was no doubt
at all that as soon as the loss was discovered the whole plan would be completely
altered.

There are many conflicting details in accounts of how it was acquired, but it
seems clear that it was taken from the office of *Bauleiter* Schnedderer in the
Avenue Bagatelle in Caen by a painter and decorator named René Duchez,
who was also a member of Resistance Group Centurie. The theft was not
planned, luck played a very large part in it, and the story is an illustration of
the quickness of reaction, resourcefulness and courage needed by an espionage
agent if he is to be successful. Yet Duchez was not a professional spy; he was a
patriot and an opportunist, always on the look-out for useful information.

At the beginning of May 1943 Duchez saw an advertisement posted up
outside the *Mairie* in Caen and it invited tenders for the redecoration of an
office in the local headquarters of the Todt Organization. Duchez applied for
the job, quoting a price low enough to make certain of getting it, simply because
it would give him a chance to look round inside the headquarters. The office
was the one occupied by *Bauleiter* Schnedderer. Duchez' bid was accepted,
taking his pattern book he went to see Schnedderer and they discussed what
would be suitable. While they were talking, a clerk came in and put several
files and papers in the *Bauleiter's* tray.

Schnedderer said he could not make up his mind between blue horsemen on
a light yellow background and silver cannon on dark blue paper. In the
meantime he had to go to a meeting but Duchez could get on with any necessary
preliminary work. The meeting would only take a few minutes. While the
Bauleiter was out of the office, Duchez looked at the papers in the tray. On the
top of the pile was one marked *Sonderzeichnungen – Streng Geheim* (Special
Blueprint – Strictly Secret) and Duchez realized it was the Todt plan for
fortifications along the Calvados coast. Acting on the spur of the moment, he
hid the map behind a large looking-glass hanging on the wall. Very soon
afterwards Schnedderer returned, chose the wallpaper he wanted and told
Duchez he could start work on the following Monday.

When he came back with all his equipment, paper and paste, Duchez was
informed that Schnedderer had gone to St Malo, no one knew anything about
papering the building manager's office and nothing could be done for at least a
week. Duchez' loud protests were heard by one of Schnedderer's deputies, a
man named Keller, who wanted to know what all the fuss was about. Duchez

explained, and offered to paper Keller's office for nothing if he could just be allowed to get on with his work. In due course he retrieved the map, concealed it in a roll of wallpaper and walked out without being searched by the guard. Within a few days the map was in Paris, where it was copied, and the master was flown to London by the MI6 communications system based on the Convent of St. Agonie. The copy remained in France to be used as the basis for the work Centurie was doing in mapping the whole of the Wall from Trouville westwards to Cherbourg. This was only a routine espionage task because it had not yet been definitely decided where the Allies would land.

Meanwhile, Schnedderer and his staff in Caen were so appalled by the loss of the secret blueprint, and the probable consequences for them all if the Gestapo were to hear about it, that they covered everything up. It was easy enough to replace the map because like most engineering drawings it had been reproduced on blue cartographic paper. MI6 doubts about its value were soon proved to be unfounded by reports from agents which were confirmed by air reconnaissance.

René Duchez' acquisition was indeed of great value to Allied Intelligence, but it was only an initial plan which could be changed, and for many reasons there could be differences between the original concept on paper and the completed work on the ground. It was therefore of extreme importance to keep a careful check on the actual building of the Wall, and this was done by the host of agents in France, working through Resistance Groups and MI6.

7
Espionage in France

Intelligence is so closely allied to deception that anyone working in a wartime intelligence organization soon develops the habit of looking for confirmation of every incident, report and fact, preferably by several independent sources, before accepting it as possibly true. Even then, he or she may still have a lurking suspicion that what seems to be genuine enough might be part of an enemy deception plan. Sources may have been 'turned', agencies may have been penetrated, and it is never wise to underestimate the skill, ingenuity, tenacity and ruthlessness of enemy intelligence and counter-intelligence services. Therefore, in gathering information about the Atlantic Wall the Allied intelligence organization did not rely solely on reports from agents in France, and collection was divided under the four general headings of espionage, beach reconnaissance, air reconnaissance and the interception of signal traffic.

Espionage in France was conducted on lines somewhat similar to the sales and collection methods of the famous Prudential Assurance Company, especially before the war, when the 'Man from the Pru' became so well known a figure. He spent much of his time going round from house to house in his appointed area, on foot or on a bicycle, selling insurance and collecting the weekly payments on the policies he had sold. He knew his area, the people in it and what went on, possibly even better than the local policeman whose beat was relatively much smaller. The French Resistance Groups collected information in much the same way as 'The Pru' collected its premiums. Sectors of the Atlantic Wall were allotted to individuals who went round regularly to all the local inhabitants encouraging them to speak of anything they had seen or heard which might perhaps be of interest to the Allies who, when the time came, would liberate France and drive the Germans back behind the Rhine.

The people interviewed could hardly be called spies. They made little or no conscious effort to gather information, for the good reason that it was an extremely dangerous pastime. The whole coastal area of the Wall had been declared a Prohibited Zone; it was patrolled by troops at all hours of the day and night, and temporary check points and road blocks were set up on major and minor roads without warning. German troops billeted in villages and isolated farm houses were soon able to recognize the locals, and any stranger was likely to be picked up for questioning. No stranger, however good and authentic his reason for being in the area, could afford to loiter for long enough to learn much about, for instance, a battery position, but the farmers who owned the land on which the batteries had been built, at places like Morsalines, St-Marcouf, Azeville, le Mesnil and Merville, saw them every day and often enough had to provide food and lodging for one or more of the gun crews who manned them.

Many of the gun crews were middle-aged men, anything from 45 to 56, who, like the farmers on whom they were billeted, had been through the horrors of the First World War and had this bond in common. In many cases it was no hardship to have a courteous old *Feldwebel* (Sergeant-major) of the Wehrmacht in the half-circle round the kitchen fire. Over a glass of calvados or marc the farmer and the soldier talked of the past, of their present troubles, of the futility of the war as a means of deciding anything, and when the man from the Resistance came round, he could be told all sorts of things; and the man from the Resistance could be the friendly neighbour apparently dropping in for a chat, the postman, the gas- or electricity-meter reader, the doctor, or even the local policeman.

Even today the people who lived close to the Wehrmacht units in the Cotentin peninsula stress that the behaviour of Wehrmacht troops was *'très correct'*– perhaps mainly because Rommel would not have it otherwise – and where there are good relationships there is normally a flow of information. (The soldiers of SS units were in quite a different category.) The middle-aged *Feldwebel* and his like probably did not regard their fireside conversations as being of any military importance at all. They spoke of the habitual drunkenness of the Battery Commander at Merville, of the difficulty of communicating with soldiers who had no other language but Russian, of the sickness rate in units manned by invalids from the eastern front, of the unfamiliar mechanism of the captured French artillery in the emplacements, and the lack of fire control equipment. They complained that the great steel protective doors for the front of the emplacements still hadn't arrived from Germany, that some of the machine gun posts sited by the Todt engineers were nothing but death-traps.

Individually, such items did not amount to very much, but they all flowed back, through the Resistance and MI6 to the intelligence cell in London's Oxford Street known as the Martians. This was the organization set up by the Chief of Staff, Supreme Allied Commander (COSSAC) and Supreme Headquarters, Allied Expeditionary Force (SHAEF) to collect, process and disseminate, strictly on the 'need to know' principle, all information and intelligence on the German defence of Europe.

To the Martians, the thousands of little items of information were all pieces of the vast jig-saw puzzle which, when assembled would provide a comprehensive picture. Although the reports of eye-witnesses and eavesdroppers are seldom entirely reliable because of the ordinary human failings of exaggeration or understatement, or because of fear and other emotional strain, and also because of a general tendency to report not what is actually seen but what one thinks one sees, when collated by experts so great a mass of material does yield remarkably accurate intelligence.

From the personal observation of all these informants — Gilles Perrault claims there were 50,000 of them, all along the Wall — it was possible to build up an extremely detailed survey of the enemy as people, with all their strengths and weaknesses, assets and shortcomings, faults and advantages, and the real importance of this was that soldiers who *know* their enemy cease to be afraid of him. The taut apprehension that so often precedes a battle is compounded more of fear of the unknown than of death, and it is fear of the unknown that can have so adverse an effect on the morale of soldiers.

For example, it was of the greatest help to the paratroopers earmarked for the silencing of the Merville battery in the early hours of D-Day not only to have intimate details of its commander and his troops, but also to be able to practise their attack and rehearse all the movements of it on an exact reconstruction of the battery set up months before on a training ground in England.

However, the analogy of building up an intelligence picture is not a particularly good one because a picture can be finished. Intelligence is continuous and therefore the picture is never complete. Moreover, it may not be entirely accurate and there may be blank spots. This was true of the D-Day picture, as will be seen. There were gaps in the information which had dire consequences.

It must not be assumed that the French Resistance, which supplied so many of the espionage agents who collected information sent to England through MI6 channels, was dedicated solely to the cause of Allied victory and the consequent liberation of France. Its aims stretched far beyond Overlord and were primarily political. The leaders of the Resistance were confident that sooner or later the Allies would drive the Germans out, and as soon as the German political administration, functioning through the so-called Vichy Government, ceased to exist, there would be a political vacuum. Whoever filled that vacuum, whoever seized the opportunity to exploit the chaos left behind when the Germans went, would rule France — perhaps for many years. There would be rich prizes for the political party which could eliminate competition and be ready, when the time came, to move in as the new government of France.

When General Charles de Gaulle was brought out of France by MI6 in 1940 the Allies assumed he was the leader of the Resistance, and no more than that. Subsequently the Vichy Government declared him to be an outlaw, a deserter and a traitor and sentenced him to death in his absence. What the Allies did not know at that time was that de Gaulle, solitary, arrogant, abrasive and ungrateful, regarded himself as the one man alive who could restore France to her former glory and greatness. He was not the personification of resistance but of renaissance. His aim was to rule France. But the Communist movement in France was just as determined to seize power as was de Gaulle, and the Communists were well aware that while they were on the spot and de Gaulle was in England, they had the advantage.

Things might have been easier for the Allies if the French Resistance had consisted of just the two factions, de Gaullistes and Communists, but there were many different types of *résistant*: the Catholics and the Protestants, loyalists, Breton secessionists, the followers of Marshal Pétain, and various others. Each party had its own aims and loyalties and there was no centralized system of control or organization. Inevitably there was confusion and dangerous duplication. For instance, Group Sosies sent an agent named La Bardonnie to collect information in the Cherbourg area without apparently knowing that Group Centurie had a *reseau* (network) of more than a hundred there already.

Some agents worked for two or more Resistance Groups simultaneously; Charles Douin, a sculptor, and a fisherman named Thomine belonged to both Centurie and Alliance without the leaders of either group being aware of it.

In effect, by ignoring the intelligence principle of centralized control, all the Resistance *reseaux* made themselves vulnerable to penetration by counter-intelligence agents employed by the Germans — usually *les collaborateurs* — and Colonel Hermann Giskes of Abwehr, whose area of responsibility was Holland, Belgium and northern France, was able to create havoc. Even so, although he managed to 'clean up' the whole of Alliance, force the remnants of Centurie to scatter and disappear, and send dozens of *résistants* to torture and execution by the Gestapo, it was not until the spring of 1944 that his counter-espionage campaign in France began to have any real success. By then it was too late; most of the espionage work had been done. The intelligence 'picture' of the Atlantic Wall was virtually complete, in relation to the static defences, and there was little more for the spies to do except keep London up to date with the dispositions of its German garrison and reserves. Previously the Germans had concentrated more on stamping out the Resistance than penetrating it.

Espionage has always been a risky business, and a spy is more likely to find his or her career coming to an abrupt end than receive much material benefit from it. Yet there never seems to be any shortage of recruits, and the motives which prompt them to undertake so hazardous an occupation are many and varied. The most common is money; many people seem to have the erroneous idea that espionage is well paid; others are motivated by jealousy, a desire for revenge, patriotism, loyalty to some political or other ideology; some are the victims of blackmail. Some become spies because they are stimulated by danger, are adventurous by nature, are reluctant to settle down to any routine task and have an entirely false idea of the glamour and excitement of espionage as portrayed by writers of fiction.

Many Frenchmen working for the Resistance found a lot of satisfaction in tricking and making fools of the Germans they hated, others simply wanted to kill the invaders, often for purely personal reasons of revenge, but virtually all of them shared a somewhat cloudy and confused aim of somehow restoring the honour and glory of France. Unfortunately, and largely because of the rival political factions seeking power when the war was over, for every loyal and brave *résistant* there was more than one *collaborateur* ready to be useful to German counter-intelligence.

In these circumstances men like René Duchez took immense risks because they were untrained amateurs operating against the ruthless professionals in Abwehr, the SD and the Gestapo. Duchez adopted the 'cover' of an obliging simpleton, anxious to help the Germans where he could and willing to demonstrate his goodwill—hence the offer to paper the walls of Keller's office for nothing. He and another agent, Henri Marigny, joined the Civil Defence organization at Ouistreham, near the mouth of the river Orne. The Germans looked on them as collaborators, but while Allied bombers were overhead and the Germans were in their air-raid shelters, René and Henri had considerable freedom of movement among German defence works.

As a freelance painter and decorator, René Duchez could spend much of his time in cafés frequented by men working for the Todt Organization. He was wont to argue about building methods, concrete mixes and reinforcement, giving his dogmatic opinion and then listening with apparent reluctance while his old-fashioned ideas were ridiculed in the light of modern processes. Often it was difficult to make him understand and so the point would have to be explained in a brief sketch drawn on an old envelope or a bit of paper Duchez happened to have in his pocket. At weekends Duchez would take a party of boys and girls for bicycle rides along the coast, and the Germans, who gave their approval for this form of healthy exercise arranged for the younger generation, knew nothing of the rolled maps concealed in the handlebars of the leader's elderly machine.

Eventually, in April 1944, Duchez was betrayed and the dreaded black.Citroen of the Gestapo drove up to his house. The story is that the secret police found only Madame Duchez trying to cope with an infuriated and insulting client of her husband who was refusing, at the top of his voice, to pay for bad workmanship. After a brief struggle, the Gestapo threw him out, not knowing it was Duchez himself, and because they could not find the man they wanted, they sent his wife to Mauthausen concentration camp.

When La Bardonnie from the Dordogne was sent by Group Sosies to Cherbourg he disguised himself as a priest because the comings and goings of priests at all hours of the day and night can be accounted for by normal religious duties, visits to the sick and dying, and so on. His disguise was penetrated, not by any hostile agent but by certain devout Catholics who suspected he was not what he said he was and so had no right to hear confession. Warned by a genuine priest he quietly disappeared.

Charles Douin, the sculptor, was a slightly deranged Royalist. He hated the English on the grounds that they had been responsible for the Revolution which destroyed the *ancien régime,* and therefore were also responsible for the execution of Louis XVI — in his opinion, the last of the real kings of France. When it was suggested to him that he could be a collector of valuable information for the Allies he rejected the whole idea. On the other hand he was perfectly prepared to be a spy for 'the King of France'. He travelled round to old churches in coastal towns and villages restoring statues and monuments, having long talks with local incumbents and gazing at the countryside from towers and steeples. His artist's eye noted with exactitude such things as newly-turned earth, fresh concrete and the gleam of barbed wire in the sun — and before the war his hobby had been cartography.

There were many of these amateurs. Doctor Sustendal had a large number of patients in the Todt Organization and so was issued with a permit allowing him to move about after curfew. He could visit anyone at any time, and he could pass on what patients told him. A certain M. Cardron owned a fishing boat that was not very seaworthy, so he had to ply his trade close to the land, and to the coastal defences. His nets were old and seemed to need constant repairs which took some time as he drifted gently along. Hidden in the nets was a camera. M. Thomine, another fisherman, owned one of the boats in the little harbour of Port-en-Bessin. Every now and again warning was given by the local German headquarters of firing practice by the coastal artillery. The range and fields of fire of the guns could be calculated from the written notices. Thomine was one of several agents who made copies of the notices which eventually arrived in London.

All along the coast of northern France, in the Prohibited Zone, men like these patiently amassed information and passed it on, and although the Germans knew what was happening they could not prevent it. Nor did they appreciate the vast extent of the intelligence attack on the Wall until their counter-espionage operation in April and May 1944. It was then that Colonel Giskes commented on 'the wealth of minute detail in the many documents we seized', and added that it made him understand not only how successful Resistance espionage had been but also that the papers which came into his possession represented only a very small fraction of the information reaching London. He knew, too, that German attempts to conceal information from thousands of watching eyes had seldom been worth the trouble.

One example was the sowing of the minefields. This was done with maximum security in conditions where the men laying the mines could be certain they were not observed. Yet every hectare of land in France is owned by someone, and every farmer whose pasture or arable land was requisitioned at once demanded a reduction of his land tax. All an agent had to do was sit in the waiting room of the local tax offices and listen to angry farmers expressing themselves freely about the disadvantages of the German occupation.

The Germans made great efforts to conceal the designation and the movement of units. All unit signs, numbers and identification symbols were removed from uniform jackets and overcoats, transport, equipment and supplies. But to a German soldier the number of his unit was as important as a personal number is to a British serviceman; it followed his name everywhere, from his paybook to his underclothes, and underclothes were sent to local laundries or washerwomen where they could be examined by agents of the Resistance.

Each unit also had a postal number and when that had been identified it was easy enough to keep a record of all unit locations and moves. Postal numbers presented no real problem because every time a unit moved — usually at very short notice, in the interests of security — the local laundry would be given the number and a forwarding address for all the soldiers' washing that had not been returned.

When a German soldier died, the body was buried in the nearest cemetery only as a temporary measure until it could be taken back to the Fatherland when the war was over. Since it was to be moved, the grave was clearly marked with the name, number and unit of the dead man.

Aware of the spies all around them, German staff officers marked false information on map displays, issued false movement orders to the French railway authorities, routed through northern France units that were being sent to Russia, and leaked news of the move of unit advanced parties to destinations on the coast but did not move the main body. These measures, aimed at causing confusion and uncertainty in the minds of compilers of the Order of Battle of

German Army Groups in northern France, did not deceive either the agents of the Resistance or the Martians in London.

If the French Resistance had been centrally controlled it is probable that the lives of many *résistants* could have been saved. No less than 90 of them, including Charles Douin and Thomine the fisherman, were executed by machine guns in the courtyard of Caen prison at six-thirty on the morning of 6 June 1944 — at the very time when British and Canadian troops were storming across Gold, Juno and Sword beaches, barely ten miles away. It would also have been possible to exploit the whole intelligence organization in France far more efficiently and economically, and at the same time make penetration of it far more difficult and hazardous. Unfortunately, the rival factions with their different aims made this impossible.

De Gaulle, professing to be the leader of the Resistance and the head of the French 'government in exile', had his own *Bureau Central de Reseignements et d'Action (Militaire)* (BCRA), run by André Dewavrin as a Central Intelligence Office, equivalent to a 'Deuxième Bureau in exile'. But de Gaulle did not speak for France, and in France his voice on the BBC radio was by no means a controlling authority, least of all to the Communists. As the self-proclaimed head of the French nation he put himself in that very dubious category of 'soldier politician', neither one nor the other and not really trusted by either soldiers or politicians. In some ways his conduct as the upholder of French pride and French honour was admirable, in other ways it was impossible. His personal pride, vindictiveness and obstinacy, and above all his distrust of the British as the historic and traditional enemies of France, made him the most temperamental and difficult of allies, and it is a pity that a man whose character and attributes contained something of greatness should have so often, and apparently deliberately, prejudiced relations with those whose main object was the liberation of his country.

In the period just before D-Day he was at his headquarters in Algiers which was known to have been penetrated by German Intelligence, and there was good reason to believe that at least one member of his staff was working for Abwehr. He was therefore regarded as a security risk, and because he could not be trusted to keep very highly classified information to himself, Churchill and President Roosevelt were forced to take the disagreeable decision to deceive him about Neptune. He was given the impression it was only part of a much larger design. De Gaulle was not slow to realize that the British and Americans were not treating him as a French statesman but as a rather untrustworthy general with lofty political ambitions. To the day he died, he neither forgot nor forgave, not did he ever miss an opportunity to confound or thwart British or American political aspirations in relation to France, the North Atlantic Treaty Organization (NATO) or the European Community.

It was the lack of any centralized control of the underground forces of resistance to the Germans in France that lay behind the formation of the British Special Operations Executive (SOE), commanded by General Sir Colin Gubbins, and the clandestine activities of America's Special Operations Branch of the Office of Strategic Services (OSS). But the functions of these two agencies were concerned primarily with guerrilla operations and not with intelligence. Their role, specifically, was to organize and equip the Resistance Groups and, within the plan for Neptune, to direct and control the sabotage and guerrilla warfare against German units, transport, supplies and communications so as to create the maximum disruption during the initial reactions of the Germans to the first phase of Overlord. In other words, they were to make it as difficult as possible for German armoured formations and reserves behind the Wall to concentrate, move or fight. For this reason the activities of SOE and OSS fall largely outside the scope of this book, but the definitive accounts are listed in the Bibliography. Intelligence acquired through SOE and OSS agents was regarded as a bonus, welcome but not expected.

The majority of espionage agents in the French Resistance collected information overtly, in their capacity as employees working in laundries, as telephone operators, as cleaners in German offices and so on. If challenged they were ready with an excuse, not with a gun. There was another type, personified by the Ponchardier brothers, Pierre and Dominique from the Auvergne, and a Communist named Pepé. These, in their own way were as ruthless as the Gestapo and perfectly prepared to murder some unsuspecting German sentry in the dark, or shoot their way out of trouble. Yet violence was a two-edged weapon, to be used sparingly because it was liable to provoke such savage and inhuman reaction from the SS. Merciless reprisals were taken against innocent men, women and children who were shot, hanged or burned alive to avenge the death of a soldier of the Reich.

In any case, the advocates of violence were primarily guerrilla fighters and saboteurs, and only on rare occasions did they fight for information. One example is the story of a raid by seven men, including Pepé, Dominique Ponchardier and a man called Pineau, on a German command post in a requisitioned factory a few miles from St-Malo. The object was to take documents, said to be highly secret and stored in the strongroom of the command post. Ponchardier, Pepé and Pineau made the actual assault, leaving the other four men to cover another entrance and create any necessary diversions. The sentry and two German officers sleeping in the building were killed, and the raiders found there was no strongroom containing files identifiable as Most Secret; instead there was a room lined with cupboards containing truckloads of papers. They had brought one sack with them, and only one of three had a slight knowledge of German. They did not know where to begin, and this sort of disorganization was typical of quite a number of 'operations' mounted without SOE or OSS assistance.

While they were stuffing into the sack papers taken at random from some of the cupboards, shooting began outside and the raiders had to make their escape, dragging a heavy sack of documents which might, or might not, be of some value. Hunted through the woods, Pineau was killed by German troops and Ponchardier was wounded. Only by superhuman efforts did he manage not only to hold on to the sack but deliver its contents to Group Sosies in Paris.

Most of the papers were of no interest but among them was a report made by Rommel after a detailed inspection of the Wall only a few weeks before – in November and December 1943. The report had been written early in January 1944. Rommel had found much to displease him. Some of the gun emplacements were too small to allow for recoil; embrasures were not wide enough in some cases and limited the fields of fire; some of the fortifications had no proper foundations, reinforcement was inadequate, concrete was crumbling, materials were inferior, workmanship was bad...the list of defects was long. Rommel, a very able, energetic and dedicated soldier, had discovered what the agents of the Resistance had known for some time. First, that the slave labour forced to build the Wall had in many places sabotaged it by the only means available to them. They had made cement with too high a proportion of sand and put sugar into the mix so that in due course the concrete would crumble. They had deliberately reduced the size of emplacements and embrasures, and they had 'economized' on reinforcement and foundations. Secondly, that none of the faults had been reported – for a good reason. The main concern of all the officials responsible for the Wall had been to avoid being sent to the Russian front. To have reported defects would have been to make trouble, and trouble attracted attention. There would be accusations and recriminations, scapegoats would be found. The comparatively peaceful air of military headquarters and the Todt Organization in the West would be most unpleasantly disturbed and there would be a great deal of unnecessary fuss and bother. Hitler would lose his temper, people would be sent to the Eastern Front and many of them would not come back. There were defects in the Wall; everyone knew that, but it was far better not to know about them.

Rommel had passed along the Wall like a whirlwind through a field of cut hay and his report had been written in anger because he knew that time was running out, but the real value of it to the Martians was that it confirmed what the spies and informants had been saying. Intelligence officers in London had sometimes been sceptical. It was possible that defects and shortcomings had been exaggerated so as to encourage the planning staff and make them think that things might not be as difficult as they feared.

Yet, because of too much sand and because of sugar in the water, there were defects in the Wall which Rommel had not seen, and many of them had been reported to London. So it can be said that as a result of the espionage organization in France the Allied Supreme Command knew more about the Atlantic Wall than the Germans who had built it. But the manned defensive positions, the strongpoints and the coastal batteries were only one aspect of it. Below the Wall were the beaches and the mined obstacles on them, designed to destroy the landing craft delivering men and armoured fighting vehicles for the assault. There is no other way to find out whether a beach will support the weight of men and tanks, or whether they will sink in mud or quicksands, except by walking on it, digging into it and analysing samples taken from it.

For obvious reasons no spy for the Resistance could even walk on a beach, let alone take samples from it under the eyes of German sentries and patrols.

It had to be done from the sea.

8
Beach and
Air Reconnaissance

At the time when the original outline plan for Overlord was discussed, at the Quebec Conference in August 1943, no detailed study had been made of the beaches selected for the invasion, and in the autumn of that year, at the request of COSSAC, Lord Louis Mountbatten's Combined Operations Headquarters (COHQ) launched a number of small raids along the coast between le Havre and Ostend, on the Cotentin peninsula and in the Channel Islands. These raids, primarily for beach reconnaissance, were all part of the design to distract the attention of the Germans from the Normandy beaches and focus it on the Pas de Calais, and at the same time collect information for Neptune.

When the Dieppe raid (Operation Jubilee) was first planned, a nationwide appeal had been made for photographs of beaches in France taken by people during their holidays or who had lived there. The response had been considerable, and pictures taken at normal eye level can be more informative than obliques taken from an aircraft because they can show the gradient of a beach, whether the surface is sand or shingle, and the height and construction of sea walls, groins and breakwaters.

There were other sources of information, and it was from a French guide book that COHQ learned of the existence of peat in commercially workable quantities on the beach in the Arromanches-Asnelles region, where it was planned to locate one of the artificial harbours. No one knew very much about the effect on the load-bearing capacity of a sandy beach of the presence of peat or clay, but it could pose a considerable threat to vehicles that had to cross it. Accordingly, on 3 November 1943, Professor Bernal, who was the Experimental Scientific Adviser at COHQ, recommended that a very detailed study should be made of the characteristics of peat. His suggestion was at once approved by COSSAC.

Professor Bernal then collected all available topographical, geological and biological data on French beaches in the Neptune area, compared them with similar beaches in England and made a hypothetical reconstruction of all the invasion beaches showing the places where peat and clay might be found. He discovered that the beach at Brancaster in Norfolk had virtually all the characteristics of the Normandy beaches, and it was here that Combined Operations Pilotage Parties (COPPs) carried out their preliminary training in December 1943.

The formation of COPPs was the result of experience gained on previous combined operations such as Torch (the invasion of North Africa) and Husky (the invasion of Sicily), and they consisted of officers and sometimes senior NCOs specially trained to carry out the reconnaissance of beaches at night. The party was kept as small as possible and always included one naval navigation specialist and one officer of the Corps of Royal Engineers. The technique was to take a COPP as close inshore as possible by submarine and let two men go the rest of the way to the beach either in a Folbot (rubber dinghy) or swimming, depending on the distance and the depth of the water. The two men going ashore carried daggers which served the dual purpose of silent weapons and probes for mines; torches, a borer for taking up samples and small bags for putting them in, a clinometer for measuring gradients, a long thin line threaded through glass beads fixed at regular intervals, and .45 Colt automatics.

Pegging one end of the line at the water's edge, they crawled up the beach probing for mines, paying out the line and taking a sample at every interval marked by a bead. The line not only marked a mine-free route back to where they had landed but enabled them to measure the width of the beach and identify the samples. At the far edge of the beach they turned back, took to the sea and indicated their whereabouts to the waiting submarine by flashing their torches. On returning to England they were usually debriefed orally, and that is why it is so difficult to find any first-hand written reports of close beach reconnaissance missions.

It all sounds quite simple, and no doubt the men training at Brancaster found it was, but a similar reconnaissance of a beach guarded by an alert and active enemy was extremely hazardous. The policy of keeping up continual hit-and-run Commando raids along the coast of France, especially in the Pas de Calais, had made the Germans defending the Atlantic Wall abnormally edgy. They never knew when men with blackened faces, moving like shadows, might emerge from the sea, knife a sentry, post grenades through the letter-box slits of strongpoint embrasures, blow up a radar or radio-interception station and disappear into the darkness. Therefore patrols moved along the beaches at night, and sentries in the strongpoints down on the shore listened for the splash of oars and the small sounds of a swimmer. Anything suspicious or unusual was illuminated by flares or searchlights and fired at by machine guns and mortars.

There was an added risk for the COPPs because the success of lightning Commando raids in killing Germans, taking prisoners for interrogation and destroying shore installations, had prompted Hitler to issue a directive in 1942, ordering that all such raiders, when captured, were to be shot.

Undeterred by the hazards, the COPPs finished their training at Brancaster in December 1943, made reconnaissances of the Neptune beaches in January 1944, and on 1 February 1944 COHQ issued a comprehensive report on the Normandy beaches which events on D-Day proved to be remarkably accurate.

The beach at Brancaster was also used for solving another problem. No one knew what effect on the disembarkation of men and vehicles aerial bombs might have if, in air attacks on the beach defences in Normandy, they fell short and cratered the foreshore. As a result of trials, only 100-lb bombs with instantaneous fuses were used during Neptune.

For two reasons the work of the COPPs was not devoted entirely to invasion beaches. Deception plans stipulated that any pre-invasion activity in Normandy would be duplicated and intensified in the Pas de Calais, and if sent to a large number of beaches the COPPs themselves would not know which the vital ones were and so, if captured, would not be of much value to interrogators.

Collecting information on the gradients, surfaces, bearing power and consistency of beaches was only part of the task given to the beach reconnaissance parties. Equally important were details of the obstacles below the high-water mark. The real object of these was not to prevent the assault waves of troops from getting ashore; the Germans always assumed they would. The function of obstacles was to hold off the reinforcing echelons of fighting troops and administrative units by making it as difficult as possible for them to land on a broad enough frontage and at the speed essential if the build-up in the bridgehead were to be fast enough to enable the first troops ashore to cope with enemy counter-attacks.

The first 24 hours after the assault troops had landed would be the critical period, and the flow of reinforcements during that time had to be smooth and uninterrupted. If only narrow lanes could be cut through the obstacles, there would be an increasing concentration of landing craft on the seaward side, and this would be extremely vulnerable to air attack and bombardment from the long-range coastal batteries. If the weather was bad and the sea rough, it would not be possible to keep to timings and landing schedules; and if the German Panzer reserves were deployed in strength against the assault troops contained in a narrow bridgehead, the whole situation might get out of hand very rapidly.

It was therefore of great importance that all details of the design, construction and components of beach obstacles were obtained so that exact replicas could be made in Britain and engineer troops could be properly trained in the destruction of them.

In a report to General Eisenhower after Husky the Commander-in-Chief Mediterranean, Admiral Sir Andrew Cunningham, praised the officers and men of the beach reconnaissance parties and added, 'the estimation of beach conditions and gradients by air photography, and the study of wave velocities, have now reached a fine pitch of efficiency, but where sand bars exist there is no present substitute for swimming reconnaissance, so the services of these gallant parties will continue to be necessary'. To sand bars must be added beach obstacles, because no spy on land could get near enough to them to give any accurate details.

The dimensions could of course be calculated from air photographs, and the photographic interpreters could tell whether they were mined or not, but there was only one way of making sure what type of mine was being used and determining the nature, thickness and strength of the metal used for the obstacles. The *Official History of Combined Operations* says that 'every form of beach obstacle encountered during any reconnaissance was reconstructed at one or another of the Combined Operations Establishments, and methods of destroying or neutralizing it were decided upon after extensive trials. This technique helped to cut down losses from beach obstacles although they were still severe.'

There are many stories behind the prosaic language of the official history. The adventures, for example, of Major Logan Scott Bowden and Sergeant Bruce Ogden Smith who, having crawled up a beach one starry night, paying out the measuring line behind them, heard a German sentry approaching, between them and the sea. He passed without seeing them and without tripping over the line. Apparently they were quite glad to see him because his presence indicated that the beach was not mined.

On another occasion a party went ashore to investigate a large obstacle known as a 'Belgian Gate' which stood nine feet high on a base of about 100 square feet. To calculate the weight, strength and resistance of the structure they needed a sample of the metal, so they removed a piece with a hacksaw and covered the gap with seaweed. Anyone who has ever cut through angle-iron with a hacksaw knows how much noise it makes.

At the beginning of 1944, COHQ developed the technique of beach reconnaissance from Midget submarines manned by COPPs, and these operated in daylight. The submarine cruised offshore and the beach was reconnoitred without surfacing, but the information obtained by this means was limited. It

Coastal Bty.   xxxxx Wire   X Road Block
(4 No of guns) +++ Coiled wire D.L Defended Locality
AA/CD(6gun)   ᴖᴖᴖ Mines   S.P. Strong Point
▲ Light Flak (3gun) U Unoccupied ▨ Hutted Camp or Barracks
● Searchlight   U.C. Under Construction ▲▲▲▲ A/Tk obstacle
                                          (wall or ditch)

1   The elaborate defence system constructed round Dieppe after the raid in August 1942.
The area outlined and arrowed at the top of the map shows details of a minefield. (*Crown copyright*)

3 A closer look at the three guns in open emplacements near the Cap Gris Nez lighthouse. (*Crown copyright*)

2 The Framzelle Floringzelle Battery at Cap Gris Nez. There are three super heavy guns mounted on concrete structures at A, with corresponding dummy positions at B. In front of the lighthouse is a three-gun battery at C, and there are six more guns in the battery at D. (*Crown copyright*)

4 Mulberry A, off Arromanches, during the first week after D-Day. (*Courtesy of the RUSI*)

5 The main harbour wall of Mulberry A. *(Courtesy of the RUSI)*

6 The same wall, made ready for winter storms. *(Courtesy of the RUSI)*

7 The effectiveness of Phoenix. Inside the inner main breakwater, reinforced by block ships, the sea is calm. *(Courtesy of the RUSI)*

8 A general view of the floating roadway of Mulberry A. *(Courtesy of the RUSI)*

9 and 10: *above* Photographic reconnaissance records enemy activity. At the super heavy coastal battery of 3 guns (arrowed) at La Tresorie, Boulogne, camouflage netting over casements fails to hide the construction work; *below* The same battery a year later. Concealed, but recorded. *(Crown copyright)*

11 and 12: Camouflage vs Infra-Red. The German airfield at Dreux Vernouillet. *Above* photographed on infra-red film; *below* using ordinary panchromatic film. The runways at A and B, coated with camouflage paint, are inconspicuous on the panchromatic print, but stand out clearly on the infra-red film. *(Crown copyright)*

13 This picture, taken from an Allied fighter, shows the reaction to air attack by German troops planting Rommel's 'devil's garden'. *(Intelligence Corps Museum)*

14 Despite Rommel's efforts the Todt Organization failed to complete all the beach defences in Normandy. This unfinished strongpoint was on Omaha Beach. *(Intelligence Corps Museum)*

had one advantage over air reconnaissance in that the observer could remain stationary and watch movement on the shore, but surveillance through the periscope of so small and cramped a craft demanded adaptability and practice.

The Combined Operations staff in Britain did however have a great advantage over their colleagues in the Far East who were planning operations against the Japanese, because they had a wealth of reliable intelligence in the form of maps, charts, Sailing Instructions, guide books, Harbour Regulations, Tide Tables and photographs. They also had the assistance of an effective meteorological service. Beach reconnaissance in Europe was an essential supplement and not, as in the Far East, an essential primary requirement.

Although air photographic reconnaissance is principally a confirmatory source, for the reasons already given, it can also be the starting point for the work of other sources. For instance, it was known in London that the Germans were manufacturing torpedoes in a factory in Toulon. Looking at pictures of this factory through his stereoscope, a photographic interpreter saw what appeared to be a torpedo in the yard, but there was something unusual about it. He could not make out the detail because of shadow thrown by a wall, and MI6 were asked to investigate. In due course an agent reported that midget submarines were being built secretly and were normally taken out of the factory at night.

Between the spring of 1942 and the beginning of June 1944, Allied airmen photographed every yard of the French coast in three different types of mission: tasked reconnaissance of specific areas, heavy bomber operations and fighter-bomber attacks. Tasked reconnaissance and heavy bomber sorties were usually recorded by cameras taking conventional stills in stereoscopic pairs — a straight run of film with a two-thirds overlap of each print — which could be interpreted in the ordinary way. The fighter-bombers and fighters had ciné-cameras mounted beside the machine guns or cannon in the wings and these made a record of what the pilot himself saw when he attacked air and ground targets. Most of these films were extremely exciting to watch but not easy to interpret. Stereoscopic pairs had to be made from them, and since the aircraft was normally diving into the attack when the cameras were switched on, angles were confusing, definition was not always good and it was difficult to assess scale with any accuracy.

Pictures taken by heavy bombers were usually of high quality but very often the target was partially obscured by smoke and dust caused by incendiaries and high explosive, and so the intelligence staff tended to rely on the product of photographic reconnaissance. These missions were flown by pilots who had been briefed in detail to bring back information on such targets as a factory — to assess damage done in a previous raid—a bridge, beach obstacles, defensive positions occupied by the enemy, or concentrations of enemy infantry or armour.

The part played by photographic reconnaissance pilots in revealing development of Hitler's secret weapons was of vital consequence to Overlord. They indicated the targets which were then destroyed by the bombers, and so Hitler could not use these weapons to interfere with the administrative build-up in Normandy, nor had he been able to disorganize and delay Allied preparations for the invasion, as he had planned, by launching 6,000 of his secret weapons each day against England.

After the Royal Air Force operation Hydra, on the night of 17/18 August 1943, when the German research establishment at Peenemünde was put out of action by more than 1,500 tons of high explosive and incendiary bombs, on Hitler's orders the manufacture of missiles was transferred to the enormous underground factory in the Harz Mountains called the Central Works, and a new proving ground was set up at Blizna in Poland—an area well covered by Polish agents run by MI6. Thus air reconnaissance could not feature in further measures against the V-2 rocket but it continued to be of crucial importance to the Allies in their efforts to cope with Hitler's other two secret weapons: the Flying Bomb (V-1) and the so-called London Gun which Hitler called the V-3.

The Flying Bomb was a pilotless aircraft driven by a ramjet engine at a maximum speed of 400 mph and carrying a warhead of about one ton of explosives. It was launched on guide rails running the length of a rising ramp made of concrete and about 160 feet long. A hook underneath the fuselage engaged with a steam-driven catapult device which pushed the aircraft along the ramp at a speed of 185 mph, and this forward motion started the motor so that at the end of the ramp, when the hook disengaged, the aircraft flew off under its own power. Flying at 2,500 feet the aircraft remained, in theory, on a straight and steady course for a period predetermined by a timing device operated by a small propeller in the nose of the aircraft. At the end of this period the fuel was cut off, the tail elevator was pushed down and the aircraft dived into the ground. The impact drove the shaft of the timing propeller into the detonator and the warhead exploded, making a small crater but with devastating blast effect.

In April 1943 British Intelligence knew the Germans were developing a weapon of this sort. Air reconnaissance, prompted by reports from agents in France, identified more than 100 concrete ramps being built in the Pas de Calais, all pointing towards London, and the interpreters at Medmenham calculated that they must be for some kind of self-propelled bomb. They were bombed.

On 16 May 1944 Hitler gave orders for the bombing of London to begin, but nothing was ready. Even by 6 June, D-Day, the situation was still chaotic;

all the 'permanent' ramps had been destroyed and none of the makeshift temporary ones were yet in action. Finally, at four o'clock on the morning of 13 June 1944, two members of the Royal Observer Corps at Dymchurch in Kent saw the first Flying Bomb approaching the coast. It fell on a railway bridge in North London.

The concept of the London Gun, known to the Germans as the *Hochdruckpumpe* or *Tausendfusil,* is almost in the realms of science fiction. It was a weapon with a barrel just over 400 feet long fitted with booster inlets at intervals which, when the booster charges ignited in sequence, would propel 55 lb of high explosive over a distance of 100 miles. There were to be two batteries, each of 25 guns, located just to the south of Calais in the area Marquise-Mimoyeques. Laid on London, a target of nearly 700 square miles, no range corrections would be necessary, the guns could be bedded in concrete and everything would be under-ground — the breech mechanisms buried nearly 450 feet below the surface. The plan was that when both batteries were firing together at maximum rate, a shell would land in the London area every six seconds.

Although the 'B 2' Section at Medmenham had heard about a *Vergeltung* weapon early in 1943 and had been keeping an eye on mysterious field works near Calais, it was not until the early summer that serious attention was paid to them. This was because MI6 had learned that the Germans were negotiating with the local electricity authority *(Société Electrique du Nord-Ouest)* for power lines and a power supply large enough for a town the size of Hereford or Basingstoke. It was then noticed that spoil from the underground workings was altering the shape of the landscape. Interpreters working on the prints from a tasked air reconnaissance sortie now noted the 50 shafts under construction and the fact that like the ramps, they were all aligned on the centre of London.

Five months later, when work was well advanced — largely because Albert Speer, Reich Minister for Armaments, had been vastly impressed by initial trials of the prototype on the Baltic test range and had given the project a high priority — bombers of the United States Ninth Air Force caused so much damage that one battery site was abandoned altogether. In the end the design came to nothing because of great technical difficulties, and the actual performance of the guns never looked like reaching what had been achieved on the test range.

Another function of air reconnaissance was to observe the activities of Field Marshal Erwin Rommel.

On 31 December 1943, immediately after Rommel's tumultuous tour of the Atlantic Wall, Hitler appointed him to command Army Group B, consisting of 15th Army in the Pas de Calais and 7th Army in Normandy. He went about the task of strengthening the Wall with characteristic energy and skill, making the coast of northern France into what he called a 'devil's garden', and it was clear he would do his best to obey Hitler's directive and let the invading force get no further than the beaches. He personally designed some of the beach obstacles. He supervised the laying of minefields, the siting of defences and the deployment of artillery. He drove his men on, knowing that the race was against time. It was of great importance to the Allies to know where he was concentrating his efforts.

Although every source of information was tapped, the one with the shortest response time was air reconnaissance. A pilot could be briefed, fly over the target, bring back photographs and make his report in less than an hour. The processing and interpretation of the prints took a little longer, but there was no quicker way of getting an answer to such a question as: 'Have the guns been mounted in the Gris Nez battery?'

Air reconnaissance in the first months of 1944 revealed that Rommel was still devoting most of his energy to the Calais area, although subsequently, in the weeks just before D-Day a very great increase of activity was seen all along the open, wide beaches of the Calvados coast. To the Allies, haunted by the 'spectre of Dieppe', it seemed that he had wind of the Neptune plan.

Against such intelligence targets as the Atlantic Wall, Hitler's secret weapons and the activities of an energetic commander like Rommel, air reconnaissance is of the greatest value, principally because it is a source of visual intelligence, and an air photograph is visual in the planes of the vertical and the oblique. The vertical photograph provides the interpreter with an immensely detailed plan on which there is no dead ground. To the expert this is far better than a map, and since on each print the altitude and focal length of the camera are given, he can calculate the scale exactly and so relate the print to the map. Oblique prints give a 'hill-top' view of the ground but they are difficult to scale and there will be areas of dead ground in valleys and behind hills and buildings. Nevertheless, a combination of verticals and obliques provides the interpreter with a comprehensive study of a target which he can see greatly magnified and three-dimensionally through his stereoscope.

No other source can provide quite this type of visual information because the pilot and his cameras see the target as a whole and in relation to its surroundings, in a way that a spy with a camera on the ground can never see it.

First reports of the Flying Bomb launching sites, and the London Gun, were very confusing, for several reasons. The sites were guarded and therefore spies could only get glimpses of what was going on, from a distance. In trying to be helpful, spies put their own interpretations on what they saw and they tended, no doubt subconsciously, to invent explanatory details to fill gaps in description. In effect, they probably only saw a small part of what appeared to be a major project and hazarded guesses about it. But this was good enough because it set in motion the system for collecting more information. Something big was happening and so an aircraft was sent to take pictures of it. Subsequently the bird's-eye view could be studied at leisure by experienced intelligence officers against the background of what they already knew from other sources.

Naturally it is a great help to pilots flying photographic missions if they can do so in conditions of air superiority, because it is very difficult to maintain straight and level runs over a target while being attacked by enemy fighters. By the beginning of 1944, when Goering was calling his fighters back to Germany to protect the Fatherland from the massive Allied air raids, there were very few German aircraft available to cope with fast, low-flying Mosquitos that came over, took pictures and were gone before they could be intercepted.

Air reconnaissance provided the Allies with detailed pictures of the Atlantic Wall and of the secret weapons on which Hitler based all his hopes of winning the war; indeed, since he was always capable of deluding himself, Hitler's opinions about the outcome of the war were compounded more of conviction than of mere hope.

Despite defeat in North Africa, the landings in Italy, the relentless crushing advance of the Russians, and the threat of a British and American force of some 85 divisions — according to *Fremde Heere West* — poised to attack his Fortress Europe, Hitler, in the spring of 1944, still believed he could win the war even though in winning it, Germany might be destroyed. He was confident that any invasion of northern France could be defeated, the Wehrmacht was still some ten million strong, the production of war *matériel* by German industry had increased since 1940 in some cases by as much as tenfold, and though there were shortages of certain raw materials and Allied bombing had put some factories out of action, there was no sign of any crisis in supplies.

His ground forces had tanks and artillery superior to anything the Allies possessed; in a short while the Kriegsmarine would have its new submarines which would sever the supply lines between England and America. The jet aircraft coming into service could outfly anything produced by the Allies. The mass production of V-1 and V-2 weapons was coming up to its peak in the Central Works under the Harz Mountains. The Flying Bombs, the high-altitude rockets which could not be intercepted, and the continuous fire of the London Guns would turn London into a devastation of smoking rubble and at the same time annihilate the invasion force known to be concentrating in south-eastern England.

This was not hope or surmise, it was belief.

He also believed that the bombardment of London from the launching sites in the Pas de Calais would have so great an effect on the morale of the people in Britain that no matter what plans might have been made for invasion elsewhere, the British and Americans would be forced to attack in the Pas de Calais in order to capture the weapon-launching sites; and here, behind the strongest sector of the Atlantic Wall, the powerful 15th Army lay in wait.

Hitler's only real worry was the Luftwaffe. The Allied operation Pointblank, the combined bomber offensive against German cities and industries that began in 1943 and went on until 14 April 1944 — when it was switched to Neptune — had two major objectives: to destroy German industry and to force the Luftwaffe to come up, fight, and also be destroyed. The cost was appalling. The United States Eighth Air Force alone lost over 10,000 men in three months just before D-Day. German industry was badly disrupted and the second objective was achieved. The heavy losses of German aircraft could be, and were, made good, but it was impossible to replace experienced aircrew. The Luftwaffe was shot down and could not rise again to defend Fortress Europe, and the air reconnaissance pilots who might have penetrated the vast Allied deception plan for Neptune could not get past the air defence of England unless they were allowed to do so.

Hitler's conviction that the Anglo-Saxons would have to attack the Pas de Calais undoubtedly made the task of Allied deception agencies easier, and his own reconnaissance aircraft were made to play their part in strengthening that conviction by contributing, unwittingly, to Fortitude.

9
Jael, Bodyguard, Fortitude and Mulberry

The *Oxford English Dictionary* defines deception as 'a piece of trickery, a cheat, sham.' The deception which was the prelude to D-Day was a vast, complex web of trickery spun right across Europe, from the North Cape to Cairo and from Moscow to Algiers, and it was designed to be effective for as long as possible after D-Day.

As has already been said, the essence of deception in war is that the enemy must be made to work out for himself the false picture that is being conveyed to him. He must assemble all the pieces of the jig-saw, discard any which seem to belong to other puzzles and, with the growing conviction that he is being remarkably astute in interpreting the design of the opposition, fit it all together so that the message is plain. It has to be done this way because of the axiom that all easily obtained intelligence is automatically suspect. Careless coat-trailing may be either disregarded as being an obvious attempt to deceive, or 'read in reverse'. In other words, a clumsy attempt to deceive the enemy into thinking you have no intention of attacking Point A may convince him that it is in fact your main objective.

In the practice of deception, this is the real problem. One minor miscalculation, one small slip, may tear down the whole skilfully woven screen of lies. The structure of deception must be erected on a foundation of credibility and, because of normal human failings, credibility is often a matter of satisfying a personal belief. It is only too easy to form an opinion based on a preconceived idea and then, in looking for confirmation of that opinion, to reject the truth because it doesn't 'fit'. So, if deception is to succeed, it must support opinions already formed in the mind of the enemy; it must emanate from sources he trusts, and yet never be obvious.

A well-known illustration of the adage about the untrustworthiness of easily obtained intelligence is the case of 'Cicero', the Turk named Elyesa Bazna, who is said to have passed to the Germans top secret information obtained from the

British Embassy in Ankara. As the personal servant of Sir Hughe Knatchbull-Hugessen, the Ambassador, Bazna apparently acquired keys to despatch boxes, photographed documents inside them and sold the films to a man named Ludwig Moyzisch who was head of the SD in Turkey. The German Ambassador in Ankara was Franz von Papen, a man whose cunning and guile as a diplomat were not in proportion to his small stature, and though at first he was uneasy about the genuineness of Bazna's material, he authorized Moyzisch to negotiate with him. Subsequently, neither von Papen nor Moyzisch seem to have had any doubt that Bazna did have access to highly classified documents of great value to the Third Reich, and even Schellenberg and Himmler lost their initial scepticism. On the other hand, Ribbentrop, the Foreign Minister, and Hitler remained convinced that 'Cicero' was a plant.

Neither of them could believe that anyone in Bazna's position could possibly get hold of the sort of papers he was photographing, and it is very probable they were right.

Harsh words have been written about the lack of security in the British Embassy and of the carelessness of the Ambassador in particular, but there is another aspect to the story. Bazna may well have been a genuine spy, but his activities and loyalties were known to the British. There is good reason to believe that Lieutenant Colonel Chidson, an Assistant Military Attaché who was also looking after MI6 affairs in Turkey, controlled him in the sense that he chose the documents that were put in the despatch boxes. The degree to which Bazna was turned, if at all, and the amount of control exercised over him may never be known—Colonel Chidson died in 1957—but the information supplied to the Germans dealt principally with the solidarity of the Grand Alliance, its immense resources and its determination to extirpate Nazism and, significantly, plans for an Anglo-American campaign in the Balkans which would lead to an advance on Vienna and then Munich, through the Ljubljana Gap.

There were also references to Overlord, but at a time when the codeword meant no more than the Allied strategy in North West Europe; there was no mention of Neptune, nor any hint of the time and place of the invasion. The proposed Balkan campaign was very definitely part of the Allied deception plan, and therefore, whether willingly or not, Bazna-Cicero was himself part of that plan. He was certainly credible to Moyzisch, von Papen, Schellenberg and Himmler, and their belief in him had an effect on Hitler because he decided to reinforce the Balkans to the extent of 25 divisions which were thus kept out of the battle for France where they might well have had a decisive influence.

And so the Cicero episode is not only an example of the scepticism inspired by easily acquired secrets but also of the workings of deceit, and the effects of it.

A democratic government, a dictator, or a commander in the field may decry a piece of intelligence as an obvious enemy ruse, but it is very difficult to be absolutely sure. It requires a very strong will not to take precautions, just in case.

Like Overlord itself, the deception operation designed to shield it was the largest of its kind ever attempted in the history of warfare. The ramifications, side issues, off-shoots, subordinate schemes and all the strange twists and turns in the dark alleyways of the secret war cannot be contained in a simple chronological narrative, and so, if any understandable pattern is to emerge, the story has to be divided into objectives, means, methods and results, and further separated into areas of actual and fictitious proposed operations. Another confusing factor is the plethora of codewords sprinkled so liberally over all accounts in official and other records — at the end of this book there is a glossary of codewords and other titles that appear in the text.

Initially, the deception plan for Overlord was called Jael, after the wife of Heber the Kenite, although the analogy seems inexact. She certainly deceived Sisera, the commander-in-chief of the Canaanite army, into thinking he was safe in her tent when he fled on foot after his disastrous defeat by Barak at the battle of Megiddo in about 1125 BC. She covered him with a mantle, gave him milk to drink, and when he fell asleep, exhausted, she drove a tentpeg through his head in one of the blackest acts of treachery and crimes against the rigid laws of hospitality in all that blood-stained history of the Old Testament. Jael should thus be synonymous with treachery, not necessarily deception, because, as the *Book of Judges* tells us, there was peace between the Canaanites and the House of Heber. It could perhaps be argued that the death of Sisera liberated the Israelites, and Jael was the instrument of that liberation, hence the codeword for a plan that was to play so great a part in the liberation of Europe — but it all seems rather far-fetched; and in December 1943 it was decided to delete Jael and substitute Bodyguard. This stemmed from Churchill's remark at the Teheran Conference in the previous month that 'in war time, truth is so precious that she should always be attended by a bodyguard of lies.'

In a guide to documents of the Second World War published by the Public Record Office, Jael is the overall deception plan for the war against Germany, and Bodyguard is listed as the deception plan for Overlord — beforehand, that the invasion would be in the Pas de Calais area; afterwards, that the main blow was still to come. Subordinate deception schemes within the main design of Bodyguard all had their own codewords, about three dozen of them, but the main divisions of Bodyguard were Fortitude and Zeppelin. Fortitude had three sub-divisions:

Fortitude North: the fictitious invasion of Norway, the bringing of Sweden into the war on the side of the Allies and a subsequent invasion of northern Germany through Denmark.

Fortitude South: the fictitious attack against the Channel coast of Belgium and northern France in the Pas de Calais.

Fortitude South II: also called Rosebud, dealing mainly with radio activity, which continued after D-Day with the object of convincing Hitler that the landings in Normandy were only a feint and the real invasion across the Pas de Calais was still to come.

Zeppelin covered all the deception plans for south and south-east Europe, in which Cicero played a part, posing such threats as an Anglo-Russian attack on Rumania from the Black Sea to cut off the vital German oil supplies from Ploesti, an Anglo-American attack on Trieste, a British attack through Greece, and the campaign into Austria and south Germany. All these were to culminate in a massive invasion of central Europe.

Bearing in mind that the principal operational objective of the Allies was the landing of an Army Group across the Normandy beaches between the base of the Cotentin peninsula and the mouth of the river Orne, on 5 June 1944, and that concealment of the place and time of the invasion was of crucial importance to the success of it, Hitler was to be deceived into believing:

1. That if the Allies were able to invade France at all in 1944, it could not be before July.
2. That land operations in 1944 would begin in the spring with a combined British, American and Russian attack on Norway.
3. That the main Allied effort in 1944 would be in the Balkans.
4. That when the invasion of France did come it would be directed against the Pas de Calais area.
5. That the ground forces available for an invasion of Norway, the main attack across the Straits of Dover, and for diversionary landings elsewhere in France, were fully trained and equipped and standing by in Britain, and that follow-up divisions were to move from America.

It must be remembered that Bodyguard was aimed at Hitler personally, because Hitler was the sole arbiter of Germany's fate. His interference in the affairs of the Wehrmacht extended beyond headquarters and formations down to individual units. He was the only judge of the right moment for the movement of reserves, and he denied his commanders all freedom of manoeuvre. Battles were to be fought in the way that he, hundreds of miles away, dictated. The Allies knew this. Ultra told them what orders he gave, and through Ultra they could follow his changes of mood and plan. They could watch for any wavering in his feelings about the threat to the Pas de Calais, or to Norway, or to the Balkans.

When the Allies had committed everything to Normandy he must be made to hold Rommel's 15th Army to the east of the Seine until it was too late to prevent the liberation of Paris and the drive eastwards to the Rhine. He must also be made to disperse his forces round the perimeter of his empire; in Norway and Denmark, Greece and Yugoslavia, Provence, Gascony and the Channel Islands, so that they were too far from the Normandy battle to be able to get there in time. This was not so difficult as it might appear, because, as von Rundstedt said contemptuously, the Bohemian corporal would try to hold everything and so in the end would lose everything.

In short, the fundamental aims of Bodyguard were to reduce Hitler to the state of knowing his enemies hemmed him in on every side and not knowing where or when they would attack, and at the same time giving him every reason to believe their main onslaught would be across the Straits of Dover.

His appreciation which had already led to this conclusion was in fact supported by von Rundstedt and Rommel and Admiral Krancke, all experienced professionals whose assessments were based on facts and not, like Hitler, primarily on intuition. Yet Hitler's intuition was not to be despised. He did have, or at least appeared to have, a remarkable 'feel' for a situation, though it is difficult to say how much of it came from good intelligence reports which he did not acknowledge.

Von Rundstedt's assessment was based on five factors which he regarded as critical to any Allied invasion plan:

1. The sea crossing must be the shortest possible; where the turn-round of landing craft and the build-up of the beach-head would be quickest.
2. Maximum air cover; time over the battle area must not be reduced by a long flight from home airfields.
3. The shortest route to the main objective, the heartland of Germany. From Calais the Rhine could be reached in four or five days, and the effect on the morale of the Wehrmacht and the German people would be over- whelming.
4. Destruction of the sites of the weapons bombarding London.
5. The need for at least one major port.

The only ports in Normandy were Le Havre and Cherbourg, and both had been prepared for demolition to the extent that they could be made useless to the Allies for a long time to come. In any case, they were both about 100 miles from the English coast; the approach of an invasion fleet over so great a distance would be seen by radar, aircraft and E-boat patrols while there was still plenty of time to blow the demolition charges, whereas in a very swift attack across the 22 miles between Calais and Dover it might be possible to capture one or more of the three great ports of Dunkirk, Calais and Boulogne.

Admiral Theodor Krancke had studied the combined operations of the Allies and had come to definite conclusions about the tactics of amphibious warfare where a landing is likely to be inhibited by beach obstacles and carefully prepared coastal defences. He was confident that the Allies would come by moonlight and at high tide, so that they could see and float over the obstacles. This would have to be in the neighbourhood of a large port and as far as possible from cliffs, reefs and awkward cross-currents. Visibility would have to be at least 5,000 yards, wind speeds no more than 30 mph and wave height no greater than seven feet.

Rommel felt that if seaborne forces were to get through his 'devil's garden', paths would have to be blasted by engineers who could only work in daylight and at low tide.

All three commanders agreed that the Allies would have to capture a major port, and this requirement influenced all German thinking—yet the idea of floating piers had been in the minds of British combined operations planners as long ago as June 1938.

In a paper (DCOS(IT) 32, dated 2 June 1938) the Deputy Chiefs of Staff instructed the Inter-Services Training and Development Centre to examine such things as beach organization, beach roadways, methods of crossing underwater obstacles, and floating piers. But another paper, dated 30 June in the following year, indicates that no material progress had been made in any of these projects. They were still more or less under discussion at the time of the Dieppe raid in 1942, and this operation not only revealed but underlined many of the shortcomings in the technique and tactics of invasion. The official report lists 19 lessons learned, yet by far the most important lesson of all is not in the list but buried in a paragraph on close support.

The words which were to have so great an effect on Overlord were simply, 'unless overwhelming close support is available, assault should be planned to develop round the flanks of a strongly defended locality rather than frontally.'

In effect, a frontal attack to seize any of the reasonably large ports on the north coast of France was not a feasible proposition. The Germans knew the Allies had to have a large port, preferably more than one of them, and had taken steps to make them unobtainable. Since they had planned the defence of northern France on the principle that ports were essential objectives, it can perhaps be said that the ability of the Allies to ignore them was one of the greatest operational deceptions of the war.

In examining the problem of supply over open beaches, the planners at Combined Operations Headquarters (COHQ) knew it would be dependent on the weather, and statistics collected over a number of years indicated clearly enough that the weather in the Channel would probably be a great asset to the Germans. Restoration of any port that might be captured might take months. Therefore some form of artificial harbour would be needed.

In his book *Crusade in Europe,* General Eisenhower says that the first time he heard of this idea was at a conference attended by a number of Service Chiefs in the spring of 1942.

'Admiral Mountbatten said, "If ports were not available, we may have to construct them in pieces and tow them in." Hoots and jeers greeted his suggestion but two years later it was to become a reality.'

The first result of a study made in the summer of 1942 was an apparatus to release compressed air under the water on the seaward side of the proposed 'calm area'. This worked reasonably well in small-scale experiments but was abandoned in favour of a plan to construct a breakwater by sinking old and virtually useless ships filled with concrete. It then became clear that if the required rate of supply was to be maintained, large ships would be needed for carrying stores, and any breakwater of ships sunk far enough offshore to enable deep draught vessels to unload alongside would in fact be submerged. At length, Brigadier Bruce White, in the Directorate of Transportation in the War Office, produced designs for concrete caissons (literally, large water-tight chests or containers) which solved the problem.

While Brigadier Bruce White was working on his design Winston Churchill wrote a brief note to Lord Louis Mountbatten. It was dated 30 May 1942.

'Piers for use on beaches. They must float up and down with the tide. The anchor problem must be mastered. Let me have the best solution worked out. The difficulties will argue for themselves. W.S.C.'

This led to the development of what were known as 'Spud Piers'.

In the spring of 1943, progress on the artificial harbour showed signs of coming to a halt because the Force Commanders had not said exactly what was wanted, and so Mountbatten convened a conference, with the codename Rattle, to be held at Largs in Scotland on 28 June 1943. It was attended by a large number of naval, army and air force commanders and staff officers from British, American and Canadian forces. The question of whether the Allies would land in

Normandy or the Pas de Calais was resolved, requirements for artificial harbours were laid down, and various aspects of Fortitude were discussed and agreed.

Rattle was followed very shortly afterwards by the Quebec Conference, codenamed Quadrant, where definite proposals for the construction of artificial harbours were tabled and approved. Two were to be built; one for the British and the other for the American sectors of the Neptune beaches, and the whole project was put in the hands of Brigadier Sir Harold Wernher. He organized a team consisting of representatives of the Admiralty, the American Corps of Engineers and various firms sponsored by the Ministry of Supply. This team brought into being the project with the codename of Mulberry.

The specification stipulated that a Mulberry harbour was to be able to withstand gales of up to Force 6 on the Beaufort Scale, and last for 90 days. The main components of the Mulberry off the little seaside town of Arromanches are still there.

Each Mulberry had its own set of codenames; Bombardon, Phoenix, Gooseberry and Whale.

Bombardon was an outer breakwater of floating structures anchored in the open sea in two rows with 400-yard intervals between them and lying parallel with, and to seaward of

Phoenix which was the inner main breakwater of concrete caissons sunk in deep water.

Gooseberry was another breakwater consisting of block ships sunk in shallow water, and

Whale was the name for the Spud Piers — 6 American and 9 British — that floated. These were connected to the beach by flexible floating roadways which were towed across the Channel in spans of 480 feet.

All this had to be taken across the Channel in a special operation conducted by the Admiralty, and the one in the British sector, off Arromanches, was a complete success. It attained a rate of discharge of 12,000 tons of cargo per day in any weather. The Mulberry off St Laurent-sur-Mer, at the eastern end of Omaha, which was to serve the American beaches of Utah and Omaha was not quite so successful. The official report says discreetly that, 'it never attained the efficiency for which it was planned owing to: (1) the rapidity with which the American Army endeavoured to erect it; and (2) the fact that proper soundings were not taken prior to the sinking of the caissons, which resulted in many of the latter being sunk out of sight.'

The labour force employed on building Mulberries was about 45,000 and the material used included 144,000 tons of concrete, 850,000 tons of sand and ballast, and 105,000 tons of steel.

After he had been captured, Grand Admiral Raeder, Commander-in-Chief of the Kriegsmarine, said the Germans knew something about the Mulberries but had no details. This was his way of avoiding a direct admission of ignorance, but there is no doubt that the idea of the Allies bringing their own harbours with them never entered the mind of any German.

Mulberry gave the Allies complete freedom, logistically, to land anywhere in northern France, and therefore was a major step towards achieving strategic and tactical surprise. The Calvados coast had been chosen for Neptune and it was now the task of the Bodyguard planners and schemers not only to distract the attention of the Germans away from it but to make them deploy and disperse their forces as far as possible from the invasion beaches.

10
Means and Methods

Espionage, air reconnaissance and radio interception, the main sources of information available to intelligence staffs not in direct contact with an enemy, are, naturally enough, the principal channels for deception; and of these, the spy is perhaps the easiest to exploit because he — or she — is the most vulnerable. The Germans had no reliable agents in Britain, but they did have several they trusted.

Trust in a spy has to be based on past performance because there is no other criterion. 'The spy,' said Napoleon, 'is a natural traitor.' Loyalty and reliability can only be judged by the quality of information supplied, and a sudden falling off in the standard can indicate that either the spy has, for one reason or another, lost his or her initial enthusiasm, or she or he has been 'turned.' Turning need not be difficult. A large proportion of spies, when caught and threatened with a trial followed a few weeks later by execution, will be glad enough to come to some arrangement, but their original handlers try to provide for this.

The spy is required to use certain checks and safeguards in his messages which will indicate to the handler that he has been caught and is no longer a free agent. Such checks are normally simple and often negative. For example, at the beginning or end of every genuine message he inserts a word, a letter or a number which is omitted if the message is not genuine. A turned spy, used as a double agent in a deception plan, will go on using the security checks to indicate that his messages are genuine, but the problems, so far as his new masters are concerned, arise when he begins to lose credibility with his former handler because the information he sends is found to be unreliable or false. This will at once reveal his change of loyalty and he is then of no use to either side.

If he is to be of any value, a double agent working against his former employers must maintain the level of trust, and this can only be done by providing information which can be corroborated by another entirely different source. Since spies traffic in secrets, this too can be a problem because unless the whole deception plan is very carefully worked out and centralized by some organization which can keep control in detail, the maintenance of trust may — and in fact sometimes does — involve the deliberate sacrifice of information of value to an enemy.

The success of deception depends on maintaining credibility by the skilful exploitation of all sources used by the enemy so that he can obtain corroboration which is in fact as worthless or deceptive as the initial report he is trying to substantiate. Centralization is therefore of crucial importance because if the lines of deception and those of the corroboration of deception become crossed, there will be chaos and disaster.

All the ramifications of Bodyguard were centralized in a secret office within Churchill's war headquarters. It was called the London Controlling Section (LCS), a title which gave nothing away, and it was run by Colonel John Bevan and Lieutenant Colonel Sir Ronald Wingate. They worked very closely with 'C', the head of MI6, with MI5, the counter-intelligence organization, and with a dependent branch of MI5 known as the XX Committee — the double cross having a special significance.

The XX Committee, under the control of Lieutenant Colonel Robertson of the Seaforth Highlanders and John C. Masterman, an Oxford don, had a specific task within the main functions of MI5. Whereas the role of MI5 was to neutralize all hostile intelligence services in Britain, that of the XX Committee was to persuade selected agents to change their allegiance, become double agents and double-cross their former handlers by supplying them with information directly related to Bodyguard.

Seen in retrospect, and even with the advantages of hindsight, the whole idea would seem to have been fraught with difficulties and involving enormous risks, because success depended very largely on being able to make an accurate assessment of that most volatile and capricious element in all Nature — the human mind. The key word was selection. Double agents had to be selected with the greatest care, and every potential recruit for the ranks of the XX Committee's special force was interrogated at length at Battersea by very skilled and experienced interrogators who were not easily deluded.

In the last decade, interrogation has become an emotive word with connotations of psychological pressure and physical torture, but this does not alter the fact, known to all interrogators with any experience, that the only way to discover the truth is by establishing a relationship — interrogators call it 'rapport' — with the man or woman being questioned and creating an atmosphere of complete co-operation and understanding. There are many people with whom this can never be achieved; there are others who can become willingly co-operative in time — sometimes a long time — but when time is valuable it cannot be wasted on 'hard cases'. The XX Committee concentrated on subjects who were likely to respond, usually for good and fairly obvious reasons, and enemy agents who were clearly of no value were handed over to the civil authorities for disposal in accordance with the law.

The Nazis themselves unwittingly propagated the growth of double agents by their aims, policies and methods. To be successful, a spy must have certain attributes; among them are intelligence, courage, common sense, resourcefulness, speed of reaction and a highly developed instinct of self-preservation. The fanatic does not make a good spy, nor does he make a good interrogator, largely because he is incapable of making an assessment from more than one point of view. Many of the agents recruited by Abwehr, and even by the SD, knew that Nazism was fundamentally evil and, especially after the turn of the tide at Alamein and Stalingrad, that the Hitler regime would eventually destroy itself and Germany. Such people were not difficult to turn.

There were others who were not German nationals and who joined Abwehr, some willingly and some as hostages or in exchange for their lives, with the object of subsequently becoming double agents. These faced the XX Committee with the problem of determining their true loyalty, because it is always possible that the spy who is apparently eager to become a double agent may be playing the dangerous game of the triple agent. The world of espionage can be very complicated.

The double agent has a double value. He can be used to supply his original masters with the material which is part of a deception plan; he can also supply his new masters with useful information about the enemy; communication systems, ciphers, codes, operating procedures and the identity of other agents. It is also possible to determine enemy intentions, and the gaps in their knowledge, from the instructions they give to their spies.

But the problems of trust and credibility remain, and it is unwise to assume that a flow of false information, no matter how carefully corroborated by other independent, or apparently independent, sources, will deceive intelligence officers as astute as von Roenne and Gehlen indefinitely. Therefore a certain amount of truth has to be blended with the lies; but deception will often have to go deeper than that.

A good, innately sceptical intelligence officer knows that most of his sources can be 'fixed'. The seed of doubt may stay in the back of his mind, ready to germinate and blossom at the first hint of deception. If this seed is to be grubbed out altogether he may have to be given concrete proof that his assessment is correct, and this may involve the sort of sacrifice that the secret war demands and yet will probably never be admitted or acknowledged by any government. Indeed, similar sacrifices may also be required to safeguard a vital source of information. For instance, it has been claimed that the city of Coventry was sacrificed to the Luftwaffe for the preservation of Ultra.

It has also been claimed that more than 50 Dutch agents were deliberately sacrificed when they parachuted into Holland to join Resistance Groups which had come under the control of Colonel Giskes of Abwehr in what he called Operation North Pole. The object, allegedly, was to sustain the belief that the Allies would land between Calais and the Scheldt. The evidence available to support all this would never convince a jury.

The story is that a Dutch Resistance radio operator named Hubert Lauwers was captured, turned by Colonel Giskes and compelled to maintain radio contact with London. Accused of treason after the war, Lauwers said he had given his code to Giskes under duress but had kept the secret of his security check. He also said he had warned London by every means available to him that he was in the hands of the Germans, but his efforts were ignored. Agents, arms and equipment in large quantities were dropped into the hands of the waiting Germans, and all but three of the agents sent in were executed. When the war was over, a Royal Commission in Holland made an investigation and the British Foreign Office issued a statement to the effect that the allegations about the betrayal of Dutch agents in the interests of deception were not only repugnant but untrue.

No definite conclusion seems to have been reached, and inevitably the story has been perpetuated. It is likely that a great deal still lies concealed under the surface of the secret war, and for many reasons it is better to leave it where it is. Every man and woman who is killed in a war is a sacrifice — although it may be difficult to agree on the cause for which the sacrifice is made — and to some extent this is a consolation to relatives. It is the waste of life that causes so much distress; and no purpose is served by revealing, years afterwards, that a hero and martyr of the Resistance was in fact nothing more than the sacrificial victim of planned deception. Truth is sometimes so unacceptable that it has to be buried in lies, and myth can be an anodyne.

Every businessman knows it may sometimes be necessary to write off £5,000 in order to save £50,000. The same principle applies to war. It is a terrible decision for any commander to have to make, but he may have to order part of his force to make what he knows is a costly and hopeless attack so that the remainder can reach their objectives without loss.

This was not Hitler's philosophy at all. His conquests were considerable and so was his determination to hold on to what he had taken. This made him sensitive to any threat to any part of his empire. Any withdrawal, any loss of ground was an humiliation, and for this reason he was likely to move units and deploy reserves without measuring the longer-term effects or even discussing them with the commanders most affected. Guided, often enough, more by impulse than intuition, he broke a basic military law and, as von Rundstedt had implied, in trying to be strong everywhere he was weak everywhere. This was a failing of which the Bodyguard deceivers were very well aware, and they did their best to exploit it.

They also knew Hitler had certain strategic obsessions. One concerned Scandinavia, and the origin was a belief that Germany had lost the First World War because her High Seas Fleet had been contained within the German Bight. If she had had access to the ice-free ports of Norway she would have been able to destroy Britain's merchant fleet. Hence his seizure of Norway in 1940 and his determination to deal immediately with any Allied threat to Scandinavia by stationing large forces in Norway. He also had an obsession about the Pas de Calais and a perpetual concern about the weakness of his southern flank. In his opinion the 'vital ground' was the Ljubljana Gap, and he was sure that the Allies would come up into Germany from Greece and the northern Adriatic. This belief was undoubtedly one of the reasons why he was deceived by Operation Mincemeat — better known as the story of The Man Who Never Was — because it seemed logical to him that after the North African campaign the Allies were more likely to strike at the Peloponnese and Sardinia than at Sicily.

Hitler's reactions to operational threats, whether real or part of Bodyguard, were made known by Ultra — a great help to the staff of the London Controlling Centre because they could see some of the effects of their activities. Through Ultra it was also possible to detect any leakage of Allied secrets and judge whether double agents being run by the XX Committee were still trusted by the Germans. The value of this was incalculable, because the success of Bodyguard depended very largely on the continued credibility of double agents, whose part in the secret war had never previously been so carefully organized, developed and controlled.

Hitherto the management of captured enemy agents had been left more or less to chance and the initiative of individuals who exploited them when the opportunity arose. The limiting factors were always security and the need to protect valuable sources, and the risks were great because the whole business was not properly centralized. The XX Committee, under the direction of the London Controlling Centre and in concert with MI6 and SOE, developed what became in practice an efficient and extremely effective weapon.

The double agents run by the XX Committee were given a dominant role in Bodyguard because they were in direct contact with Abwehr handlers who gave them their instructions. In addition to providing the information they were asked to obtain, they were able to 'volunteer' information on other matters and thus initiate Bodyguard projects. One of the secondary sources was radio interception, which confirmed the espionage reports.

The German Y Service was always on watch and missed very little, and because of this, Bodyguard took every advantage of the alert ears on the other side of the Channel. British radio security was in fact of a high standard and the Germans were well aware of this, so it was not easy to exploit radio as a means of deception without arousing suspicion. The solution was to make use of those ciphers which were being read by the Germans, and Ultra revealed which these were.

Where there is no contact between ground forces, and consequently no ground observation and reconnaissance, there are considerable problems in trying to use radio as a primary means of instigating deception, mainly because even the most astute enemy may have some difficulty in finding out what is going on. All he is likely to discover is that there is an increase of traffic in the area indicated by his direction-finding apparatus. He records the call signs and from the volume of traffic coming from them estimates the level of command — whether the head-quarters is that of an army, a corps, a division or a brigade. Gradually he complies an Order of Battle, but it takes time, patience, skill and experience.

He can, of course, send over reconnaissance aircraft, but if they are harassed by opposing fighters and forced to fly above 30,000 feet, he may not be much the wiser. It is all so much easier if one of his trusted agents tells him what to expect, and also if he can get confirmation from the source which Tsar Nicholas I found so helpful in the Crimean War.

'We have no need of spies,' said Nicholas. 'We have *The Times.*'

Newspapers can contain all sorts of information useful to an enemy and are often freely available in neutral countries. If not, relevant clippings can be sent by post through neutral countries to enemy spymasters. Provincial newspapers can be especially valuable when they print news of soldiers from the local area, with the names of regiments and their whereabouts, or they include announcements of engagements and marriages of servicemen and women, giving unit designations. Correspondence columns have been known to contain letters from angry local residents complaining about the behaviour of soldiers of a certain regiment; other letters have commented on the effect of large concentrations of troops arriving in a local area, and so on. Newspapers can be a useful and apparently undirected and independent confirmatory source, but, like every source of information, they can be exploited for deception.

Since Overlord was to be an Anglo-American operation, Bodyguard had to be too, and in trying to unearth the secrets of Allied invasion plans, Abwehr and the SD did their best to place agents in America. MI5, MI6, SOE and the London Controlling Centre all had their American counterparts and there was close liaison between most of them. The American counter-intelligence organization was the Federal Bureau of Investigation (FBI) run by J. Edgar Hoover who had been in a position of great authority for so many years that he had become a little inflexible and autocratic. He wanted no help from outside in his task of catching spies, and said so. When the British sent Dusko Popov, the Yugoslavian businessman and one of their best double agents, across to America in August 1941, it was made clear to him that Hoover would have nothing to do with the agents of a foreign power, and attempts to interest the FBI in the activities of the XX Committee did not succeed until much later in the war.

The American Office of Strategic Services (OSS), founded by Major General 'Wild Bill' Donovan, was the approximate equivalent of MI6 and SOE, and the American Joint Security Control (JSC), formed in May 1942, had virtually the same functions as the London Controlling Section. The JSC directed the affairs of the OSS and the FBI in deception projects in much the same way as the London Controlling Section gave guidance to the XX Committee, MI6 and SOE. The American department dealing with XX Committee matters was known as X2 and was part of the OSS.

When the Overlord planning committee, known as COSSAC and in effect the headquarters of the Combined Chiefs of Staff, was formed in 1943 it had a branch known as Ops B, or the Committee of Special Means, and deception was its main responsiblity. Thus the basic structure of Allied Intelligence and Deception was, at the top, the Joint Committee of Special Means (Anglo-American); subordinate to it, on one side, were the British London Controlling Section, MI5, the XX Committee, MI6 and SOE, and on the other side, the American Joint Security Control, OSS, X2 and the FBI. Below them were the intelligence services of the navy, army and airforce of each nation.

The components of this structure covered the four principal activities of the secret war; the acquisition of intelligence, counter-intelligence and security, special operations and deception. There was also a fifth activity known as psychological operations — shortened nowadays to 'psyops' — which in Britain during the war was the responsibility of the Political Warfare Executive (PWE). In America the equivalent was the Office of War Information (OWI). Political/psychological warfare was, and is, an attack on the hearts and minds of the enemy. Its product is 'disinformation', its main weapon is rumour, and its objectives are disillusion and defeatism. It can become a boomerang. Words, however barbed, are only words, and propaganda can have an effect disappointingly different from what is intended. For instance, attempts to ridicule and undermine the authority of a leader may merely strengthen the loyalty of his followers.

The principal successes of PWE were in the Balkans.

The German intelligence attack against America was just as unsuccessful as the one against Britain, but whereas in England the agents of no value to the XX Committee were tried as spies and about 30 of them were executed with very little delay, in America, where the legal system seems to be rather more complex, other things were wont to happen. In March 1941 a senior Abwehr agent named Ulrich von der Osten arrived in Los Angeles and claimed to be Don Julio Lopez Lido. The FBI put a shadow on him. A few days later he was the victim of a slightly unusual traffic accident in New York. It could of course have been coincidence; and odd things happened in England too. The body of a man was found in a air raid shelter in Cambridge. He had been shot. Beside him was a suitcase containing a radio transmitter and papers in his coat pocket bore the name of Jan Villen Ter Braak. That was all the public ever learned about him.

Following the example set by MI5, J. Edgar Hoover's FBI rapidly brought all German agents in America under control, and some were used to advantage by X2, but if the story of the mission with the codename Pastorius is typical, spycatching in the United States was made comparatively simple by the Germans themselves.

In 1942 Hitler ordered a large-scale attack on the American armaments industry, though no one was quite sure how this could be done. Kaltenbrunner, recently made head of the SD after the assassination of Heydrich, called for volunteers from the SS to undertake a mission in which sabotage and espionage would be of equal importance. Since the SD had very little experience of overseas espionage, eight men were trained at the Abwehr school in Hamburg. From there they went to Paris where they feasted, drank — and talked — rather in the manner of gladiators about to die. By the time they left Paris en route for the submarine base at Lorient, details of their mission had been passed by the Resistance to MI6 and thence to the FBI.

According to the story, only seven men went to Lorient; one had been detained in Paris with venereal disease. At Lorient they were given American money in notes, some of which were no longer legal tender in the United States and others had been overprinted in Japanese. Apparently one of the gladiators was intelligent enough to protest and was told that suitable notes would be obtained and sent on as soon as possible. Although carefully chosen for their unswerving loyalty to Nazism and the Third Reich, two of them defected almost immediately on landing in the United States, and they denounced the others, which was probably just as well because it seems unlikely they would have been very effective. None of them had any real command of the English or American languages, and it is said that when one of them went into a drugstore to buy a razor, he clicked his heels, gave the Nazi salute and said 'Heil Hitler' purely from force of habit.

Since they had no loyal spies in England or America the Germans could not —though they did not know it—check the intelligence obtained from their Y Service or air reconnaissance, and the whole field of deception was open to the Allies. Yet there were two ever-present dangers; a breach of Allied security might sound the alarm, or a double agent might arouse suspicion, fall into the hands of the Gestapo and be made to talk; and the most vital secret in the whole deception plan was that trusted German agents were under the control of the XX Committee.

The XX Committee did in fact lose one of their double agents, a man who had been given the codename of Artist. He held high rank in Abwehr and had been sent to Lisbon in the summer of 1943. He was also a close friend of Dusko Popov, and it was because Popov assured MI6 that Artist was an anti-Nazi who wanted to work against Hitler that he was enlisted by the XX Committee. Two MI5 men checked on him in Lisbon, reported favourably, and he joined the 'Yugoslav Ring' in which Popov was the chief figure; but the XX Committee had misgivings because if Artist was not what he said he was he put the whole ring at risk.

The defection of Erich Vermehren and his wife in Ankara, which led to the compulsory retirement of Canaris, also sealed the fate of Artist. Erich Vermehren's mother lived in Lisbon and Artist spent a lot of time in her house. He therefore automatically came under suspicion by Schellenberg and the SD who were doing everything they could to discredit Abwehr. Artist was also suspect of misappropriating Abwehr funds. He was kidnapped by SD agents in Lisbon early in May 1944, about a month before D-Day, drugged and packed in a trunk which was taken back to Germany overland as diplomatic baggage. He was interrogated in the notorious Gestapo building in Prinzlbrechtstrasse in Berlin, and while he was being tortured the whole of Fortitude South (to convince Hitler the invasion would be in the Pas de Calais) was in jeopardy; and there was nothing anyone could do about it.

If, through Artist, the SD discovered that Popov was a double agent, they could assume that all the information he had passed them was false, and Popov had been one of the main sources of information about the build-up of the invasion force in south-east England. It was during this agonizing period, for COSSAC as well as Artist, that Ultra provided really alarming information.

Hitler had ordered the move of certain reserve formations to Normandy, although he had made no changes in the troop dispositions in the Pas de Calais.

Artist had not talked. He was either executed or died under torture soon after D-Day without revealing his or Popov's connections with the XX Committee. Apparently the SD knew nothing of any possible defection and were really only concerned with the allegations of financial fiddling. They still had no cause to doubt the integrity or credibility of their agents in England, who were working for the XX Committee.

Yet, even if Artist had 'blown' Popov and discredited him, the great deception which kept the 15th German Army waiting for the main Allied attack to come between Calais and the Somme would not necessarily have been seriously compromised because of von Roenne's false estimate of the number of divisions on the Allied Order of Battle.

11
Plans and Personalities

Fortitude, the overall cover and deception plan for Overlord in northern Europe, made use of all the channels for conveying information to the enemy, but Fortitude North, relating to Scandinavia, was based initially mainly on radio deception. The plan had a number of closely related objectives; to keep the garrison of Norway where it was — it consisted of a German force of nearly half a million men with tanks, artillery and air support — to persuade Sweden to join the Allies and thus deprive the Ruhr steelworks of vital supplies of iron ore; to isolate German forces in Finland; and finally, to threaten an invasion of north Germany through Denmark. It was hoped that if conveyed convincingly enough, all this would compel Hitler to retain in Denmark and Norway the large forces that could otherwise be used against Neptune.

The main threat to Norway was to be offered by the British 4th Army, located in Scotland with its headquarters in Edinburgh. This was an entirely fictitious force simulated by wireless traffic. The scheme was given the codename Skye and was operated by Colonel R. M. MacLeod, late of the Royal Horse Artillery. The officer formally gazetted to command this non-existent army was General Sir Andrew Thorne who had made his name as a divisional commander in Flanders in 1940 and was well known to the Germans because he had been a Military Attaché in Berlin before the war.

With a handful of officers and a number of wireless operators, Colonel MacLeod set up the 4th Army headquarters in Edinburgh Castle, 2 British Corps headquarters at Stirling, and 7 British Corps headquarters at Dundee. The Army headquarters was rapidly located by the direction finders of the German Y Service and a single aircraft came over and bombed it, without much effect. Two of the double agents in the XX Committee's team — their codenames were Mutt and Jeff — confirmed the existence of the various headquarters, even to the details of the 4th Army insignia, and Mutt told his German handler that the Russian intelligence officer Klementi Budyenny had arrived in Scotland to co-ordinate the Russian contribution to the campaign. The Germans were also told that the interests of the American 15 Corps, in Northern Ireland but earmarked for the Norwegian operation, were represented in Edinburgh by a small liaison staff.

By the end of March 1944, Colonel MacLeod had created what the Germans believed to be a force consisting of the two corps headquarters with corps troops, an armoured division and an armoured brigade, four infantry divisions, an airborne division and an organic tactical air support cell. Radio messages put out by these 'formations' contained references to the training and equipment required for rock-climbing, skiing and operations in cold climates, and the local press carried announcements, articles and reports of the sporting and social activities and fixtures of the formations and units of 4th Army.

In the meantime British agents in Norway were plied with questions about local conditions, communications and the locations and combat efficiency of German garrison units. The German Y Service became well aware of what was going on even though many of the messages were in a cipher they could not read. The Russians, playing their agreed part in Bodyguard, began leaking information about shipping concentrating for the forthcoming attack on Petsamo, and the formation of the army that was to carry it out in June 1944.

The Germans questioned their two most reliable agents in Britain, Dusko Popov and a Spaniard, codenamed Garbo, both of whom had been working for the XX Committee for years, and received confirmation of all the material they had collected. Popov, codenamed Tricycle, also reported the existence of Budyenny's military and naval mission in Edinburgh, first notified by Mutt. For the benefit of air reconnaissance, dummy aircraft appeared on Scottish airfields and real British warships assembled in sea lochs and firths; but the ships were part of 'S' Task Force, destined for Sword beach in Normandy.

The channels of espionage, radio interception and air reconnaissance might well have been adequate, but evidence of a more concrete kind was provided in abundance. Throughout the spring of 1944 a series of Commando and other raids was made against the German garrison of Norway and against all types of industrial installation. These, unmistakably, were pre-invasion tactics. Shipping was attacked. The German battleship *Tirpitz* was mined, the troopship *Donau* and the merchant vessels *Tugela* and *Ortelsburg* were sunk. Railways were sabotaged. British and American air reconnaissance sorties increased. Russian submarines reconnoitred coasts. SOE sent messages which were interpreted by the SD as instructions to the Norwegian and Danish Resistance. An Anglo-American military mission arrived in Sweden and began to make inquiries and take photographs indicating a great interest in the problem of moving large forces of infantry and armour through Sweden and down into the Baltic.

It seems that von Roenne collated all this material with care but was never entirely convinced that operations in 1944 would begin with an Allied invasion of Norway. On the other hand, Hitler was quite sure they would. Von Roenne's confidence in his own judgement was shaken by a report from an Abwehr agent named Kraemer, operating in Stockholm, about the Russian mission in Edinburgh. He was even more concerned when he heard, through Kraemer, that Anthony Eden the British Foreign Secretary had been to Moscow and agreed the details for the attack on Norway by the Grand Alliance. (Eden had not in fact been to Moscow.) Kraemer originally obtained his information from a pro-German member of Swedish Intelligence who had access to reports sent from London by the Swedish naval and air attachés, who had no knowledge of what was going on. British agents in Lisbon discovered the source of Kraemer's information, the London Controlling Section was informed and it was arranged that thereafter the attachés' reports to Stockholm would play a part in Fortitude North by stressing the likelihood of an Allied invasion of Norway.

Von Roenne was, however, convinced that the British 4th Army existed, and this helped to ease his conscience, and when reports from England indicated that the 4th Army was about to move to join the (equally fictitious) First United States Army Group (FUSAG) assembling in south-east England as the invasion force for the Pas de Calais, he regarded the news as confirmation of the existence of FUSAG.

Fortitude North was a complete success. Large German forces remained in Norway awaiting the invasion that never came; but in due course, when the war was over, the Allies did come—to accept their surrender.

The First United States Army Group was the lynch-pin of Fortitude South, and the scheme for raising it had the codename Quicksilver. The first moves were made, appropriately enough, in America, by a Dutchman known as Albert van Loop. He is of some interest because although J. Edgar Hoover considered him to be a reliable double agent, it transpired subsequently that he was the comparatively rare bird, a triple agent. He was not a very effective one mainly because the German intelligence organization was not properly centralized.

Van Loop had been a member of Colonel Nicolai's intelligence service in the First World War, collecting information on General John Joseph Pershing's American Expeditionary Force in Europe. Canaris took him back into Abwehr in 1941, as an expert on the American Army. After retraining at the school in Hamburg he went to Madrid, where he told the United States Embassy that he had been forced to join Abwehr and really wanted to go to America and work for the OSS or the FBI. As proof of his sincerity he handed over two ciphers and all his transmission instructions which included his call sign, security checks and so on. In doing this he appeared to be double-crossing Abwehr because he had been told to hand over only one of his ciphers. The Americans in Madrid came to the conclusion he was a German spy, whatever else he might say he was, but as such he might be useful to the FBI.

He was sent to New York where the material he had brought with him was taken over by an expert of the Radio Intelligence Service who impersonated him, sending to Hamburg messages containing information about the move to England of American formations which the Germans would be bound to hear of in due course from sources such as the press. After the war, when Abwehr records were captured and examined, it was discovered that van Loop had made his own contact with Hamburg using a cipher he had not surrendered to the FBI, and by this means had sent more messages than those despatched by his impersonator. It seems probable he did not know he was being impersonated, and did not bother to tell Hamburg it might happen. In any case, the Germans seem to have accepted the information about Quicksilver which came from the FBI impersonator, probably because in the administrative chaos resulting from the absorption of Abwehr by Schellenberg's SD they were incapable of sorting out the intricate tangle of single, double or triple agents in Portugal, Spain, Sweden, England and America. This, no doubt, is also the reason why Schellenberg knew nothing of Artist's defection.

In England, Quicksilver was given the full treatment of radio transmissions press 'leakages' and dummy installations to be photographed from the air but, as the London Controlling Section and the XX Committee knew very well, anyone as experienced as von Roenne would want proper substantiation from his trusted agents. They were the only source that could reveal this type of deception because the building-up of a fictitious force is not quite the same as creating the threat of a fictitious invasion.

At the beginning of 1944 the XX Committee had 20 double agents under control, nine of whom were in radio communication with handlers in Portugal or Germany. The remainder used various methods of secret writing and the ordinary postal services to neutral countries. The London Controlling Section and MI6 also had their own means of passing messages to the enemy through their own agents who had penetrated Abwehr and the SD. There was no difficulty in providing the Germans with false information, but the question of whether or not it would achieve anything depended, as always, on credibility and trust. The whole intricate tapestry of Fortitude hung from these two slender threads, either of which could snap so easily and bring everything down in ruin.

In deception on the scale of Bodyguard there is, perhaps somewhat paradoxically, no safety in numbers. The means and the methods must be very carefully chosen, and the fewer there are, the less likelihood there is of discovery and disaster. This applied particularly to double agents because if one of them is 'blown,' or even suspected, the messages he passes may well be read in reverse. Therefore the XX Committee chose only four, and they were to be the espionage element of Skye in Edinburgh and Quicksilver in Kent and East Anglia. They were Dusko Popov — Tricycle; Garbo; Brutus, an ex-officer of the Polish General Staff; and a Frenchwoman, the daughter of Russian émigrés — Treasure.

Popov was recruited into the Abwehr organization by his friend Artist when they were both at Freiburg University before the war; at least, it was Artist who suggested that spying for the Germans against the British could be an entertaining and lucrative pastime. Approached again by the German Consulate in Belgrade in 1940, Popov made contact with a member of MI6 and asked for advice because, as an ardent anti-Nazi about to become an Abwehr recruit, he felt he might be of value to the British. He was told to show interest in the German offers. Abwehr then asked him to go to England to collect secret material from their agent in the Yugoslav Embassy. He arrived in London in December 1940 and was soon regarded by the XX Committee as an agent of unusually high quality. He had connections with the Yugoslav court; he could mix naturally and easily at any level of society; he was in the shipping business which provided good reasons for travel to neutral countries and, through Artist, he was in good standing with Abwehr.

In due course Popov brought other Yugoslavs into his circle, which also included Artist when he had lost his faith in Hitler and Nazism, and in February 1944, when Popov went to Lisbon to give his Abwehr handler, Karsthoff, the Quicksilver Order of Battle, the 'Yugoslav Ring' consisted of agents with curious codenames such as Freak, The Worm, Gelatine, Balloon and Meteor.

The trip to Lisbon was a calculated risk because it was the supreme test of Abwehr's trust in Popov. If Karsthoff believed what Popov told him, the pattern of FUSAG that von Roenne was putting together from all the radio interceptions, press 'leaks', air photographs and reports from other agents controlled by the XX Committee, would begin to take definite shape and the deception project would be fairly launched. If he did not, Quicksilver would have failed almost before it had got under way.

For no apparent reason Karsthoff accused Popov of trying to pass off a lot of rumour and conjecture as valuable intelligence. Popov, with his usual blend of authority, personality and resourcefulness, insisted that the information be sent to Berlin and thence to Zossen where, fortunately for the future of Quicksilver, von Roenne considered it was of great value in confirming the operational picture being put together by *Fremde Heere West*. Thus, in March 1944, Hitler and his intelligence staff accepted the existence of FUSAG. Subsequently, in May, when Artist was kidnapped in Lisbon and taken to Berlin, the Yugoslav Ring had to be taken out of the Quicksilver project, but there were others to continue the work. Garbo was one of them.

Of all the singular characters who worked for the XX Committee, Garbo is perhaps the most remarkable. The Germans paid him some £20,000 to finance an entirely mythical spy ring which provided detailed information about an equally mythical Army Group. He hated Nazism and Communism, mainly because of his experiences in the Spanish Civil War, and at the beginning of 1941 he approached MI6 in Madrid with an offer to spy for the British. When this was not accepted he went to the head of Abwehr in Spain and Portugal, a man named Wilhelm Leissner who operated under the alias of Gustav Lenz. After some delay while Garbo's background was being vetted, he was recruited into Abwehr in July 1941, provided with money, espionage contacts and a list of the items of information required, and told to go to London. He went no further than Lisbon where, with the aid of perfectly overt sources such as maps, guidebooks, and journals and magazines dealing with technical subjects — as well as a fertile imagination and considerable literary talent — he began to provide Leissner with excellent intelligence reports about the British Isles. After a short time he told Leissner he had recruited three valuable agents of his own in various parts of England. He included their reports, which he had written himself, with his own.

In February 1942 the British learned from Ultra that the Germans were making special efforts to intercept and destroy a large convoy which they had been told was moving between Liverpool and Malta, but it was not until some time later that MI6 and the XX Committee discovered that the inventor of this convoy was Garbo. In his one-man campaign against Nazism he was doing his best to make the Germans waste their efforts to no purpose.

In his book *The Double Cross System in the War of 1939-45,* John Masterman says that at this stage it became clear to the XX Committee that 'Garbo was more fitted to be a worthy collaborator than an unconscious competitor,' and he was brought to London.

By April 1944 Garbo had increased the number of non-existent members of his spy ring from 3 to 14. Leissner also believed he had about a dozen carefully placed contacts, two radio operators and reporting posts at a number of vantage points in the Quicksilver area. At the same time the network had become international because he had told the Germans he had a spy in Canada and another in the headquarters of the Supreme Allied Commander, South-East Asia (SACSEA) in Peradenyia in Ceylon. The labour involved in fabricating the reports of all these ghosts was enormous, but Garbo was an indefatigable worker, and the Germans apparently trusted him implicitly. They sent him a cipher which they used themselves for signals between Madrid, Hamburg and Tangier, and notified him whenever they changed the key—thus giving the 'Bomb' at Bletchley more time for other work.

Garbo's achievement is all the more striking when one bears in mind that he was dealing with German intelligence experts who measured trust against performance; but his value to the Germans remained constant because once the OKW believed FUSAG was genuine, and that the British 4th Army really existed, he reported what the Supreme Headquarters more or less expected to hear.

Brutus, the Polish officer, had been a member of the intelligence organization that had been instrumental in enabling Britain to acquire Enigma before the war. When Poland was overrun by the Wehrmacht he escaped to Paris where he went underground, took the codename of Paul, and founded the MI6 *reseau* known as Interallié. He was betrayed to Abwehr by a girl who was working for him and had become jealous of his association with another young woman. Colonel Rohleder, head of Abwehr in Paris, was looking for British agents who could be turned, and he arranged for Paul to make an elaborately stage-managed 'escape' from Abwehr to the French Resistance, and thence across the Pyrenees to Madrid, Lisbon and finally London.

Brutus/Paul had agreed to work for Abwehr on condition that the hundred members of Interallié who had been picked up by Anwehr at the time when he was betrayed should not be executed but treated as prisoners of war. He crossed the Pyrenees on a British escape route operated by a British officer with the codename of Monday, whom he met in Madrid. Monday drove him to Lisbon and on the way heard the whole story of the engineered escape from Abwehr.

Brutus reached London in January 1943 and was screened at Battersea, but the XX Committee was reluctant to employ him because he had worked for MI6 before; the Germans knew this and might therefore expect him to offer to do so again. However, possibly because of the hundred Interallié hostages, Abwehr apparently did trust him. It was therefore arranged that he would tell Rohleder he had become a liaison officer between the RAF and the Polish Air Force in Britain, and thus had access to information about Allied plans for the invasion of France. His role in Quicksilver increased in importance when the abduction of Artist put Popov's Yugoslav Ring temporarily out of action.

Treasure, aged 26 and the fourth member of the Quicksilver team of double agents, had a Tsarist background and upbringing, and her feelings about the Germans were much the same as those of Popov, Garbo and Brutus. When the war began, she was in the Lebanon, and she went to Paris with the object of joining MI6. Before she could make contact, Paris was occupied by the Wehrmacht, so she went to Abwehr. Canaris disapproved of female agents in principle. If he had ever seen it, he would have agreed with what Colonel David Henderson — Director of Military Intelligence (DMI) in South Africa during the Boer War — had written about women in Intelligence in the first official British pamphlet *Field Intelligence, Its Principles and Practice,* published in London in 1904: 'they are variable, easily offended, seldom sufficiently reticent, and apt to be reckless. Usually they will work more consistently for a person than a principle.'

Treasure was not given a radio transmitter or any ciphers and was told to use secret writing when communicating with her handler in Lisbon, Major Kliemann. Her real reason for joining Abwehr in Paris had been to obtain the necessary papers and money so that she could get to Spain or Portugal. In Madrid she went to the British Embassy and said who she was and what she wanted to do. Her passage from Lisbon to England by air was arranged in June 1943, her loyalties were established during interrogation at Battersea and she was offered 'secret work'. The XX Committee appear to have shared at least some of Canaris's views about employing women because she was not told how her work fitted into the Bodyguard plan, nor was she told that the XX Committee existed. Her German and British handlers both seem to have found her temperamental, not always easy to control and, because she believed she would die of leukaemia in a few months, reckless of her own safety — but, according to Anthony Cave Browne, she was still alive in 1971.

Using secret ink and a 'letter box' in Lisbon, she reported to Kliemann that she had joined the Auxiliary Territorial Service (ATS), the women's branch of the British Army, which she did, but later, and that she had an intimate friend who was a staff officer stationed at Bristol with the headquarters of the American 14th Army. The 14th Army was fictitious and part of FUSAG, but Bristol was in fact the headquarters of the real American 1st Army, earmarked for Neptune. Subsequently she said that the 14th Army headquarters had moved to Essex, where FUSAG was assembling. She also reported the moves of real and imaginary units being used to build up the Quicksilver picture, giving details which supplemented other information sent by Popov, Garbo and Brutus. Moreover, when Treasure gave the location of a unit, especially a false one, its position could be verified by the German Y Service from the signal traffic.

These four principal double agents took great pains to help von Roenne compile the Overlord Order of Battle, and all their reports were substantiated by the countless ramifications of Bodyguard, each designed to add convincing touches to the mass of information being collated by the intelligence staff of

Fremde Heere West at Zossen. One such convincing touch was the appointment of the commander of FUSAG.

Although Montgomery was an expert at keeping in the public eye, his teetotal vegetarianism, his sincere religious faith and his knowledge of military history combined to create the image of a somewhat puritanical and academic soldier. His complete opposite was General George Patton, old 'Blood and Guts', the fighting soldier, the master tactician, the rigid disciplinarian, the brilliant exponent of mobile war who liked to lead his army from in front. Patton's creed was uncomplicated: go after the enemy and destroy him. He was a large, tough, immaculately dressed and rather frightening man whose indiscretions and unbridled tongue were the delight of journalists all round the world. He was very well known to the Germans, who seem to have had far more respect for him than for Montgomery as the protagonist of the Principle of Offensive Action, and when he was appointed Commander of FUSAG they had no doubt that the main weight of the Allied attack would be across the Pas de Calais.

Another, much smaller, touch was the arrival on von Roenne's desk of the information that someone in Geneva, trying to be surreptitious, had bought up all the available copies of Michelin Map No. 51, Boulogne-Lille.

General George S. Patton's First United States Army Group began to take definite shape on air photographs. There were landing craft in the harbours, estuaries and inlets along the east coast of Britain. Something that looked like a large oil refinery was being built in Dover harbour, obviously to provide the main invasion force with fuel when it gained a foothold on the Far Shore. Woods in East Anglia and Kent were being used to conceal military installations and dumps; concentrations of armour and wheeled vehicles began to appear and were easily discernible because of the tracks they made; and all the time the German Y Service in the listening posts along the coast from Calais to Cherbourg could hear and record the ceaseless flow of signal traffic generated by the formations and units located by their direction finders.

Yet eastern England had become the land of the dummy. The washing hung upon lines slung across landing craft in creeks along the shore fluttered above ingenious constructions of canvas and plywood. The fuel installation in Dover had been made by stage and scene builders recruited from theatres and film studios, working to the plans of professional illusionists such as Major Jasper Maskelyne and film-set designers like Colonel Geoffrey Barkas. The making of tracks to create the impression that a wood was full of stores became a military skill. The tanks seen along a hedgerow or in the lee of a wood were inflatable and the tracks behind them had been made by dragging a 'track simulator' across the field. When the German direction finders located Montgomery's 21st Army

Group headquarters in Kent they did not know his headquarters was in fact just outside Portsmouth and that radio messages sent from it went first to Kent by land-line.

Supporting the evidence of the camera, the spy and the radio-interception analyst was operational activity on a far larger scale than the 'pre-invasion' tactics in Norway. Air attacks, commando raids and COPPs all helped to convince the watchers on the Far Shore that the invasion would be between Calais and the mouth of the Somme.

These means and methods did convince Hitler, the OKW, von Roenne and von Rundstedt. Rommel was not so sure. He had inspected every metre of the Wall. He had stood in the command posts on the cliffs, above the famous 'Elephant's Trunk' at Etretat, at the spot marked *le Chaos* on the Michelin map to the west of Arromanches, at the Pointe du Hoc, and on the battlements of the ancient fortress at St-Vaast-la-Hogue. He knew that Montgomery, his adversary in the Desert War, had to achieve surprise, and like every professional soldier he knew that the elements of surprise are secrecy, deception, concealment, originality and audacity.

He reasoned that the Allies were probably creating an impression of strength far greater than they possessed so that they would be deemed capable of invading at several widely separated points. Hitler would be encouraged to believe that an invasion other than in the Pas de Calais was a feint designed to make him draw troops away from the area of the main threat. But because of his obsession about the Pas de Calais Hitler would not be deceived and would not be lured into committing any reserves.

Rommel pursued this line of thought as he walked with Speidel his Chief of Staff, and Staubwasser his intelligence officer, on May evenings in the garden of the Château de la Roche Guyon. Staubwasser also felt that *Fremde Heere West* had overestimated the number of Allied divisions; and he had been working on the Allied Order of Battle until Colonel Michel took over from him.

If the OKW estimate was wrong, Rommel calculated that there would probably be only one invasion. The Allies would be guided by the Principle of the Concentration of Force, and if they were going to land enough men and equipment and supplies fast enough to be able to maintain and expand their bridgehead, they would need wide beaches on a wide front. From what he had seen of the coastline from Dunkirk to Biarritz there was only one area really suitable for such a landing, and that was Normandy. The flaw in this argument was the lack of a port—Cherbourg would be neutralized at the first sign of invasion—and there was also the Allied problem of adequate fighter and fighter-bomber air cover more than 100 miles from English airfields. Therefore the Pas de Calais must not be ruled out, and there was a possibility that a feint attack would be made in Normandy; unwittingly and to a limited extent, he had pierced some of the fog of deception enveloping Neptune.

OKW and OB West, von Rundstedt's headquarters, had both come to the conclusion there would be several landings and other diversionary operations. They were also agreed that the Allies would launch their attack with airborne forces dropped either at dusk or in daylight—while it was light enough to see what they were doing—and these drops would be followed up by seaborne forces coming in at night when the tide was high. Rommel disagreed with this too. He became convinced there would only be one invasion, and though he could not be sure where it would come, the date could be calculated from factors as uncompromising as the moon and the tide.

After a discussion with Staubwasser on 31 May 1944, Rommel came to the conclusion that the most likely dates were the 5, 6 and 7 June, always assuming the weather, the most important factor of all, was suitable. He and Staubwasser also agreed that in order to deal with the devil's garden the ground troops would land just after daybreak, soon after low tide. The airborne forces would have dropped by moonlight, several hours previously.

Despite the lack of a large port, Rommel also decided that the threat to the Normandy beaches was real enough to justify a direct approach to Hitler, to convince him and persuade him to hand over control of the four powerful Panzer divisions which were the OKW reserve in the West.

His application, and Hitler's rejection of it, was followed with interest by the Allies through Ultra, and Rommel then realized he would have to go personally to reason with the Fuehrer at Berchtesgaden. It was a trip which could fit in very conveniently with a visit to his wife on her birthday, 6 June, at their house in Herrelingen, not far from Ulm. But, like the Allied invasion, this would depend on the weather. He could not possibly leave his headquarters if the weather in the first week of June was fine.

To the Allies, reading the Ultra signals, Hitler's refusal to commit his reserves to Rommel was complete justification for Fortitude South—although there was still a great deal of uneasiness about the sudden increase of activity among the Normandy defences. The exchange of signals between Rommel and Hitler did however reveal that although Rommel was very uneasy about Normandy he did not know where the invasion would come; Hitler was determined to be ready to meet the full-scale attack across the Pas de Calais. Yet, because of Zeppelin, by the end of May 1944 his reserves of armour in the West had dwindled considerably.

12
The Southern Flank

Zeppelin was the codename for deception plans and operations in the general area of the Balkans in 1943 and 1944; and the task of the London Controlling Section was made easier by the growing reluctance of Hungary and Rumania to continue to support Hitler in a war he was not, apparently, going to win. On the other hand, Hitler depended on his allies, Bulgaria, Hungary and Rumania, for manpower, especially to replace the fearful losses on the Eastern front, and for oil. A third of Germany's oil supplies came from Rumania.

The Bodyguard plan for the Balkans was aimed at encouraging the people of the three main States to sabotage the German war effort and persuade their governments to take them out of the war. If the governments proved to be recalcitrant, they were to be overthrown by revolution. The main object was not to induce these States to leave the Axis alliance and make separate peace, but to compel Hitler to withdraw troops from the West as garrisons to keep them under his control.

In practice, persuading the governments of Bulgaria, Hungary and Rumania to abandon Hitler presented no difficulties. By the summer of 1943 they had all, separately, come to the conclusion that with the huge Russian army rolling towards them it was the only sensible thing to do.

In Bulgaria, Hitler's troubles began in August 1943, when Czar Boris III visited him at Berchtesgaden and told him Bulgaria was leaving the Axis. After a series of emotional upheavals Hitler persuaded him to change his mind, but a few days later Boris died very suddenly and unexpectedly in his palace in Sofia. He had been poisoned, or at least, Goebbels said he had, but the actual circumstances of his assassination or suicide seem to be a complete mystery. If he had been murdered, it was very difficult to decide who had done it, although the motive was clear enough. Boris III was the only man capable of holding his country together; without him, though never very strong, the government was determined to end Bulgaria's part in the war. SOE and OSS agents went to work, inciting the people to revolt against Hitler, who had to make special efforts to keep the government loyal to the undertaking given by Boris at Berchtesgaden just before his death.

Finally, a few months later, Hitler was forced to increase the German garrison. His efforts to keep the Balkans under control were not helped by the sudden defection of Italy on 3 September 1943, when Marshal Pietro Badoglio, head of a provisional government set up after the fall of Benito Mussolini, the Italian dictator, negotiated an armistice for the Italians. But the circumstances in Italy were quite different from those in the Balkan States. Hitler's fears for his southern flank kept large German forces in Italy opposing the Allies right up until the collapse of Germany.

The ruler of Hungary, Admiral Nicholas Horthy, lost his faith in Hitler when he failed to keep his promise to conquer Russia before the winter of 1941. Feeling he had made a bad mistake in ever getting involved with Hitler, in the spring of 1942 Horthy asked an anglophile compatriot, Nicholas Kallay, to become Prime Minister. Kallay's first public announcement in office implied that he intended to extricate Hungary from the war as rapidly as possible. After the 1st Hungarian Army had been destroyed by the Russians in the Stalingrad battle which lasted from 23 August 1942 until 2 February 1943, Kallay tried to approach the Allies through the Vatican, in the hope of making a separate peace. He got no sympathy from Britain, and the complicated story of negotiations and missions which achieved nothing for Hungary illustrates the determination of the Bodyguard planners not to let any of Hitler's allies slip out of his control.

To keep Kallay's hopes alive, what purported to be a secret Anglo-American diplomatic mission landed by parachute near Budapest, but its members belonged to SOE, OSS and MI6, and when Kallay realized what they were, he ordered them out of the country. Meanwhile various things had been happening. News of the secret mission had been leaked through MI6 channels to the Germans. Hitler was also allowed to discover that preparations were being made for an attack on Trieste by Patton's 7th Army (by this time it was in the Bodyguard Order of Battle of fictitious formations), and that OSS and SOE were active in the area of the Ljubljana Gap.

At the end of 1943 Rommel was sent to the Balkans to organize counter measures against the American 7th Army threat; and when it did not materialize Hitler recalled him and sent him on the tour of the Atlantic Wall. It was the report on this tour that fell into the hands of Dominique Ponchardier during the raid on the command post near St-Malo.

Although the Americans did not attack Trieste, by March 1944 there were definite signs of impending revolution in Hungary, and Hitler, completely confused by Zeppelin and the secret diplomacy of Kallay, sent his troops in. It had not been easy to find the necessary units. There were none to spare from the Russian front. He had just had to send five divisions, earmarked for France, to contain the Allied landing at Anzio in Italy, and reserves in Germany were barely enough for internal security duties if the army of foreign slave labourers gave trouble. The OKW raised a few infantry divisions, mainly from Rumania and Bulgaria, but there was no armour—the spearhead of every German invasion since the attack on Poland—unless it was taken from the reserves behind the Atlantic Wall; and it was.

The Panzer Lehr Division and 2 SS Panzer Corps were moved from France to Hungary.

Very few shots were fired during the invasion of Hungary. The Germans took over the administration and Kallay sought asylum in the Turkish Embassy, much to the embarrassment of the Turks. He subsequently surrendered, because the SS made it clear that if he did not choose to come out, they would come in and get him. He was sent to the concentration camp at Mauthausen—where he may perhaps have met the wife of René Duchez. He survived, and died in exile after the war.

As Head of State, Marshal Antonescu decided early in 1944 that Rumania must sever its connections with Hitler and the Axis alliance. This was largely because his intelligence service warned him that the Russians were about to invade through the Black Sea port of Constantsa, about 150 miles from Bucharest. The report was in fact the result of joint efforts by the Russians, the London Controlling Section and Colonel William H. Baumer of the American Joint Security Control, all acting in the interests of Bodyguard, but it caused very great alarm in Rumania.

By a show of force, making the point that an army actually seen to be ready and willing to attack is likely to be more dangerous than one which has not yet appeared, Hitler kept Rumania and her vital oil supplies on his side, but the cost of asserting himself in the Balkans was high; four of his best divisions had been withdrawn from France—these were 9 and 10 SS Panzer, making up 2 SS Panzer Corps, the Panzer Lehr and one infantry division of high combat efficiency. About three months after D-Day Hitler said that if the SS Panzer Corps had been available as a counter-attack force when the Allies invaded, the Normandy landings would not have been successful. It would certainly have made the task of the Allies more difficult.

So far, Bodyguard had achieved a great deal. In the spring of 1944 the German garrison in Norway was awaiting attack by the British 4th Army, the American 15 Corps and a Russian force; Hitler, OKW and von Rundstedt were waiting for Patton and FUSAG to storm across the Pas de Calais, and some of the best troops in France had gone off to prevent a major political and military disaster in south-east Europe.

One may well ask how it was that Hitler, with his own perception and with intelligence staff officers of the quality of von Roenne and Gehlen, could apparently have been so deceived. There are two reasons. The first is that as the Grand Alliance of Britain, America and Russia began to close in for the kill, Hitler moved further away into his own world in which problems could be solved by ignoring them, the war would be won by his secret weapons and failure was not to be considered because it was too unpleasant to contemplate. Bad news was related to failure and so must not be believed.

The second reason is that Schellenberg's battle to take over Abwehr resulted in the loss of the whole Abwehr system at the one moment in German history when the fate of the whole nation depended on accurate, reliable and timely intelligence; because it is only by good intelligence that good deception can be revealed. When Canaris was pushed into limbo his organization went out of business almost overnight, and the SD were quite incapable of replacing it and certainly could not sort out the mess made by the conflict.

Gehlen and von Roenne were first-class operational intelligence officers who interpreted the reports they received in terms of enemy capabilities and intentions, and though they could task the Wehrmacht intelligence services of the ground, naval and air forces, they had no control over Schellenberg's SD which had put Abwehr—the Wehrmacht espionage service—out of action. Thus, whereas Gehlen could obtain accurate operational intelligence from units in contact with the enemy on the eastern front, von Roenne had to rely for his intelligence on an organization controlled by MI6 and the XX Committee; and because Canaris was in retirement, no one in the intelligence staff at Zossen really knew what was happening in the Balkans. Even so, it is doubtful whether the shortcomings of the German intelligence system in the West were a serious disadvantage to Hitler who believed only what he wanted to believe.

Zeppelin worked well, but Copperhead, another deception scheme related to Hitler's southern flank, seems to have had little effect, despite all the trouble taken over it. The object of it was to turn the attention of the Germans away from an invasion in northern France and concentrate it on the threat of an Allied landing in strength in the south of France. After the war the story became well known as that of 'Monty's Double', but attached to it, certainly in some Service circles at the time, were undertones indicating that the description given later in a book and a film, both entitled *I Was Monty's Double*, was not entirely accurate.

Lieutenant M. E. Clifton James of the Royal Army Pay Corps, in peacetime an actor, closely resembled General Montgomery. The likeness was noted by Colonel Jervis-Reid of the Committee of Special Means (Ops B) when the *News Chronicle* published a photograph of Clifton James impersonating Montgomery in an entertainment for the Forces given by the RAPC Drama and Variety Group on the stage of the Comedy Theatre in London. Jervis-Reid felt that if British servicemen could be deceived by the likeness it could perhaps be exploited for other purposes. Accordingly, on 22 April 1944, Clifton James, stationed at Leicester, received a letter signed by Lieutenant Colonel David Niven, then an Assistant Director of Army Kinematography, referring somewhat imprecisely to the making of propaganda films. Clifton James was interviewed by Jervis-Reid in London.

There were problems. Montgomery exuded authority and self-confidence. Clifton James had virtually no personality at all. Montgomery never smoked and would not touch alcohol. Clifton James was a heavy smoker and every now and again was apt to go off on an alcoholic 'blind'. The physical resemblance was real enough but in every other way the two men were so far apart that any hope of successful deception on the lines Jervis-Reid had in mind seemed very remote. Clifton James was given a cover story relating now to training films and not propaganda, and told to study Montgomery's speech, gait, mannerisms and so on. When it became apparent that as a professional actor he could acquire Montgomery's air of command as well as imitate his voice and movements, it was decided to go ahead.

The plan was that just before D-Day, when the Germans would have every reason to believe Montgomery was in England and preoccupied with the final preparations for invasion, he would appear first in Gibraltar, then Algiers and finally in Cairo, and be seen to be planning operations in the Mediterranean area. It was hoped this would have three results; first, if Montgomery was moving around the Mediterranean at the end of April, German Intelligence would assume there could be no invasion of France in the first week of June, consequently — and secondly — they would believe that when the invasion fleet sailed it was merely on another exercise. Thirdly, this corroborative evidence of the threat to southern France would make Hitler keep four Panzer divisions, two of which were SS, to the south of the Loire and not deploy them as reinforcements against Neptune.

Monty's Double arrived in Gibraltar on the morning of 26 May and gave an excellent performance ably assisted by the Governor, General Sir Ralph Eastwood, who was not only 'in the know' but had known the real Montgomery ever since they had been at Sandhurst together. In the presence of civilians, some of whom were believed to be German agents, Clifton James talked incisively about a 'Plan 303' and appears to have been very convincing. At Algiers on the following day he was met by General Sir Henry Maitland Wilson whose combined British, American and French staff were lined up to meet the distinguished visitor. Clifton James was then taken off to rooms made ready for him in the St George Hotel and in a very short time all Algiers knew that 'Montgomery' had arrived on some urgent operational mission.

It was at this stage that something went very wrong, and rumours circulating soon afterwards implied that despite the care taken by Jervis-Reid to keep him away from alcohol, Clifton James not only made himself drunk but was seen to be drunk while wearing the famous double-badged beret, uniform, insignia and medals of the teetotal Montgomery. At all events, Copperhead was abruptly switched off and Monty's Double disappeared. He was taken back to England in a transport aircraft, after D-Day, told to return to his desk at Leicester and warned that if he opened his mouth he would be court-martialled. His book, or rather, the book about his adventures, was published in 1954, when he was at last allowed to tell his story, and it made lavish claims for the success of Copperhead. In fact there was nothing in Ultra messages or in German documents examined after the war to indicate that any account had been taken of Montgomery's visit to the Mediterranean.

The probable reasons were that Quicksilver and Fortitude South had built up Patton and FUSAG as a far greater menace than Montgomery, and the Germans were far more concerned about quite another deception plan called Royal Flush in the Mediterranean.

One facet of Royal Flush was the making of inquiries at Ambassador to Foreign Minister level to discover whether the Spanish would grant facilities in the port of Barcelona for the evacuation and treatment of Allied casualties in any forthcoming operations. At the same time diplomatic staffs began to investigate the capacity of the port for handling stores and providing accommodation for large medical staffs, and it was clear that the Allies were hoping to use Barcelona as a base hospital area for a major campaign on the French Riviera. The Caudillo, General Franco, gave his permission, and it was this, in conjunction with the movements of the American 91 Infantry Division and the expansion of the French 1st Army in North Africa, as well as the constant activity of reconnaissance aircraft and naval vessels in the Golfe du Lion, that made Hitler decide to keep the German Army of the Riviera in its present locations for the time being.

All this came under the general heading of the codeword Vendetta which incorporated Royal Flush, was directly concerned with deception in southern France and was itself part of Fortitude South.

Thus, by the end of April 1944 it seemed that everything was working out just as the Bodyguard planners had hoped, especially in Norway, the Balkans and the south of France. German reinforcements had been sent to Italy, 164 Axis divisions faced the Russians in the East, and at this time the most hopeful sign of all was that the defences along the Calvados coast in the Neptune area were still comparatively light and manned by only two under-strength infantry divisions, 709 and 716, spread thinly between Cherbourg and le Havre. Both divisions were poorly equipped, and 709 in particular relied on horses and mules for the movement of its guns and supplies.

Even so, with the exception of Montgomery who had his own very right ideas about the confidence of a commander being infectious and inspiring, several of the Allied Commanders were apprehensive to the point of extreme pessimism about being able to hold a beach-head against determined counter-attacks by Panzers. There was a tendency to relate what might happen on the Far Shore with what was actually happening in Italy, where the figure of casualties in the eight months since the landings at the beginning of September 1943 were now approaching 150,000. It was felt that conditions were likely to be far worse in Normandy, where the Germans could bring up a far greater number of troops and where they had had four years, since the Dunkirk evacuation, in which to build fortifications.

In the armed forces of the Allies there was a strange atmosphere of inevitability. The return to France, and all that it entailed, could not be avoided. Everyone was caught up in a vast, inexorable process that nothing could now divert or stop. Amongst American troops morale was not high, but there was no suggestion that they would not carry the task through. They expected heavy casualties, and seemed to look on death or mutilation with the same resignation and indifference as Japanese soldiers. This is a bad sign in troops who do not normally have an oriental fatalism, because the soldier who thinks he is going to be killed often lacks the fighting spirit which could be his salvation. One of the problems was that many of the American troops had not been in action before and had no real idea of what to expect.

On the other hand, morale among more experienced British soldiers was remarkably high. Lieutenant Colonel (later General Sir Richard) Goodwin wrote of his own battalion of the Suffolks that 'I have never in my life seen troops so tough and fit. Despite the extreme cold and wet, their enthusiasm on these exercises [just before D-Day] was quite outstanding'. The morale of Canadian troops was high too. Perhaps the difference between the Americans and their allies was that the British and Canadians were determined to avenge Dunkirk and Dieppe. They had well-defined incentives.

Montgomery was almost alone in having no doubts about the outcome; or if he had, he never expressed them. Sustained by his faith he was quite sure the Almighty would not allow Hitler, the personification of evil if not the Devil Incarnate, to triumph over the forces of righteousness, freedom and truth, but at the same time he took every possible precaution to ensure that if the God of Battles should happen to be looking in another direction at a critical moment, those forces could look after themselves for the time being. He spoke about his confidence over and over again to the men who had to fight the battle on the beaches, and his personal influence on his soldiers, from formation commanders downwards, was perhaps his greatest attribute as a commander. Military historians may well argue for years to come about his merits as a tactician, but there was never any doubt about his leadership. He inspired confidence and trust, which in battle are far more important than affection, and he was one of the very few in the high command who did not appear to be unduly perturbed when very disquieting news from across the Channel indicated that almost at the last moment Bodyguard might have failed and the secrets of Neptune were known to the Germans.

In the first week of May 1944, air photographs taken on reconnaissance missions showed that a great deal of work had suddenly begun on the beach obstacles and defences on the Calvados coast, hitherto poorly protected. In addition, agents in France reported the movement of reinforcements, notably that of the Panzer Lehr which had been brought back from Hungary and stationed in the area of Argentan, and of 21 Panzer Division which had come from Brittany to just south of Caen—within easy reach of the beaches where the British and Canadians were to land. Even more significant was the move to the Cotentin peninsula of 91 Air Landing Division, which specialized in anti-paratroop operations, into the triangle of Bricquebec, St-Sauveur-le-Vicomte and Ste-Mère-Église, and this area happened to be the drop zone of 82 and 101 American paratroop divisions. The German 6 Parachute Regiment had also moved up to the south west of Carentan. There was now a considerable concentration of enemy troops in the Neptune area.

The only ray of light on an horizon now ominously dark was the fact that by far the most powerful Panzer formation in the West, 1 SS Panzer Corps 'Adolf Hitler', commanded by *Obergruppenführer* Sepp Dietrich, had *not* moved. Its 'Das Reich' Division was still at Toulouse, largely as the result of Vendetta, and the 'Adolf Hitler' Division was still deployed between Antwerp and Brussels as a counter-attack force for the Allied invasion of the Pas de Calais. It was reasonable to assume that if Fortitude South had been fully penetrated, both these armoured divisions would have been moved towards the Calvados coast, if only because Hitler was determined that the future of the Third Reich would be decided in the West.

When they heard this news, those Allied Commanders who were already pessimistic began to think about what had happened at Dieppe and to wonder whether Neptune was now feasible, but in fact the situation on the Far Shore was not as bad as it seemed. Fortitude had not been penetrated and Bodyguard was still intact.

Ever since February 1944 Hitler had been brooding over the options available to the Allies. In March he came to the conclusion that in common with Norway, the Balkans, Trieste, the Ljubljana Gap, the French Riviera and the Pas de Calais, the coast of Normandy in the Bay of the Seine was also threatened. His intuition was active again. He had not visited von Rundstedt's or Rommel's headquarters. He had not seen the ground. It had just occurred to him that the defences in the Bay of the Seine were thin, and like a chess player moving pieces on a board he had thickened them up a little, not because he thought the main attack would be made there but because he was sure the Allies would do what he had planned to do in Operation Sealion (the invasion of Britain), and launch diversionary attacks. In making these moves he had in effect dispersed some of the 'mass of manoeuvre' which could have had far more influence on the battle at a later stage.

In his headquarters in Paris, Admiral Krancke had already made an appreciation that was wrong in all respects, and so his Kriegsmarine had been briefed to expect the enemy in a set of conditions that did not feature in the Neptune plan. According to Speidel, he advised OKW that 18 May was the 'certain date' for the invasion, and when that day came, and went, he forecast that the attack would be in August. He thought it extremely unlikely that the Allies would risk a landing in the mouth of the Seine or on the Calvados coast because of strong currents and rock-strewn shallows. It was for this reason that, as Speidel says, 'the coastal defences on this part of the Normandy coast were not formidable'. It would be more correct to say they were not quite so formidable as those in the Pas de Calais.

Von Rundstedt could not make up his mind where or when the Allies would land. He studied the pattern of Allied bombing during May and came to the conclusion that its object was to sever communications and inhibit the movement of reinforcements to the area under seaborne attack. The destruction of the bridges across the Seine led him to think the Allies might land in Normandy, possibly in the area of the Cotentin peninsula because of their need for a port, but in general he agreed with Hitler that their main effort would be in the Pas de Calais.

Rommel was considerably relieved when Hitler decided to reinforce Normany because the wide, inviting beaches along the Calvados coast made him uneasy. The defences were not as strong as they ought to be. He set to work, and it was his driving energy that inspired his troops to work long hours on the beach obstacles, barbed-wire fences, trench systems and 'asparagus' that suddenly began to appear on the air photographs taken by Allied pilots on reconnaissance missions. 'Asparagus' was the name given to the stout stakes, with anti-personnel mines lashed to the tops of them, which were driven into fields and clearings in woods to discourage airborne landings.

The Todt Building Organization began to construct more concrete strong-points to cover the great sweep of beach that was to be known as Omaha, but, as Rommel knew, time was running out.

13

Pigeons and Bigots

There is a story, still current among people who live near the Neptune beaches in Normandy, that 3,000 American soldiers died on Omaha Beach — Bloody Omaha — because two carrier pigeons were shot. In his book *Invasion — They're Coming!*, Paul Carell gives the German account of the invasion and the battle for France, and he describes the shooting down of what he calls the 'flying postmen' by troops armed with French shotguns who lay in wait for them along cliffs and among sand dunes. It is said that the two fateful birds were carrying the information that the German 352 Infantry Division, of three regiments, was moving up to the coast between the mouth of the river Vire and the little harbour of Port-en-Bessin; the effect of this was that they would be in a position to oppose the landing of 1 and 29 Divisions of the American 5 Corps.

352 Division had fought in Russia. It was an efficient, battle-hardened formation, and its arrival meant that instead of there being only two under-strength and under-equipped German infantry divisions, 709 and 716, to defend the Calvados coast, there were now three; and the third, though desperately short of vehicles, consisted of first-class troops.

According to the story, the local Resistance group reported all this to London, by pigeon, but the French Resistance and the MI6 network in France did not rely entirely on pigeons for transmitting vital information because they were well equipped with radio sets and always used them in an emergency. Furthermore, although there were gaps in SHAEF intelligence, the move of 352 Division was not one of them.

Exactly a fortnight before D-Day, Brigadier E. T. Williams, Montgomery's senior intelligence officer in 21st Army Group, gave warning of the possible move up of this Division to thicken up the defences of the Wall between 709 and 716 Divisions. His warning was printed in *21 Army Group Weekly Neptune Intelligence Review* issued on 3 June, and though on a very limited circulation, it was distributed to senior American commanders. It has been suggested that the information was withheld from the lower levels of command because of a possibly adverse effect on morale, and if this was true, it was not the first occasion on which the troops of an attacking force have not been given a complete picture of the opposition. The first day of the battle of the Somme, 18 July 1916, is a classic example. The assaulting infantry were told that the preliminary bombardment lasting 14 days had 'left not a soul alive' in the German positions. They were not told that air photographs showed large areas of the trench system still intact and protected by uncut wire.

The Resistance Group may well have sent the information by pigeon, duplicating it as a precaution, and both birds may have been shot, but the loss of them was not the main cause of the slaughter at Omaha Beach.

The advantages of a pigeon service are obvious. It is swift and silent. The birds tend to fly high and fast, in good conditions at speeds up to 60 mph over long distances, and it is extremely difficult to intercept them. 'Homing' birds of various species have been used for carrying messages for literally thousands of years—the Chinese in the second millenium BC are said to have trained swallows—but in 1908, when wireless telegraphy was first introduced, the general opinion was that pigeons would no longer be needed in any wartime communication system. This was soon proved to be unfounded, and pigeons were used extensively throughout the First World War. One application of the pigeon service was the dropping of birds, accompanied by questionnaires and instructions, by parachute in enemy-occupied territory, and it yielded a mass of valuable information. Agents parachuting and ballooning into enemy country used pigeons to report their safe arrival, and it was the general practice for SOE agents in the Second World War to take a pigeon with them at the start of a mission. The pigeon was normally released as soon as possible after the landing.

The snag with using pigeons for communications is that they will only fly in one direction—back to the loft they came from. Therefore they have to be taken to the point of despatch. This is not a problem in the case of an agent merely reporting his arrival, but there are obvious difficulties in providing agents on the ground, or Resistance Groups, with birds to send off as and when a need arises. Not the least of these difficulties was the German tendency to shoot without question or trial anyone possessing caged pigeons—and exactly the same situation had arisen during the First World War. The very real dangers attached to the pigeon service in Occupied Europe prompted the issue of what became known as an Alanbrooke Certificate, in official recognition of the courage of people who used pigeons to convey information about the enemy.

The only means of supplying pigeons to agents and Resistance Groups on the other side of the Channel was by air, and at present it is not possible to obtain exact details. There was, however, an Operation Columba in existence from 13 March 1942 until 20 August 1944, based on the RAF Station at Tempsford, and W. H. Osman's little book *Pigeons in World War II*, published in 1950, gives a great deal of information. Pigeons were especially valuable in areas where German direction finding endangered the lives of radio operators and, repeating the system developed in the First World War, for acquiring information from the local population in areas not easily accessible. Birds were dropped singly, by parachute, but the losses were heavy. A great many birds may not have been found, and others were found by Germans, collaborators and people deterred from making use of them by the savage penalties under German regulations. However, over a period of three and half years, 16,554 pigeons were dropped and 1,842 returned to the United Kingdom. They carried information, photographs and diagrams relating to the Atlantic Wall, German installations and secret-weapons sites, and in comparison with radio messages, their real advantage was that they could carry visual information — sketch or map — which a radio operator might not have been able to convey so concisely or accurately.

The first pigeon to be used for bringing secret information out of enemy-occupied France was named Kenley Lass. The record does not state whether the Kenley is the one in Shropshire or the one in Surrey. She was carried by an agent who dropped by parachute and then had to walk nine miles in darkness across country with the bird hidden in his coat. There was then a delay of eleven days while the agent collected the information he had been sent to obtain, and during this time she was concealed in a house. She was eventually released at 8.20 am on 20 October 1940 and arrived at her loft in Kenley at 3 pm on the same day — a distance of well over 300 miles in 6 hours 40 minutes.

From this date and until the end of the war the Air Ministry Pigeon Section handled 7,556 messages. Three of these were the earliest D-Day reports, 20 were of known enemy origin, 31 were of suspected enemy origin and 9 carried German messages. Pigeons were also carried by all bomber crews and were directly responsible for the saving of many lives from ditched or crashed aircraft — but this was nothing to do with intelligence or deception. They were also used by the crews of light naval craft.

During the month of May 1944 there was a growing sense of tension throughout England; a feeling of approaching climax. After long preparation the huge forces gathered for the liberation of Europe were being wound up like some great clockwork mechanism, ready, on the release of a single catch, to spring forward.

From hundreds of small towns and villages, whose inhabitants had become accustomed to seeing soldiers of many different nationalities in the shops and churches and pubs, the troops suddenly disappeared without warning. In the countries of the south and west the 21st Army Group assembled silently in places where there was easy access to the ports; in Kent and Essex, Cambridgeshire, Suffolk and Norfolk the fictitious but voluble First United States Army Group of General George Patton kept the German Y Service busy at its radio receivers, and lights not too carefully shaded gave the impression of a great deal of movement along roads and much loading activity at all jetties in all ports and harbours at night.

Garbo, Brutus and Treasure sent a flood of reports to their handlers bearing out the intercepted radio intelligence and the photographs and reports of reconnaissance pilots, and their chorus had now been augmented by a girl given the name of Bronx.

In the middle of May she informed German Intelligence that she now had definite information. The Allied landings would be in the Bay of Biscay on or about 15 June. Treasure told her handler, Major Kliemann, that through her friend Nelly who was on terms of the greatest intimacy with the Free French General Koenig, she had discovered the invasion would quite certainly be in the Pas de Calais in the second week of July.

Schellenberg, nominally in control of Abwehr for the last three months, sat in his enormous office, so very different from Canaris's old room on the top floor of 74-76 Tirpitzufer, and tried to evaluate the messages—250 of them in the period just before D-Day—each of which told him when and where the invasion would be. He had plenty of choice; they covered every possible area and a wide range of dates: Denmark, before 18 June; Belgium between 19 and 25 May; the Pas de Calais between Dunkirk and St-Valery, on the night of 18 May; and so on. One of the messages, from a French officer in Algiers, was accurate. He said the invasion would be on the coast of Normandy on the 5, 6 or 7 June; but his reputation for reliability was such that his message was read in reverse. It convinced Schellenberg that the invasion would be on any day except 5, 6 or 7 June, and anywhere except on the coast of Normandy.

There is still some argument whether this French colonel really was a traitor who had somehow obtained the information from de Gaulle's headquarters in London, or whether he was a double agent with whom the XX Committee took a calculated risk. Perhaps the Committee felt the Germans would come to their own conclusions if, in the mass of espionage reports, certain dates on which the moon and tides were suitable, were not mentioned.

Admiral Krancke's categorical statement, which convinced OKW, that the

Allies would attack on 18 May was of considerable assistance to the Allies because, from this date, the defenders of the Atlantic Wall began to lose a great deal of sleep in one General Alert after another. Furthermore, all through the month of May the weather was hot and dry, there was no wind and the sea was smooth — perfect invasion weather. It seemed obvious that if the Allies were coming they would come very soon, before the weather broke.

As always, frequent cries of 'Wolf!' promote indifference to real danger. Soldiers made to 'stand to' night after night while radars scan the empty sea and nothing moves in the devil's garden on the beaches, tend to lose interest in alarms and forecasts which always turn out to be false. This was true of Rommel's troops, especially those in Normandy, because every day and all day they were driven hard to strengthen the fortifications, put up obstacles, hammer in the 'asparagus', dig trenches and weapon-pits and lay minefields. They needed their sleep.

As the glorious summer days succeeded one another and the Allies did not come, scepticism replaced the feeling of urgency. The Allies would not come at all. What was said to be happening in England was nothing more than a gigantic bluff designed to tie down German forces in the West while the Russian steamroller crushed those in the East. There would be no invasion. The Allied deception plan was becoming clear. They would let the Russians sap the strength of the Wehrmacht and there would be no attack across the Channel until all the German formations in the West had been withdrawn to deal with the menace in the East.

Even Hitler himself began to have his doubts about an attack in the West, and the general atmosphere of confusion and uncertainty was made more tense by a strange and ominous quiescence in the areas of active operations. Nothing seemed to be happening in Italy and there was little or no movement on the Russian front. The reasons, unknown to Hitler, were that in Italy the Allies were making their preparations for Operation Diadem — linking up the main front with the Anzio beach-head and advancing on Rome — and in the East the Red Army was getting ready for the summer offensive, timed to give all possible help to Neptune.

Yet this apparent hiatus was filled with itense clandestine activity, designed to make every German soldier feel he was surrounded by ruthless, implacable enemies determined to take revenge for all the crimes committed by the occupation forces. Factories and dumps were blown up, trains were derailed, explosions wrecked repair shops and fuel-storage tanks, individual soldiers returning to their billets at night disappeared without trace, partisan commando raids destroyed radar and radio-interception stations. The number of incidents ran into thousands, and they seemed to be going on everywhere, in places as far apart as Denmark and Crete, in Norway, Rhodes and the Balkans, and all over France. The Germans reacted savagely, but no longer as the conquerors of Europe. Their fear of the *maquis* was genuine and their response revealed a nervousness amounting to hysteria. They sought out and slaughtered the men and women of the Resistance, they took hostages and murdered them in horrible ways, yet all they succeeded in doing was swell the tide of hatred and revenge. Every *maquisard* they killed was at once replaced by others in rapidly increasing numbers, and although on the military fronts the calm might be a prelude to a storm, elsewhere the inflammation of Resistance was the gathering of a boil which sooner or later had to burst.

Meanwhile, in Britain, the invasion forces moved into their assembly areas under the cover of Quicksilver, and the Committee of Special Means and the London Controlling Section added yet another voice to the choir singing so persuasively to Schellenberg and von Roenne. It was known from Ultra that Hitler was persuading himself the Allied preparations might be a hoax, and there was always a danger that his intelligence staff might begin to wonder whether the intelligence obtained from air reconnaissance and radio interception was geniune, and whether their agents in England were being deceived. It was therefore decided that an eye-witness of irreproachable integrity should be sent to Germany, a man whose word would not, in any circumstances, be doubted.

His name was Hans Kramer, his rank was General der Panzertruppen, he held the Knight's Cross of the Iron Cross with Oak Leaves, and his last assignment had been Commander of the Afrika Korps. He had been a prisoner of war in England ever since the defeat of the Axis forces in North Africa in May 1943 and his ill health provided an excellent opportunity to send him back to his home under a repatriation scheme organized by the Swedish Red Cross.

In the middle of May 1944 he was driven from a prisoner of war camp in South Wales by a roundabout route to the Detailed Interrogation Centre in Kensington. On the way he saw the invasion assembly areas, the concentrations of shipping and the apparently endless ranks of aircraft. He was introduced to General Patton, 'the Commander-in-Chief of the First United States Army Group'. He was allowed to meet divisional commanders who made it clear that their destination was Calais. He did not, however, know where he had been. He was told that General Patton and his Army Group were in Kent and East Sussex; he was given to understand he had been driven through these counties, but he had no means of confirming the information so freely imparted because all signposts and place names had been removed as long ago as 1940.

General Kramer returned to Germany in the Swedish vessel *Gripsholm.* He arrived in Berlin on 23 May and reported first to the German General Staff and then OKW. He was given a few days leave and posted to Paris, to the headquarters of General Baron Geyr von Schweppenburg, commanding the Panzer forces in the West. His account of all he had seen in England apparently created a certain amount of alarm and despondency, and he was accused of 'adopting a defeatist attitude'— by Goering—but the main effect of his return to Germany was to dispel any doubt about the reality of the invasion threat. There was no longer any question of a hoax. The Allies were going to invade; but in spite of all the assessments and guesses of German commanders and intelligence staffs, and the intuition of the Fuehrer there was no one on the Far Shore who knew the answers to the two vital questions: When? and Where?

Hitler had no doubt where the attack would come, nor had von Rundstedt, but no one could be sure. Kramer's report seemed to confirm the Fuehrer's beliefs but Rommel was not entirely convinced. He was still resolved to see Hitler and insist on being given control of the Panzer reserve, in case of a landing in Normandy.

The idea behind General Kramer's conducted tour was not new. In 1066 Harold Godwin of England sent spies across the Channel—their voyage is recorded in the Bayeux Tapestry—to bring back information on Duke William the Bastard's army assembling at the mouth of the river Dives. They were caught almost at once and taken to Duke William. He gave them all the details of his large force and sent them back to Harold, to persuade him he could not win.

The beautiful May weather persisted, and while the sentries in the command posts and defence works on the far side of the Channel waited, apparently in vain, Eisenhower issued the last of the orders marking the end of the preparations for Neptune.

The Allied planning staff had come to the same conclusion as Rommel. On three days only, 5, 6 and 7 June, would factors such as tides and currents, phase of the moon and hours of daylight be right for Neptune. Y-Day, codenamed Halcyon, the day on which all preparations for the assault must be completed, was set for 1 June. D-Day was to be Halcyon plus 4—5 June— although if the weather on that day was bad it would still be possible to launch the operation on 6 or 7 June. If for any reason, the weather being the most likely one, none of these days was suitable, the next opportunity would be between 19 and 22 June.

Movement towards the embarkation points actually began on 18 May. The largest combined operation ever undertaken had now been set in motion, and it is a military truism that the larger an operation, the more difficult it is to make any change of plan. Everything now depended on the weather, for bad weather could nullify all the essential conditions of tides and moonlight, and any change of plan necessitated by it could very well have a serious effect on deception and security. Deception on so vast a scale as Bodyguard was perpetually at risk, and it demanded the same degree and standard of security as the operational plan for Neptune. Any delay imposed on the operational plan created great difficulties for the deceivers because, unlike operational plans which within limits must be flexible enough to enable the unforeseen to be contained or exploited, deception, if it is to be successful, must be worked out step-by-step in advance and all possible side-effects or repercussions calculated at every stage. It is only a flimsy screen put up to conceal genuine intentions, and some apparently trivial error or miscalculation can be the chink through which the enemy can see all that lies behind.

Surprise can be a vital ingredient of success, and though it depends to a very large extent on deception it can only be preserved by security. Thus, although an operational plan must be based on good intelligence and seconded by deception, the measure of its success is directly related to the standard of security which prevents the enemy from finding out what it is.

The British are not, by nature, security-minded. It is sometimes surprising to discover what intimate details of their lives they will reveal in casual conversation to complete strangers. It is not always easy to decide whether these details are in fact truth or mere fantasy, but on the whole there is a lack of reticence. It is therefore even more surprising to note how reticent, cautious and observant so many of them became during the war when proper regard was paid to the need for security, not only in keeping secrets from the enemy but being constantly on the watch for spies. All this was very largely the result of intensive publicity campaigns mounted by the government and summarized in the slogan 'Careless Talk Costs Lives'. It was very difficult for any enemy agent, even one unknown to the double agents working for the XX Committee, to survive for long in an island whose inhabitants were constantly reminded, on large hoardings, in buses, trains and offices, in hospitals, cinemas and even church porches, that they must be always on guard, always suspicious, and swift to report the activities of an incongruous or inquisitive stranger.

The censorship of mail and the monitoring of telephone exchanges became accepted as irksome but necessary wartime restrictions. Travel was strictly controlled and large areas of the countryside, particularly near coasts, were put out of bounds to all but those who had good reason for visiting them. When

General Eisenhower arrived to take up the appointment of Supreme Commander he issued instructions to every man and woman under his command telling them there was to be no relaxation of the security rules and that anyone who broke them would be the subject of the most stringent disciplinary action. Even so, when one considered the magnitude of the Overlord concept, the thousands of people involved in it, and consequently the thousands of potential breaches of security, it is astonishing that Bodyguard and Neptune were so successful. There were, inevitably, several bad moments and nasty scares.

Since the time and place of the invasion were the two secrets most eagerly sought by German Intelligence, a special procedure was devised for safe-guarding all documents bearing upon them. The word 'Bigot' was used as the highest security classification, and papers stamped with it could be seen only by 'Bigots'—carefully selected people who had been 'positively vetted' and 'cleared' to receive information at this level. Positive vetting involved extremely detailed checking of every aspect of character and background, parents and associates, education, political leanings, professional or business affiliations, and so on, and once admitted into the small circle of Bigots, his or her 'behaviour pattern' was also closely watched. Deviation in a behaviour pattern has been the undoing of many a spy or informer; a man known to be living on a beer income who suddenly starts drinking whisky is likely to attract the attention of people interested in finding out where the extra money is coming from.

One of the first of the Bigot scares was what has been described as the Case of the Chicago Parcel. In March 1944 the FBI informed the chief of army intelligence in Washington that a parcel containing papers marked Bigot had been broken open, apparently by accident, at an army mail sorting office in Chicago. At least a dozen people had seen the papers. The parcel had been despatched by Sergeant Thomas P. Kane, secretary to the head of the Ordnance Supply Section in Supreme Headquarters in London, and although the intended recipient of the parcel was marked as 'The Ordnance Division G-4' the address was that of Kane's sister in Chicago. Kane and his sister were of German origin and they lived in a predominantly German district of the city. Since the papers gave the date and place of the invasion and details of the planned build-up and expansion of the beach-head, inquiries into the mis-direction were conducted with some care. The explanation was simple enough. Kane was over-worked and worried about his sister who was ill. In a moment of mental aberration he had written the wrong address on the sealed parcel. Nevertheless, he and his sister and all the sorters who had seen, but possibly not read, the papers, were kept under surveillance until after D-Day.

In the middle of April a certain Major-General Henry Miller, an extremely able officer and a close friend of General Eisenhower, Quartermaster of the United States Ninth Air Force and a Bigot, announced at a dinner party given in a public dining room at Claridges that the invasion would take place before June the fifteenth. Regardless of the ties of friendship, Eisenhower reduced Miller to his substantive rank of lieutenant colonel and sent him back to the United States on the next boat. Only his excellent record saved him from a court martial.

Even before Miller had left the country a British staff officer to Brigadier Harris, who was in charge of SHAEF telecommunications, reported the loss of the SHAEF communications plan for Neptune while on his way home. He could not recall where he might have lost it, which was odd, because the document was a thick and heavy book. It contained all the radio nets and ciphers for the assault. Before Harris could take any action the Lost Property Office at Scotland Yard telephoned to say that a briefcase containing papers marked Bigot and Top Secret had been handed in by a taxi driver who found them after dropping a passenger at Waterloo Station. Brigadier Harris collected the briefcase himself.

In May, another American officer, Captain Edward Miles of the United States Navy, was the subject of a report by Air Chief Marshal Sir Trafford Leigh-Mallory, commanding the Tactical Air Force for Neptune. In the report, sent to General Eisenhower, Leigh-Mallory said that Captain Miles had drunk too much at a party and had revealed Top Secret information. Miles was sent home, but it is possible, as he himself claimed, that he was the victim of an intrigue. No other disciplinary action was taken against him and he subsequently served with great distinction at Okinawa and in the Philippines.

Eisenhower, on whose shoulders lay the heavy burden of all the major decisions for Neptune and Overlord, was badly shaken by these breaches of security. As the Supreme Commander he saw the whole picture and had no illusions about the risks. He was confident that the great force he commanded would be able to get ashore, the real problem would be to keep it there. If any Bigot-labelled information reached the Far Shore, or if any member of the Bigot circle fell into enemy hands and was interrogated by the Gestapo, whose methods were often effective, a concentration of all the available German resources could contain the beach-head and possibly force a withdrawal. He was chosen for the Supreme Command largely because of his equable temperament, but he admitted that the cases of General Miller and Captain Miles gave him 'the shakes'.

Perhaps the worst security scare of all stemmed from a most unfortunate incident on the night of 27 April 1944 when a force of nine German E-boats sailed from Cherbourg to attack a convoy off Lyme Bay on the coast of Devon and Dorset, and apparently by coincidence, intercepted Exercise Tiger. This was the American dress rehearsal for the landing on Utah Beach, and eight 5,000-ton LSTs (Landing Ship Tank) were on their way from Plymouth to the exercise area of Slapton Sands where conditions were much the same as those on the south-east coast of the Cotentin peninsula. The brief action was a major disaster, and it was all over in about 15 minutes. Two LSTs were sunk, taking a brigade of amphibious tanks with them, and one was badly damaged by 'homing' torpedoes fired from the E-boats. Nearly 650 men were killed or drowned and there were many more casulaties. The damage to morale was serious, and the loss of the LSTs meant there was now no LST reserve for Neptune. All this was bad enough, but to make matters worse, before breaking off the engagement one E-boat had switched on a searchlight, obviously looking for something, and another had cruised slowly among survivors in the water.

The vital question was whether they had picked up prisoners. There had been several Bigots in the LSTs. All the Bigots were eventually accounted for, but among the many missing there were plenty of men who knew enough about Neptune, and the tactics to be employed, to be of great value to the Germans.

The SHAEF Intelligence and Security staffs gave instructions that every missing man must be found, and divers had a gruesome task in retrieving identity discs from corpses in the sunken LSTs. It was not possible to account for everyone on the list—tides in the bay must have taken some out to sea—but an Admiralty inquiry came to the conclusion, disputed by some, that no prisoners could have been taken. Even so, the SHAEF planners spent some time trying to work out how Neptune could be altered in the light of information which they assumed the enemy now possessed.

This assumption seemed to be justified when, only a week later, Hitler issued his orders about devoting more attention to the defence of Normandy. This was followed soon after by reports from agents in France about the move of reinforcements; the sudden diversion of 91 Air Landing Division, en route from Germany to southern Brittany, to the area of La Haye-du-Puits; the deployment on the coast of 101 Regiment equipped with flame-throwers; the arrival near the Cap de la Hague of 17 Machine-Gun Battalion, of young, fit and well-trained men; and that 795 Georgian Battalion near Carentan had been joined by 100 Armoured Car Battalion. All these units had been warned to prepare for enemy airborne landings and they were now in the drop zones planned for the American 82 and 101 Airborne Divisions.

As a result of this information the drop zone of 82 Airborne Division was moved from St-Sauveur-le-Vicomte to the area of Ste-Mére-Église, and this was all that could be done. So great an operation, in which the timings were all inter-dependent and which involved so many thousands of men, ships and aircraft, could not be amended piecemeal. Apart from this minor adjustment the whole plan had to be either carried out or cancelled.

We know now that these moves of German units were not based on intelligence obtained from breaches of security, but the Allied Commanders did not know this, and in fact Ultra, the source of most of their information on Hitler's intentions, indicated there might have been some leakage. The Germans were in fact reacting to information — and also to Hitler's intuition — but the information had been acquired from sources over which SHAEF had little control. One was the signal traffic between SOE and its operatives in France which was very difficult to monitor and therefore even more difficult to keep secure, and the other was the German Y Service whose deductive analysis was, as always, outstandingly skilful.

The *Funkabwehr* analysts of the German signals intelligence system were considerably disconcerted by the security restrictions imposed on all British, American and Canadian radio nets in the period just before D-Day. So they concentrated on the distinctive patterns of transmissions, from which they gained little more than a general impression of the Allied Order of Battle — which included all the simulated radio traffic from fictitious Quicksilver units and formations. They were, however, able to identify air liaison traffic coming from formations to which an RAF liaison cell had been attached for ground-air co-operation, and they rightly assumed that such formations not only had an assault role but, because they had RAF cells, were preparing for active operations. By plotting the air liaison traffic they were able to identify the assault divisions in southern and south-western England, and the location of them so far away from the Pas de Calais indicated that their landing area would probably be somewhere between Le Havre and Cherbourg.

However, as so often happens in Intelligence, it is one thing to come to accurate conclusions and quite another to persuade others, especially commanders with fixed ideas, to accept them. Hitler distrusted signal intelligence on principle. He felt, with some justification, it was such an obvious form of deception, but he believed the evidence of the threat to Normandy because it coincided with his own assessment. It did not affect his firm opinion that the main weight of the Allied invasion would fall in the Pas de Calais but merely confirmed what he had been saying for some time; there would be diversionary attacks designed to make him draw troops away from the defences between Dunkirk and the mouth of the Somme. Confirmation of this opinion, if he needed it, lay in the volume of signal traffic coming from General Patton's FUSAG in Kent and East Anglia. Therefore he did not alter his main dispositions and merely deployed enough units in Normandy to hold what he was convinced would be only a feint attack. The need of the Allies for major ports still dominated German intelligence estimates.

Some indication of the extreme security-mindedness in Britain at this time can be gained from the story of the crossword puzzles in what was then *The Daily Telegraph and Morning Post*. A senior British officer was in the habit of doing the crossword every morning as he travelled by train to his office in SHAEF. In a series of five puzzles, spread over more than five days, he found that each of them contained a secret codeword as the answer to one of the clues. These codewords were Utah and Omaha—two of the Neptune beaches in the American sector—Overlord, Neptune and Mulberry. The clues were not very difficult; the one for Mulberry, for example, was 'This bush is the centre of nursery revolutions', and that for Neptune, 'Britannia and he hold to the same thing'. Investigations revealed that the puzzles had been compiled by two schoolmasters, Leonard Dawe and Neville Jones, and Leonard Dawe had been the newspaper's senior crossword compiler for more than 20 years. Both men were subjected to stringent security checks which, if anything, established their innocence. Dawe pointed out that puzzles were often composed six months before they were printed, possibly before anyone had thought of the codewords. No action was taken because there was none to take, yet quite recently there has been speculation in America whether those 'rustic British schoolteachers were really so naïve and innocent.' That such a question could still be asked is really rather ludicrous.

It has been suggested that General Eisenhower himself was a security risk because of his association with an Irish divorcée named Mrs Summersby who, having joined the ATS, became his secretary, driver and companion. It must be remembered that a relationship of this sort is normally only of interest to security staffs when there is a possibility of exploitation by blackmail. This did not arise. It could perhaps be said that Goebbels might have tried to make capital out of it, if he had found out, but since he had come to be regarded as a congenital liar, any personal attack by him on the Allied Supreme Commander would not have had much effect. In any case Mrs Summersby and General Eisenhower made no secret of the fact that they enjoyed each other's company; they were fully aware of the issues involved and the loyalty and discretion of

Mrs Summersby were never in question. Rather like the crossword-puzzle scare, the concern aroused by their association was another indication of pre-invasion nerves and anxiety.

Indiscretions and carelessness certainly caused anxiety at a time when there was already a great deal of apprehension about the feasibility of the whole operation, but Churchill himself was a considerable threat to security. He was a compulsive telephoner and spent a lot of time talking to President Roosevelt from his underground headquarters in the War Bunker at the east end of the Mall in London. He used a private radio telephone on which all conversation was 'scrambled' by a device known as the Bell A-3 system. The Germans learned of it and built an interception and unscrambling station on the Dutch coast near the Hague. Despite the fact that the telephone operators changed the frequency irregularly, at random and often, the Germans were able to listen to conversations up to the beginning of 1944, but from their point of view it was not quite so valuable a source as it might have been.

For one thing, the Americans, in testing the security of the system, came to the conclusion it might be insecure for part of the time it was in use and so both Churchill and Roosevelt were guarded in their speech and always used codewords when discussing operational matters. Subsequently Ultra disclosed that the Germans had information which could only have come from these trans-Atlantic telephone calls. This leak was effectively plugged in February 1944 when a new scrambler came into operation and the interception station in Holland was destroyed by the Royal Air Force. Yet Schellenberg himself wrote that it was possible to make a number of useful deductions from the pattern and timing of conversations, especially in connection with the impending invasion. He was not able to discover the date or place of it although he did deduce that the main threat in 1944 was to France and not, as Zeppelin tried to imply, to the Balkans.

It is an axiom of Intelligence and Security that excessive secrecy defeats its own ends, because if intelligence is to be of any value it must be disseminated to those who need it, in time for them to be able to make proper use of it. The Germans were greatly inhibited by a security instruction issued by Hitler in January 1940, though the reasons for it probably seemed good enough at the time. On 10 January 1940, during the 'Phoney War' before the *Blitzkrieg* was launched against Belgium, Holland and France, a certain Major Helmut Reinberger of the Luftwaffe, who carried in his briefcase all the operational plans for the surprise attack on Belgium, was travelling in an aircraft which made a forced landing near Mechelen-sur-Meuse because the pilot had lost his bearings in the fog. It seems that as soon as Reinberger realized he had landed in Belgium he got into a panic and tried to burn the documents behind a hedge. He was prevented from doing much more than char them because a Belgian patrol came up to investigate. This led to a major diplomatic incident, and though it had little effect on Hitler, who merely postponed the date of his attack which was to have been on 17 January, he decreed that in future no German officer or soldier was to have any knowledge of any operation in which he was not personally and directly concerned.

As General Speidel has complained, the result of this was that commanders of Wehrmacht formations and units were given the minimum amount of information about anything, and they certainly knew nothing of events outside their own immediate areas of interest. This had political advantages entirely unforeseen by Hitler when he issued the order, because when one disaster followed another in North Africa and Russia, and subsequently in north-west Europe, German officers and men of all three Services fighting against hopeless odds did not know how bad things were elsewhere; otherwise they might have abandoned Hitler and Nazism and made their own peace. Apart from intelligence reports which were purely local and made little or no mention of the Resistance, the only source of information was Dr Josef Goebbels, to whom 'news' was a political instrument not by any means necessarily related to the truth. It is not surprising that more and more German officers began to listen to BBC foreign broadcasts.

The consequences of Hitler's security policy were sometimes fatal. On several occasions, because no one had a clear idea of what anyone else was doing, German ground forces shot down Luftwaffe aircraft and the Luftwaffe bombed German ground forces; reinforcements pushed forward to restore a tactical situation opened fire on friendly units because they thought they were the enemy.

One of the greatest security problems of the war was keeping the secret of Mulberry. It was impossible to hide the huge concrete caissons—the size of a block of flats—moored off Tilbury, and it was known that they had been photographed by German reconnaissance aircraft. If the purpose of them was guessed accurately, German intelligence assessments of likely assault beaches would be radically altered. So, when Lord Haw Haw, William Joyce, said in a broadcast on Berlin radio on 21 April 1944 that the Germans knew exactly what the caissons were for, he caused great dismay. The whole strategy of Neptune depended on the security of Mulberry.

'You think you are going to sink them on our coasts in the assault,' said Joyce. 'We'll save you the trouble. When you come to get under way, we're going to sink them for you.'

The obvious conclusion to be drawn from the broadcast was that the Germans had indeed worked out what they were for, and extra precautions were taken to defend them and, if necessary, rescue the men working on them if they were attacked. But this did nothing to allay the fear in SHAEF that the Germans now knew a great deal more than they ought to know. News of the move of reinforcements to the Calvados coast had been alarming enough, this was very nearly the last straw. There could be very little hope of success for Neptune against an alert and formidable enemy deployed in readiness.

Fortunately, for the peace of mind of planners and commanders so far as Mulberry was concerned, relief was provided by General Hiroshi Baron Oshima, the Japanese Ambassador in Berlin. Ultra had provided the Allies with copies of all the reports sent by Baron Oshima to his government ever since Hitler declared war on the United States, and the Baron was a very industrious and conscientious man. In October 1943 he had toured the whole of the Atlantic Wall and sent long detailed reports to Tokyo at regular intervals. They arrived at their destination at about the same time as transcripts reached London and Washington, and they contained a great deal of information about shortages and shortcomings. In April 1944 Baron Oshima toured the Wall again and was given a very full briefing by von Rundstedt, who told him about the massive concrete structures seen by Luftwaffe pilots; von Rundstedt said it was his considered opinion they were anti-aircraft gun towers.

It transpired subsequently that the original German interpretation of them was that they were replacements for harbour moles, jetties and pierheads in ports destroyed by demolition or in the initial assault. This view was endorsed by Hitler and strengthened the German belief that the Allies would try and capture major ports.

There was further relief in the lack of any troop movements on the Far Shore which could indicate that the Mulberry secret was known.

And so, in the last few days before D-Day, although it was apparent that for some reason Hitler had seen fit to redispose some of his forces in the Neptune area, there was no reason to believe that Bodyguard had failed or that Neptune would fail.

14
Les Violons d'Automne

The Glorious First of June, 1944, was another hot and cloudless day. Between
the Isle of Wight and the Bay of the Seine the Channel was like smooth grey
silk. The soldiers on the Far Shore, who had lost a great deal of sleep since
Admiral Krancke's announcement, were drifting into apathy. They had become
accustomed to the constant air raids, the attacks on their fortifications,
communication centres, radar posts, and bridges over rivers and railways. They
had also had to suffer the burden of heavy air strikes on the sites of the secret
weapon Hitler said would win the war. All but one of the 93 Mark I launching
sites, designed to hold a large number of flying-bomb components to be
assembled on the spot, had been completely destroyed, and there was now
intense activity in woods and forests where hundreds of makeshift ramps were
being built under cover of foliage hiding them from photographic interpreters
in Britain. These too, soon attracted attention. Being built on the edge of
woods, so that the flying bombs would have a clear flight beyond the end of
the ramp, the misfires — and there were many — made craters in the open ground
in a direct line with the hidden ramp.

The troops manning the Wall had very little idea of what was happening.
Admiral Krancke had said there could not now be any invasion before August.
OKW had decided the Allies would not strike before the Russians resumed
their offensive in the East, and since the thaw in Russia had been much later
than usual the Red Army would not be able to move before the end of June.
Krancke and Lieutenant General Günther Blumentritt, Rundstedt's Chief of
Staff, reckoned that the delay and all the false alarms connected with the
Allied invasion could mean only one thing; the Allies did not intend to attack
until the losses inflicted on the Wehrmacht by the Russians made it reasonably
safe for them to do so. General Kramer's gloomy report was all part of a
deception plan designed to keep Rommel's Army Group alert but inactive
while the apparently unlimited forces of the Soviet Union flowed into eastern
Germany.

What seemed to clinch this argument was the weather, which all through May had been ideal. There was a general feeling that the Allies had missed their chance, but this was the effect of the strain of watching and waiting. The tension and reaction of frequent alerts had brought the German troops in the West to the point where they believed that because Eisenhower had not taken advantage of the good weather, he and his divisions would not come at all. It did not apparently occur to them that a plan made for June could not be changed just because the seas in May were calm.

The days passed. The moves of units up to the coast and into the Cotentin peninsula had been completed. There was nothing more to do, nothing to relieve the boredom, and the strain, of waiting for an enemy who did not come.

Rommel had no doubt the Allies would invade, but General Kramer's information, combined with the Allied air activity over the Pas de Calais, had made him less sure it would be in Normandy. He was, however, quite sure that when they came they would be able to break through the Wall and overcome what General Speidel describes as 'the classic crisis that comes in the first three days of a landing, while the foothold is being consolidated.' Hitler had promised there would be an adequate Panzer reserve, in the area of Paris, and Rommel presided at a number of staff studies which took this into consideration when examining possible enemy courses of action and suitable counter-measures. He and his staff concluded that a landing north of the Somme was doubtful because the combination of steep cliffs and relatively narrow beaches did not provide the width of front the enemy would need; but if there were enemy landings between the Somme and the Seine, or between the Seine and the Loire, the best thing to do would be to withdraw to a tactically defensible line, preferably on a river, and then counter-attack with Panzers, infantry and close air support on a massive scale in a set-piece battle. Piecemeal resistance, with reserve units being pushed into the battle at random to cope with a local crisis, would be disastrous.

At these staff studies Rommel stressed that the resources of his Army Group, plus the promised Panzer reserve, could defeat the invasion provided he, as the Army Group Commander, was given complete freedom of manoeuvre — as he had had in the Western Desert — and that General von Schweppenburg, commanding the *Panzerarmee* in the West, had up to eight armoured and seven motorized divisions under his direct control as the strategic reserve to the east of Paris. Even if Hitler continued to insist on obedience to the directive he had issued — that the decisive action must be fought on the Wall itself — the situation might not be so hopeless as it seemed if 21 and 12 SS Panzer divisions, the

Panzer Lehr and the Adolf Hitler Panzer division were all placed under the command of Army Group B now, so that they could be deployed well forward and used to counter-attack the Allies before they gained a foothold.

Rommel protested angrily to Hitler about the command and dispositions of these armoured formations, and since the fate of Neptune might well hang on Hitler's reply, as has been said, the Allies took considerable interest in the exchange of signals, made available by Ultra. Hitler remained adamant. He would control the battle. There would be no freedom of manoeuvre. He would dispose of the armoured reserves and, for the moment, they would stay where they were. Rommel felt that only by laying indisputable facts in front of Hitler personally could he make him see that the future of the Third Reich really lay in the hands of the military commander on the spot. A desperate battle for survival cannot be conducted from a headquarters more than 600 miles away.

Furthermore, there was no time to be lost. He and Staubwasser had calculated that the invasion would be between either the 5 and 7 or 12 and 14 June. If the weather stayed fine there could be no question of going to Berchtesgaden during the first critical period, but if it should break, and by the evening of 1 June there were signs that it might, he would leave the Château de la Roche Guyon early on 5 June, spend the night at home with his wife at Herrelingen, and then go on to see Hitler. He would have to go by car because senior officers were forbidden to use aircraft for ordinary travel. Speidel says 'It was impossible to protect them against the Allied air forces.'

Rommel telephoned to von Rundstedt, telling him what he proposed to do. Then he rang Lieutenant General Rudolph Schmundt, Hitler's Army Adjutant, and exercising a Marshal's right of direct access to the Fuehrer, arranged a personal interview for 6 June.

Thus, in the last few days before D-Day there were considerable differences of opinion among commanders and intelligence staffs on the Far Shore. Admirals Doenitz and Krancke and their Kriegsmarine intelligence service did not expect the Allies before August. Goering does not appear to have given the matter much thought because his main concern was the air defence of Germany, and the manpower position was becoming serious. Though his fighters and ground defences were taking a fearful toll of Allied bombers he was losing far too many experienced men in the air battles, and they could not be replaced. Von Rundstedt felt Hitler and OKW might be right, the next Russian offensive would determine the course of events in the West. Invasion was not imminent. Kramer had been deceived, and the recent security measures imposed in Britain—the complete control of all movement and travel and the unprecedented restrictions on all diplomatic communications—were all part of a deception plan.

Rommel seems to have been the only senior commander anticipating an attack in June, and his efforts to impart any sense of urgency to the formations and units under his command had been sabotaged by the false alarms put out by OKW and OB West, which were mainly the results of Schellenberg's reactions to Fortitude South.

Alarms, alerts and orders to 'stand to' had now become part of the routine of the soldiers on the Wall, and in some places very little attention was paid to them because nothing ever happened. It was obvious the enemy would try to achieve surprise, and there was every reason for a sentry to keep his eyes and ears open in the dark stillness just before dawn, when the only sound was the faint rustle of little waves washing through the devil's garden on the beach, but the sentry himself knew he might well be the last person to be told the battle was about to begin. Reconnaissance aircraft and E-boats patrolled the Channel; there was a long line of radar posts all along the shore from Holland to Brittany. These would be the first to see an invasion fleet. No enemy could cross the Channel without the Kriegsmarine, the Luftwaffe and the ground surveillance stations knowing they were coming. The sentry would be told, in due course — unless it was just another false alarm.

The only reliable guide was the weather, albeit a negative one. The wind was now rising, and away out to the west, over the Atlantic, clouds were forming. Normandy farmers, reading familiar signs, said storms were coming, as they very often did, just at the beginning of June. It was often a bad time for gales and rain; the last bit of bad weather before the real summer set in. As the wind sighed in the hedges and copses of the bocage country, and as rain splattered against the gunshields in the batteries at Azeville and Morsalines, Marcouf, le Mesnil and Merville, the elderly gunners, the semi-invalids transferred from the Eastern front, the Russian conscripts and all the other soldiers in the German 7th Army on the Calvados coast felt a sense of relief. The Anglo-Saxons could not attack in a storm.

On the other side of the Channel the weather had created a very serious problem. Soon after Eisenhower had ordered the sending of the signal 'Halcyon plus 4'— meaning that the invasion would be on 5 June — a weather report from North America stated that conditions along the eastern seaboard were changing rapidly. This was later confirmed by weather stations covering the whole area of the North Atlantic, from Greenland to Bermuda and the Azores to Northern Ireland. Eisenhower's meteorologist was Group Captain John Stagg, Royal Air Force, and his deputy was Colonel D. N. Yates of the United States Air Force. Their information came from naval and air forces, the US Weather Services and the British Weather Centre at Dunstable.

Anyone who has to form a definite and concise opinion based on information supplied by a number of different and quite separate experts has a difficult task because, as every barrister knows, it is usually possible to find an expert who will readily refute the evidence given by other experts. The weather is a particularly fruitful topic for discord and, to add to his burdens, Stagg soon discovered that although he was required to provide accurate forecasts covering the next five days, the weather in the Channel is so unpredictable that it is rarely possible to estimate much more than 24, or at best, 48 hours ahead.

On Thursday 1 June it was apparent that the prospects for good weather on the 5, 6 or 7 June were becoming remote. During the next three days, while the whole Atlantic gradually filled with a series of depressions and it became clear that the Normandy coast would be affected by winds up to Force 5 (Beaufort Scale), high seas, low cloud and driving rain, Stagg realized that although responsibility for making the decision whether to launch or postpone the invasion rested with Eisenhower, the decision would be based on his forecast which, in turn, had to be founded on the opinions of experts who could not agree. He was not in a very happy position.

On the evening of Saturday 3 June Eisenhower realized he might have to delay D-Day by 24 hours, but he postponed the formal decision until a meeting called for 4.15 am the next day, by which time Stagg would have had an opportunity to consider any changes that might occur during the night.

On Sunday morning there was no change in the forecast of bad weather and so Eisenhower issued the signal 'Ripcord plus 24', postponing D-Day until Tuesday 6 June.

At this stage every one of the 5,333 ships in the assault force was in position, and behind them lay another thousand vessels of the initial build-up. More than two million men and women of all arms and services had just come to the end of the final preparation and the Neptune armada was, in military language, committed. Now, suddenly, everything had to stop, even though several convoys were already under way and steaming for the Far Shore. These included the elderly merchantmen which were to form the Gooseberry breakwater of the Mulberry harbours, ships making for Omaha and Utah beaches from ports in Devon and Cornwall, minesweepers, which were only 35 miles off the Calvados coast when they received the order to go about in the stormy night, and one convoy of nearly 140 ships, carrying American troops of 4 Infantry Division, which was out of radio contact.

By nine o'clock on Sunday morning, nearly five hours after the Ripcord signal had gone out, this convoy was 25 miles south of the Isle of Wight and making eight knots in a rough sea. It was at last found, in the evening, by one of several amphibious Walrus aircraft which had been searching for it all day in appalling flying conditions of howling gusty winds and a cloudbase down to about 100 feet.

It was getting dark when the pilot of the Walrus flew low over the commodore's ship and dropped a canister with a streamer. In the canister was a signal from naval headquarters ordering the commodore to turn back. The pilot saw it fall into the water and sink. He then wrote a message on his knee pad, put it in another canister and this time saw it land on board. Nothing happened. The convoy steamed on and the pilot assumed his informal, scrawled note had failed to convey the sense of approaching disaster — and it would have been disaster. The convoy would have arrived off the invasion coast entirely unsupported and compromising beyond redemption the security and surprise of the whole Neptune operation. Finally, after a considerable delay, the pilot must have been enormously relieved to see the convoy put about and steam north.

That night, like many June storms in the Channel, the wind rose to hurricane strength and showed no signs of abating. It blew small branches off the lime trees in the avenue leading up to the Château de la Roche Guyon, and Rommel, dining with his Staff, listened to the rain lashing against the windows. He sent a message to his driver, Corporal Daniel. He would leave for Herrlingen at seven o'clock in the morning. A weather report from Admiral Hennecke in Cherbourg assured him there was no likelihood, in the foreseeable future, of five consecutive days of fine weather which the Allies would need for consolidating a beach-head.

During those first few days of June the strain on Group Captain Stagg must have been oppressive. He knew he had been right in advising the postponement of Neptune by 24 hours, but if the weather showed no signs of improving there would have to be another delay — this time for 14 days. He did not have to be reminded of Dieppe and of the effect of first postponing and then abandoning Rutter, which was remounted as Jubilee. Neptune was an infinitely greater undertaking, and by now the majority of troops would have been briefed on their objectives and timings. It had been hard enough to keep the secrets in the little circle of Bigots, it would be impossible to keep them if they were known to an Army Group.

All this may well have been in his mind when later on that Sunday, 4 June, he examined the latest weather charts of the Atlantic. From them he noted that an eastward movement of a cold front, combined with a drop in the rate of progress of a depression off Newfoundland, could bring, as he wrote later, 'an interlude of improved weather, and this... might just allow the first two critical sets of assault landings to be launched, at dawn and at dusk, on the same day, and that day could be Tuesday'.

There was always the possibility that German meterologists would also see and interpret the significance of the cold front and the depression, but if they did not, they would probably forecast a prolonged period of bad weather in which there could be no invasion.

Although Group Captain Stagg and Colonel Yates agreed that a brief period of better weather was approaching, and assumed their discovery would be confirmed by the other weather intelligence agencies, they had not taken into account the extraordinary intransigence of experts confronted with a proposition they have not thought of themselves. Far from agreeing, they argued against it, with passion, but at length arrived at a compromise. From the afternoon of Monday 5 June until the afternoon of Tuesday 6 June, Neptune was a possibility.

At 9.30 that Sunday evening, in the conference room of Eisenhower's headquarters at Southwick House, just outside Portsmouth, Stagg gave his final meteorological briefing in which he said that although the weather would not by any means be ideal, Neptune could go ahead.

There was a short discussion, mainly of the consequences of calling off the invasion, and the air commanders, Leigh-Mallory and Tedder expressed misgivings about the success of air operations in the cloud conditions predicted. At length Eisenhower put a direct question to Montgomery.

'Do you see any reason why we should not go on Tuesday?'

'No,' said Montgomery. 'I would say, go.'

Then, only 15 minutes after the meeting had begun, Eisenhower made the great decision, saying he was positive the order had to be given, that he didn't like it but 'I don't see how we can do anything else.'

Both Eisenhower and Montgomery must have realized that in the light of the intelligence they possessed on every aspect of the Atlantic Wall and its defenders, weather was probably the decisive factor in achieving surprise. Indeed, the whole story of Group Captain Stagg and his forecasts underlines the crucial importance of weather in tactical operations. It has not always been appreciated, and on many occasions in military history, operations planned without giving a thought to the climate have been very disappointing.

Fortunately the importance of accurate and timely information about the weather was accepted early on in the war, and a carefully planned campaign was undertaken to deny it to the enemy. German weather-reporting stations in Iceland, Greenland, the Norwegian island of Jan Mayen in the Arctic Circle,

Spitzbergen, Vaagö and the Lofoten Islands were all taken over or destroyed. The Germans then fitted out ocean-going trawlers as weather ships and these too were hunted down in a relentless, bitterly cold war fought mainly by the Americans in the green and white world of the Arctic. German weather ships and stations were located by Ultra and High Frequency Direction Finding (HFDF), and the jamming techniques of electronic warfare were used against those out of reach of raiding parties or on neutral territory.

This was a counter-intelligence campaign in that its object was to prevent the enemy from gaining the intelligence he needed, and it was successful. It is reasonable to assume that if the Germans had had access to the information on which Group Captain Stagg and Colonel Yates made their forecast, Rommel would not have driven away to Herrlingen; von Rundstedt might not have misinterpreted the indications of approaching crisis clearly conveyed in orders from London to the French Resistance; and instead of trying to relax the tension because it was having a bad effect on their men, subordinate commanders on the Calvados coast would have ordered increased vigilance.

The decision made by Eisenhower at 9.45 on the night of Sunday 4 June was not in fact final. Rain was beating on the windows at the time and the sound of the wind could be heard in the conference room. If anything happened in the night to show that Stagg's forecast was wrong, a second postponement would have to be sent out, and so another meeting was arranged for 4.15 on the next morning. At the beginning of that meeting, tension was extreme but the atmosphere became quite different when Stagg said the only change was 'in the direction of optimism'. It was his opinion that for most of Tuesday 6 June the weather would be just suitable for launching Neptune, and though he could not be entirely sure what it would be like on Wednesday, it should not interfere seriously with the build-up operation.

Eisenhower then sent to all concerned the signal reading 'Halcyon plus 5 finally and definitely confirmed'.

Bodyguard gained strategic surprise in that it deceived Hitler into adopting the wrong strategy and deploying his resources in the wrong places. The weather, the one unpredictable element in operational planning, enabled the Allies to achieve tactical surprise, even though it posed a serious threat to the whole operation.

On Monday 5 June, about an hour and a half after Eisenhower had confirmed that D-Day would be on the following day, Rommel signed the weekly situation report which was to be sent to OB West, von Rundstedt's headquarters built into the side of a hill at Saint Germain-en-Laye, about 28 miles away to the south east. The report laid emphasis on the increasing weight of Allied air attacks, the laying of mines in the approaches to ports, and the apparent concentration of air strikes on coastal defences between Dunkirk and Dieppe. All this indicated that the Allies had reached a high state of readiness, and though there had also been an increase in the number of coded messages broadcast by the BBC to the French Resistance, this had happened before and did not necessarily mean invasion was imminent. In the report Rommel also made the point that although air reconnaissance had not revealed any great increase in the number of landing craft in the Dover area, it was not known how many there were in other ports along the south coast of England because no flights had been made over them. He recommended that this should be put to the Luftwaffe as soon as possible.

A few minutes after signing this report he was handed two other papers, the Luftwaffe intelligence report and the weather forecast, the latter being the work of Professor Walther Stoebe, the Luftwaffe meteorologist in Paris. The intelligence report said that the enemy's determination to prevent all air and surface reconnaissance of approaches to the south coast of England indicated he was probably concentrating shipping for the invasion. The weather forecast predicted winds of Force 6 in the Pas de Calais and Force 7 at Cherbourg. The cloud base would not be higher than 1,800 feet and there would be heavy rain. Reassured by this, Rommel set out on the long drive to Herrlingen.

There was, however, one small, disquieting fact in his mind. The Anglo-Saxons were maintaining radio silence on the other side of the Channel and from his experience of fighting the British in North Africa he knew this was often the prelude to an attack. But, like the messages to the Resistance, this had often happened before and had obviously been a ruse to keep soldiers standing-to and away from the urgent task of thickening up the beach defences. As he drove away, accompanied by Colonel von Tempelhof his senior Operations staff officer and Captain Helmut Lang his aide-de-camp, General Speidel informed the two Armies in the Army Group that because of the bad weather the troops were to stand down and get some rest after the long period of tension.

In Le Mans, at the headquarters of 7th Army, Colonel General Friedrich Dollmann gave orders that the proposed 'Officer's Day' — a Commanders' Conference followed by a *Kriegspiel* (an indoor exercise) — would now take place in Rennes at 10 am on 6 June as planned. It was to be attended by all divisional commanders who were to bring at least two of their regimental commanders with them. The operational setting of the indoor exercise would be 'Enemy Landings in Normandy, preceded by Parachute Drops'.

In Cherbourg, the naval commander, Rear-Admiral Walther Hennecke, received a message from Paris telling him that of the three *Gruppen* (each *Gruppe* had about 30 aircraft) of 26 Fighter *Geschwader*, hitherto responsible for the defence of Cherbourg, one had been ordered to the south of France for a rest and the other two were on their way to Rheims and Metz. Goering had said that fighter aircraft were not to be kept idle in France when they were needed for the defence of the Reich.

Thus, on 5 June, Marshal Sperrle, who commanded the 3rd Air Fleet stationed in northern France, was left with a total force of 88 bombers, 172 fighters and 59 reconnaissance aircraft. Because of the weather, all air and sea operations were cancelled and so there were no E-boats, submarines or aircraft on watch to detect the approach of the huge invasion fleet. Air attacks on the coastal radar stations had put the majority out of action and, again because of the weather and the weather forecast, there was no great vigilance at the few that were operational. In any case, there was no reason for anyone to be on the alert when every commander and staff officer in the West was quite certain that even though the Allies might have planned to invade in the first week of June, the weather was now too bad to make it possible. It was announced that officers could use this opportunity to take local leave.

In making one of his periodic assessments of the operational situation von Rundstedt stated on 5 June that although the Allies would invade at some point between the mouth of the Scheldt and Normandy, it was not clear where that point would be. He stressed that there was no immediate prospect of the invasion.

Yet in fact he had been given a clear warning that invasion was imminent.

When planning Neptune the Allies had to take into consideration the civilian population in the invasion area, and do their best to prevent undue loss of life among non-combatants, especially during preliminary air and sea bombardment. They also wanted to take advantage of the forces of the Resistance in a position to render valuable aid. The two vital functions only they could carry out were, first, the cutting of all local communications so that the Germans, mainly dependent on the French Posts and Telegraphs, would not be able to find out what was happening, and secondly, the disruption of road and rail movement so that Panzer and other reinforcements would have great difficulty in getting into the operational area. The resources on the Far Shore had to be very carefully co-ordinated, and this meant that an effective warning and alerting system had to be devised.

The parachuting of the three-man teams — one Briton, one American and one Frenchman — known as Jedburghs, whose task was to organize the *maquis*, and the Brissex and Ossex (British and American) teams dropped to carry out special operations directly related to the Allied landings, are all part of what has been described as the 'French labyrinth'. They have very little to do with intelligence or deception and are therefore outside the scope of this book, but the warning system and the German reaction to it illustrate an interesting combination of deception and disbelief.

Warnings and instructions were transmitted by the BBC to Resistance Groups and agents, MI6 networks and SOE personnel through what were known as *message personnels* which, though sent 'in clear', were unintelligible to anyone not in the know. For instance, one of the better known (now) of the *message personnels,* the signal for the start of guerrilla activity in Brittany and broadcast in the Breton language which is more like Welsh than French, was 'Napoleon's hat, is it still at Perros Guirec?' Even if Abwehr, the SD or the Gestapo knew that a peculiarly shaped pink granite rock at this seaside resort on the north coast was called Napoleon's Hat, they still would not be very much the wiser. Other significant messages, usually relating to the blowing-up of sabotage targets or attacks on German troops, sounded equally meaningless to the uninitiated: 'The tomatoes should be picked', 'It is hot in Suez', 'The crocodile is thirsty', and so on.

There was, however, one *message personnel* of paramount importance because it revealed when the invasion would take place. It consisted of the first two lines of a poem by Paul Verlaine called 'Chanson d'Automne':

Les sanglots longs des violons d'automne

(The long sobs of autumn violins)

Bercent mon coeur d'une langueur monotone

(Soothe my heart with dull languor)

The first line was an alert, a warning to stand by. The second was an action signal. The sabotaging of communications, road and railways, and all other planned operations in support of Neptune were to start at midnight on the night when the message was transmitted.

The significance of this couplet became known to the Germans through an SOE F Section *reseau* run by a veteran agent named François Garel, whose codename was Butler. (F Section was the department of SOE dealing with British-organized special operations against the Germans in all French territory.) Butler had parachuted into the le Mans area in the spring of 1943, and his task was to select railway and telephone targets to be blown up at the time of the invasion. He, his wireless operator Marcel Rousset and a courier named Marcel Fox were caught by the Germans, and Rousset subsequently agreed to co-operate with the SD radio expert Josef Goetz because he would then be able to warn London that the Butler *reseau* was in German hands. Rousset told Goetz that his radio security check consisted of transmitting Butler's messages to London in English and those of Fox in French, where the reverse was true.

Goetz then sent a message to London in English in which Butler asked for money. Instead of reacting to the check the London operator merely asked why the system had been changed.

This is by no means the only case of a radio operator apparently deliberately ignoring the attempt of an agent to give this type of warning through a previously arranged security check system. It can only be said that intelligence and deception in the secret war are apt to be so intricately interwoven with all sorts of designs and motives which existed only in the minds of certain individuals at the time, that it is not possible, more than 30 years later, to cut a straight path through the tangled undergrowth of cross purposes.

A few weeks later Rousset managed to escape and tried without success to warn London that his radio was now being operated by the SD, and it was through this radio set that Goetz learned of the Verlaine couplet. He did not, however, discover the full significance or the distribution of it, but his deductions were reasonably accurate. All formation commanders responsible for the defence of the Atlantic Wall were informed that the first line was an alert signal, and when the second line was broadcast the Allies would land within the next 48 hours.

On the eve of D-Day, 5 June, it was decided in London that all the *messages personnels,* a total of 325, should be broadcast despite the risk that this might have the effect of creating a general uprising in France, with consequent reprisals by the Germans. There were three good reasons. First, country-wide sabotage would help to conceal the actual place of the invasion until the last moment. Secondly, maximum damage would be done to communications simultaneously, thereby hindering to the greatest possible extent the attempts of Germans to concentrate their resources at the point of danger and mount counter-attacks. Thirdly, the effect of widespread and apparently indiscriminate action by the Resistance would be extremely demoralizing for the Germans.

The danger of a sudden uprising was not perhaps as serious as it might have seemed because the Jedburgh teams, the Jeds, and the Brissex and Ossex teams had established some measure of control over Resistance Groups, so far as operational tasks were concerned, and provided the orders already issued were obeyed, the signals putting these orders into effect should not cause serious repercussions. But the risk was there. It was possible that the broadcasting of all the *messages personnels,* instead of those for selected areas, would lead to the killing of a great many men, women and children all over France, and for this reason the decision was referred to the French Committee of National Liberation in London. Aware of the possible consequences, General Koenig agreed to the full broadcast. It went out, slowly and carefully, with every syllable emphasized.

and was repeated several times.

In the War Diary of Colonel General Salmuth's headquarters of the German 15th Army at Turcoing it was recorded that the Army Y Service monitored the first line of the couplet on 1, 2 and 3 June. The second line was intercepted at 2115 hours on 5 June — according to another entry in the War Diary — but it had been broadcast no less than 15 times during the day. From this repetition alone the Germans might reasonably have assumed something was in the wind, especially since they knew the significance of the second line, and it had not been broadcast before.

Messages personnels broadcast to the Resistance had been intercepted many times before, and *Les sanglots longs des violons d'automne* had been repeated several times on 1 May. Nothing had happened, and the weather at that time had been ideal for invasion. A storm was now raging and the German meteorologists considered it would be some weeks before the Allies could attack. The conclusion drawn was that the broadcasts intercepted since 1 June were all part of the Allies' war of nerves. Even so, since the previously unheard second line of the couplet had now been broadcast, and since Hitler, OKW and OB West all regarded the Pas de Calais as the most likely invasion area, General Salmuth, who was responsible for it, did in fact on his own initiative put his Army on the alert.

Both OB West and the headquarters of Army Group B at the Château de la Roche Guyon were told by 15th Army that the action line of the Verlaine couplet had been intercepted, but apparently no action was taken to alert the German 7th Army which was in the invasion area, whose divisional and regimental commanders were to attend the *Kriegspiel* in Rennes at ten o'clock next morning, whose officers were able to take local leave if they wanted to, and whose soldiers had been allowed to stand down and get some rest.

Several historians have made efforts to find out what went wrong. Colonel Anton Staubwasser was Duty Officer at the Château de la Roche Guyon on the night of 5 June. He was informed about the Verlaine 'action' line by a staff officer in 15th Army. Staubwasser told General Speidel and was instructed to contact von Rundstedt's headquarters. He did, and was told specifically not to alert subordinate formations and units.

There have been all sorts of stories about the penetration of OB West by a British agent, from whom this order came, and the whole business, viewed with hindsight, has been made to appear very strange and mysterious. It must, obviously, be borne in mind that none of the few senior German officers who survived the war and the massacre after the failure of the *Schwarze Kapelle* to assassinate Hitler, and who were involved in any failure to alert the defenders of the Atlantic Wall, would be outspoken about their shortcomings. But General Speidel, who did survive, makes no mystery of what happened — or did not happen. He says that at 10 pm on 5 June the 15th Army received a codeword (Verlaine's second line) warning of imminent invasion, and as a matter of course alerted its own formations and the Army Group headquarters. This would be routine staff procedure. He goes on to say that when von Rundstedt was informed, he decided not to alert the whole front.

There is nothing very strange about this. The invasion was expected in the Pas de Calais, as the result of Bodyguard and its subsidiary deceptions, and the army there was on the alert. Bearing in mind the weather conditions and forecast, knowing nothing of any approaching break in the storm, and taking into account the fact that the BBC had been broadcasting coded messages to the French Resistance for weeks, von Rundstedt probably, and with good reason, felt the Verlaine action message was just another false alarm. He saw no reason why he should dance to the Allies' tune and keep tired soldiers awake to no purpose. If he is judged in the light of the information available to him at the time, and not with all the advantages of hindsight, he did no more, and no less, than most senior commanders would have done in similar circumstances.

So it was that except for the normal duty officers and sentries, the German 7th Army, soon to be called upon to throw the Allies back from the beaches called Utah, Omaha, Gold, Juno and Sword, went to the cafés in garrison towns, attended birthday parties — like those of General Erich Marcks commanding 84 Corps at St-Lo, of the two young officers of 902 Regiment of the Panzer Lehr at Vibraye, or of Sergeant-Signaller Klaus Lück of 22 Panzer Regiment at Falaise — read letters from home, wrote to their wives or simply went to sleep. Meanwhile the greatest air and seaborne force ever assembled was moving through the night towards them.

The weather had proved to be the decisive instrument of deception.

15
Taxable,
Glimmer and Titanic

After General Eisenhower had given the order for Neptune to go ahead there was little for Allied Intelligence to do except listen to German radio traffic for any information on the moves of German units which might indicate knowledge of the time and place of the invasion. An MI6 report stated the Panzer Lehr Division was apparently about to move, but no one knew where. Throughout the night of 5/6 June Ultra remained silent, but it was impossible to tell whether this was because no signals were being sent or because radio silence was in force.

The Allied Intelligence organization had done everything it could to provide the invasion force with all the information and intelligence it needed, but inevitably there were gaps and miscalculations, which merely prove that because time and the enemy do not stand still, no intelligence picture can ever be complete. Even so, as Eisenhower said, it was unlikely that any army had ever gone into battle better informed.

Unlike Intelligence, Deception was now reaching its peak, because Hitler must remain convinced the main threat was still to the Pas de Calais. Furthermore, by creating the impression that airborne forces were landing in France over a very wide area, the Germans might be persuaded to dissipate their counter-attack forces in fruitless pursuit of imaginary enemies. These deception operations were given the codenames of Taxable, Glimmer and Titanic and took place in the Pas de Calais and in Normandy.

The Public Record Office guide describes Taxable as 'Bomber Command "surface convoy" deception operation off Cap d'Antifer to induce Germans to believe large convoy crossing north-west part of Channel to north of Overlord'. Glimmer is 'Diversionary sea-convoy, near Boulogne, in connection with Overlord,' and under the heading of Titanic is 'Airborne diversions for Overlord, including use of Window.'

Window was the British codeword—the American one was Chaff—for thin strips of tinfoil ejected from an aircraft to create a snowstorm effect on enemy radar screens and make the identification of any target extremely difficult if not impossible. The Germans had also discovered this, but the German and the Allied High Commands were both reluctant to use Window for fear the other side would use it too and render all radars, vital for air defence, ineffective. Finally the British used it in the raid on Hamburg in July 1943 and thereafter, but in 1942 Dr Joan Curran, a brilliant electronics scientist, had invented a device which she called Moonshine. This could be carried by aircraft and simulated on enemy radar screens the movement of large numbers of ships or aircraft. Tests showed that a few aircraft equipped with Moonshine gave the appearance of a large bomber fleet, and subsequently the invention was used with success to lure Luftwaffe fighters away from genuine bomber formations.

The next development in radar deception was the fitting of radar reflectors inside the type of balloon flown from naval vessels as a protection against low-level air attack. This device was called Filbert. When towed behind small ships the combination of Filbert with aircraft equipped with Moonshine and dropping Window in a scientifically controlled experiment showed on the monitoring radar screens what appeared to be an enormous fleet dispersed over an area of some 200 square miles and moving at a speed of between eight and ten knots. All this was the basis of Taxable and Glimmer.

At 2300 hours on 5 June, one hour before D-Day, Lancaster bombers of Group Captain Leonard Cheshire's famous 617 Squadron, 'The Dambusters', and others of 218 Squadron took off on what must have been the most peaceful mission they had ever undertaken, but their task demanded an exceptionally high standard of skill and precision flying. The aircraft headed for the coast of France between Le Havre and Dieppe. Reaching the coast they turned north-east, following the line of the shore, and flew in patterns calculated with extreme nicety, discharging Window at equally precise intervals. Far below, in the Channel, 18 naval and RAF launches, each towing a barrage balloon fitted with a Filbert radar reflector, pitched and rolled so heavily in the steep and stormy sea that practically everyone in the crews was seasick. Off Beachy Head the little fleet split in two. Nine vessels made for Cap d'Antifer, a little to the west of Etretat — the Taxable fleet — and the remainder, Glimmer, set course towards Boulogne.

It soon became clear to the German radar posts in the 15th Army area that a very large invasion fleet was lying off the Channel coast between Boulogne and Etretat. Response was rapid. Naval units put to sea, searchlights on the shore swept the coastal waters and shore batteries opened fire. There was no reaction to the genuine invasion fleet in the Bay of the Seine and no German gun fired in that area before H-Hour — when Allied troops began to land. German naval vessels sent out to intercept the Taxable and Glimmer fleets found nothing.

Titanic involved the dropping of hundreds of dummy paratroops through a Window screen, the object of the Window being to alert enemy radar operators to the fact that something serious was happening. When the dummies, later called 'dolls' by the Germans, hit the ground the impact detonated 'battle simulators' which made the sounds of small-arms automatic fire, shots from rifles and pistols and the explosions of grenades and 2-in mortar bombs. Some emitted the same sort of smoke that is in mortar canisters and has a characteristic 'battlefield' smell. The aircraft that had unloaded the dummies also dropped pintail bombs that fired parachute flares and coloured Verey lights up into the sky when they struck the ground, and these were accompanied by additional rifle and machine gun simulators. Thus, for about half an hour after a Titanic drop, a small but fierce little battle appeared to be raging, and if this suddenly happened in, for instance, wooded areas which are difficult to search, not too far from enemy units whose role is to deal with airborne attacks—but as far as possible from genuine paratroop and glider drop zones—it may be possible to distract the enemy's attention for a considerable time. During this interval the real airborne units might have an opportunity to find their objectives and consolidate.

The first Titanic drop was made on D-Day, a few minutes after midnight, near the village of Marigny, between Coutances and St Lo, in the operational area of the German 6 Parachute Regiment. Others were made in a wide sweep inland from the invasion beaches on a line running from Lessay, almost on the west coast of the Cotentin peninsula, south to Villedieu-les-Poeles, east to Lisieux and Évreux and then north to Yvetot. Inside this area there were also drops in the Forêt de Cérisy, between St Lo and Bayeux, and at Harfleur, just to the east of Le Havre. The effect of them was out of all proportion to the effort involved, since it was because of Titanic that Lieutenant General Helmut Kraiss, commanding 352 Infantry Division, was unable to prevent the American 1 Division from gaining a foothold on Omaha Beach.

For a long time on D-Day it seemed that the landing on Omaha Beach might be a repetition of the disaster at Dieppe. At low tide there is nearly half a mile of level sand before the beach shelves steeply into deep water. Shorewards, from the high-water line is a narrow belt of shingle running up to a low bank, three or four feet high. This bank, on which a road has now been built, is some ten yards wide, and beyond it the ground drops into a marshy strip perhaps 50 yards across at its widest part. On the far side of this low ground is a steep ridge, 60 to 80 feet high, running the whole four mile length of the beach and dominating it. For men attacking across this great width of beach, strewn with obstacles, there was no cover of any sort except right in under the lee of the low bank or in the dead ground immediately at the foot of the ridge.

The American combat teams were not expecting to meet experienced, battle-hardened troops well dug in along the dominating ridge, and they had not been neutralized by the preliminary Allied naval and air bombardment because the main weight of it had fallen behind them. Moreover, early morning mist and the dust haze from the air bombing made it difficult for the warships to bring observed fire to bear on the enemy positions.

The well-directed and sustained fire of General Kraiss's two forward regiments gave the beach its nickname of Bloody Omaha, but against the resources deployed by the Americans — even without their full complement of amphibious tanks and with no close-support artillery — a static defence line can only inflict casualties, it can seldom stop a determined assault. A counter-attack force was essential if the Americans, pinned to the beach by fire from the ridge, were to be forced to abandon their attempt, but, because of Titanic, General Kraiss had no reserve; he could not counter-attack.

At two o'clock that morning he had received several reports of landings by enemy paratroops in considerable strength — the Titanic drops in the area south of real landings by the American 101 Airborne Division. He at once placed his division on full alert and ordered his 915 Infantry Regiment, under the command of Colonel Mayer, to locate and destroy the enemy parachutists. Having no military transport, the Regiment, 1,750 strong, set off on its mission at 0400 hours in ancient requisitioned French vehicles of various kinds, on bicycles and on foot, to search the woods, fields and hedgerows of the close and difficult bocage country for an airborne enemy who did not exist.

Nervous about committing his only reserve in case anything else happened, Kraiss ordered Mayer to keep in constant touch by radio, and when it became obvious that 915 Regiment must be recalled immediately if the American seaborne landing were to be repulsed, he could not get in touch; probably because radios at that time could be very unreliable in close country. However, contact was regained at about 0930 hours and Kraiss ordered Mayer to collect up his two battalions, now dispersed in small parties over some 20 square miles of countryside, and send one to deal with enemy landing in the area of Arromanches (Gold Beach) and the other to Divisional headquarters behind Omaha. Mayer spent the next two hours trying to contact his sub-units by sending out orderlies on bicycles, and just before noon the ground mist which had been making things even more difficult for him, cleared at last. Almost immediately he and all his troops were attacked by clouds of fighters and fighter-bombers in countless low-level attacks which made movement virtually impossible. Three hours later

Mayer reported that his forward units were under fire from enemy tanks and could not move. He himself was killed a short while afterwards.

By about 1600 hours on the afternoon of D-Day the desperate situation on Omaha had been resolved. The Atlantic Wall had been breached. Salvaging what he could of his Division, General Kraiss had fallen back and the Americans had moved more than a mile inland. The cost of the landing on Omaha Beach had been high but, because of Titanic, it was, in the end, a success and not another Dieppe.

That it was so nearly a disaster can be attributed to a gap in intelligence which had nothing to do with the last-minute appearance of General Kraiss's 352 Division.

It was not known that because of Allied air attacks on the Atlantic Wall the guns had been removed from the emplacements in battery positions at Pointe du Hoc and Morsalines. Unlike the guns at St Marcouf, Azeville and le Mesnil they lacked the overhead protection of 13 feet of concrete, and though on his first inspection Rommel felt their excellent camouflage would safeguard them, he did not at that time realize how detailed was the information being sent across the Channel. Grass and earth, bushes and netting offered very poor protection from accurate bombing and so he later gave orders for the guns to be hauled back under cover a mile or so from their prepared positions. There was bound to be at least 24 hours' warning of an invasion and this would allow plenty of time to bring them back.

There was no warning, and the battery on Pointe du Hoc, six 155 mm guns set midway between Utah and Omaha Beaches and commanding the whole area of the bay in front of them, could not come into action against the Allied fleet. Yet their existence was a major factor in General Omar Bradley's plan for the Omaha and Utah landings. He detailed a combat team of Rangers, led by Lieutenant Colonel Rudder, to scale the sheer cliff, 120 feet high, using rocket-launchers to fire grapnels attached to climbing ropes and rope ladders. The elimination of the Pointe du Hoc battery was a priority objective, and because of it, Bradley kept his transport ships 11½ miles from the shore. In that long run-in across a very choppy sea 27 of the Omaha assault wave's 32 amphibious tanks and all its supporting artillery sank. As the surviving landing craft approached the shore everything seemed to be quiet. There was no sign of movement on the ridge behind the beach although it was indistinct in the misty light of dawn. Not until the first craft came up to the beach obstacles did General Kraiss's troops open fire, with devastating effect.

The attack on the Pointe du Hoc was like some scene in a mediaeval siege. The German defenders on the cliff top, cratered like a moon landscape by the air strikes, cut the climbing ropes and ladders and rolled boulders and grenades down on the Rangers below. Yet the Americans took their objective, at a cost of 135 men. Then they discovered that what had looked like gun barrels on the air photographs were telegraph poles. They found the real guns a mile away and blew them up. Accurate intelligence about the Pointe du Hoc could have had a considerable effect on the Omaha landing. There would not have been so long a run-in and the infantry could have had the close support of tanks and artillery, but with General Kraiss's division well entrenched above them, the casualties would still have been heavy.

An agent for the French Resistance said later that London had been told about the guns being moved, and the information had been sent by pigeon. Perhaps it was the shooting of this bird that is the foundation of the story about pigeons and Bloody Omaha.

An operation somewhat on the lines of Colonel Rudder's attack on Point du Hoc was undertaken to silence the battery at Merville, commanded by the German colonel reported as being a drunkard and manned by troops who were mostly Russian. This battery appeared to be in a very strong position, near the coast and the mouth of the river Orne, and it was believed its guns could cause havoc to landing craft out in the bay and to the British and Canadian troops storming the beaches. It had been heavily bombed; there were more than 50 hits in the battery area but only two on the casemates and these had not been penetrated. Like Pointe du Hoc it was a vital objective, and it was attacked by paratroopers who had been trained on a replica, built on a training area in England. The assault force, led by Lieutenant Colonel Otway commanding 9 Parachute Battalion of the British 6th Airborne Division, landed at 0330 hours on D-Day. Despite a certain amount of initial confusion caused by 88 mm anti-aircraft fire, which forced pilots to take evasive action and drop their sticks of parachutists in the wrong place, the battery was overrun and captured in an attack lasting only 30 minutes. Otway lost 66 men and the Germans about 100.

It was then discovered that the guns in the casemates were not 155 mm, as had been reported; they were French 75s, only capable of doing a certain amount of damage to the eastern end of Sword beach. The mistake in estimating the calibre of the guns had been easy enough to make. When constructing strongpoints and battery casemates the Todt Organization worked to a fixed scale of specifications. The thickness of the concrete was directly related to the type of gun, the casemates were of a set design, and the guns were usually mounted in them at night or in conditions of strict security so that agents of the Resistance could not see what was going on. The casemates at Merville had been built for 155 mm guns. The details were reported by agents and checked by air reconnaissance.

The battery, when equipped, was in a prohibited area and no spy had been able to get near enough to see that because there was a shortage of 155 mm guns the Germans had had to make do with old French 75s.

The Allied invasion force landing on the beaches on the eastern flank of the Cotentin peninsula (Utah), between Vierville-sur-Mer and St Laurent-sur-Mer (Omaha), and from Arromanches eastward to the mouth of the Orne (Gold, Juno and Sword), had a mixed reception.

The American 4 Infantry Division at Utah had surprisingly little trouble. All but one of their amphibious tanks and all their artillery got ashore, engineers swiftly cleared a way through Rommel's devil's garden, and even three and half hours later, when the move to link up with the airborne forces began, there was still no serious German resistance. By evening, contact had been made with 101 Airborne Division and in some places penetration was more than five and a half miles.

At Omaha, as has already been described, the Germans were ready, and it transpired later that by sheer coincidence, all part of the fortunes of war, the German 352 Infantry Division happened to be holding an anti-invasion exercise. That was why two of its regiments were actually manning the defences. For many hours it seemed the landing might fail and the survivors, if any, would have to be withdrawn, but an apparently disastrous situation was redeemed by American determination and gallantry. Follow-up combat teams got ashore, stormed the ridge and, largely because General Kraiss had no reserve battalions, by last light the American 5 Corps had established itself a mile inland on a line running from Vierville to Colville. Forward units were almost as far as Formigny, two miles from the coast, on the high ground which was the scene of the battle on 15 April 1450, where the French artillery of Charles VII destroyed the bowmen of England and drove the English out of northern France at the end of the Hundred Years' War.

In the area of the British 2nd Army, the task of 50 British Division landing on Gold Beach was to take the town of Bayeux and the high ground in the area of St Leger, covering the main road from Bayeux to Caen. Assault teams of 79 Armoured Division and a Royal Marine Commando, landing behind the right-hand brigade, were to turn west along the coast and take Port-en-Bessin. Considerable opposition was encountered from units of the German 716 Infantry Division at le Hamel, but this was eventually overcome and the leading British brigade reached its objective overlooking the Bayeux-Caen road.

Neither Bayeux nor Port-en-Bessin had been captured by nightfall, and though contact had been made with the Canadians who had landed at Juno, 50 Division was still out of touch with the American 5 Corps on their right flank, to the west.

A number of German strongpoints opposite Juno Beach were not put out of action by the preliminary bombardment, and it took some time for the assaulting units of 3 Canadian Division to clear the exits from the beaches on either side of Courseulles-sur-Mer; but by the evening the main divisional line had been established through the villages of Lantheuil, le Fresne, Camilly and Villons-les-Buissons, two and a half miles inland.

The task of 3 British Division, landing on Sword Beach to the east of Lion-sur-Mer, was to move up to Caen and secure a bridgehead over the Orne. This proved to be too ambitious because of the strength of German opposition but, by late afternoon, Biéville, about a mile from the outskirts of Caen, had been reached. Here a German counter-attack by infantry and about 20 Panzers was repulsed. By evening the Division had secured the line Biéville, Blainville and Herouville (east of the river Orne). Divisional units had also consolidated their hold on the swing-bridge over the Orne close to Benouville, which had been captured intact by 6 Airborne Division in the early hours of the morning—hence its name of Pegasus Bridge, which it bears to this day.

By the end of D-Day all the assaulting divisions were ashore. Great gaps had been punched through the Atlantic Wall all along the Neptune front and in the words of Montgomery, 'Our losses had been much lower than had ever seemed possible'. Because of the weather, tactical surprise had been achieved everywhere except at Omaha, where an unfortunate coincidence and not deliberate German counter measures caused losses which were heavy, but nothing like so heavy as had been anticipated.

The Atlantic Wall had in fact proved to be the myth that von Rundstedt always said it was, despite Rommel's great efforts to strengthen it at the last moment. Montgomery said that 'in spite of the enemy's intentions to defeat us on the beaches, we found no surprises awaiting us in Normandy,' and this was true enough. There had been much talk of Hitler's secret weapons which would destroy the invasion force, but there were no new submarines in the Bay of the Seine, no new jet aircraft attempted to intercept the air armada, and no flying bombs appeared. It was one of Hitler's many great mistakes that when at last, six days after D-Day, the first V-1 took off, it landed on London and not in the far more sensitive area of the Mulberry harbours. Disruption of the Allied logistical system at that critical stage of the Normandy battle could have had a serious effect.

It is also true that there were gaps in the intelligence picture, at Merville and Pointe du Hoc for example, but these were small in relation to the vast scope of the Neptune project. On the other hand, the quality of the intelligence collected before D-Day made possible the production of large scale maps, issued down to squadron and company commanders, which gave exact and accurate details of every German position and obstacle. Nowhere is this better illustrated than in the perhaps familiar story of the surrender of the strongpoint known as Osteck by Major Frederich Wilhelm Küppers, the commander of Artillery Group Montebourg.

Osteck was one of the main forts on the eastern side of the strong defensive system round the port of Cherbourg. It consisted of embrasures, bunkers, observation posts and a complete underground communication system surrounded by anti-tank ditches, wire fences and a minefield. It had certain shortcomings, for example quite a lot of the mines were harmless because not enough detonators had been issued, but it was a formidable objective for the troops of the American 7 Corps who, having taken Cherbourg — the harbour had been reduced to rubble by German demolitions — attacked Osteck on 27 June. Although surrounded by enemy in overwhelming strength, Küppers' attitude was that even though defeat might be inevitable there would be no disgrace attached to it if he fought to the end.

A combat team of 4 American Division was repulsed in fierce fighting which went on all day, and by evening the ammunition for Küppers' guns had been reduced to 20 smoke shells. He refused an invitation to surrender. Next morning the American Divisional Commander, Major-General Barton, came up under flag of truce. Küppers took him into the Osteck command post where the General unfolded a map on which the plan for the final assault had been marked. Küppers asked if he could look at it. Marked in far greater detail than on the German maps was the layout of Osteck fort. It listed every weapon and the amount of ammunition allotted to it, every officer, the designation of his unit, the number of men under his command and the addresses of their billets in neighbouring villages. Also on the map were similar details for Westeck fort on the western side of the Cherbourg defences. Küppers noted that all the facts recorded against Osteck were accurate, but at Westeck there was one error. The commander of 11 Battery, 1709 Artillery Regiment was shown as Lieutenant Ralf Neste, but he had been killed a few weeks ago, on 5 May, in an accident with an anti-tank gun.

Before they had seen that map, Küppers and his officers were prepared to face the American assault, more for the honour of the Wehrmacht than anything else, but the discovery that the Americans knew everything about them completely destroyed their morale and left them feeling totally unprotected. Küppers asked how and where all the facts had been obtained and was told that every detail of German defences had been acquired by the Allied intelligence organization directly from the original German maps and plans. In an understandable state of hopelessness and depression, Küppers surrendered.

Good intelligence at Osteck saved lives; the lack of it at Merville and Pointe du Hoc wasted lives.

The Allies, like all attackers, had the initiative, but against prepared defences manned by an enemy as redoubtable as the Germans, possession of the initiative alone was not enough. The attackers had to know their enemy and they had to be able to take him by surprise. With these advantages the Allies were able to land on the Calvados coast and to expand and build up their beach-head, but the vital question of whether they would ever be able to break out of it was not resolved for several weeks. Everything depended on the redeployment of the German 15th Army, still waiting for the First United States Army Group to attack across the Pas de Calais. The fact that Hitler did not allow it to take part in the battle for France until the decisive moment had passed, and it could not stem the flood of defeat, can be credited to Fortitude, because the deception plan continued long after D-Day.

Not until 28 July, when the Americans at last broke out of the base of the Cotentin peninsula, did Hitler allow von Rundstedt to move some — not all — of the infantry units of 15th Army from the Pas de Calais. The Fuehrer had at last come to the conclusion there would not be another Allied invasion across the Channel.

Intelligence had played a vital part in the landing of the Allies on the Far Shore; Deception was instrumental in keeping them there.

Yet wars are not won by Intelligence or Deception, any more than they are won by Logistics or Commanders — although bad commanders can be directly responsible for losing them. Wars are won by ordinary soldiers and sailors and airmen. No matter how brilliant the plan of an Army Commander may be, he cannot win the battle if his soldiers, in the rifle section and the tank, will not or cannot carry it out. Conversely, no matter how steadfast and brave the ordinary soldiers may be, they cannot win the battle if the commander's plan is fundamentally bad.

One of the most valuable weapons in the Allied armoury was Hitler himself. In the Normandy battle his strategy and tactics revealed an extraordinary military incompetence, especially in his predilection for reinforcing failure. This may have been largely because he personally would never go near a battle and tried to direct this one from Berchtesgaden. He was completely deceived by tricks as old as warfare itself. His Wehrmacht, the mighty war machine in which the whole German nation took such pride, was defeated because he imagined he was the greatest military genius in the history of war and, from 1942 onwards, virtually all his intuitive decisions were wrong. The ordinary German soldier of the Wehrmacht who, with great courage and incredible tenacity, fought on even when all hope had gone, deserved a better Fuehrer.

Glossary

Glossary of
Titles and Codenames

Abwehr   literally 'Defence': the intelligence and counter-intelligence service controlled by the German Staff

Amt Mil   the military intelligence section of the German General Staff, formed after Abwehr had been absorbed by the SD

Artist   a double agent in the Yugoslav Ring

ATS   Auxiliary Territorial Service, wartime forerunner of the Womens Royal Army Corps (WRAC)

Balloon   codename of an agent in the Yugoslav Ring

BCRA   Bureau Central de Reseignemants et d'Action, General de Gaulle's intelligence organization

Blitzkrieg   lightning war, mobile operations spearheaded by tanks and dive-bombers

Bodyguard   the deception plan and operations for Overlord

Bombardon   a concrete caisson forming an outer breakwater of the Mulberry harbours

Bronx   a female agent working for the XX Committee

Brutus   a double agent

'C'   traditional name for the head of MI6; originally Captain Mansfield Smith-Cumming

Chaff   the American codeword for strips of tinfoil used to baffle radars

Citadel   German operation against Kursk

COHQ   Combined Operations Headquarters

Collaborateurs   members of the population in Occupied Europe who were prepared to co-operate with the Germans

Columba   secret operation, dropping carrier pigeons in Occupied Europe

Copperhead   the 'I Was Monty's Double' deception plan

COPPs   Combined Operations Pilotage Parties

COSSAC   Chief of Staff, Supreme Allied Commander

CSM   Committe of Special Means, also called Ops B, the department in SHAEF dealing with deception

Der Tag   the Day; the day when Germany would take revenge for her defeat in the First World War

DF   Direction Finding, the locating of enemy radio transmitters

Diadem   the Allied operation in Italy, May 1944, to link the main front with the Anzio beach-head and advance on Rome

Enigma   the enciphering machine used by the Wehrmacht and Axis allies

Fahneneid   the oath of loyalty taken by German officers

FBI   Federal Bureau of Investigation (American)

FHO   *Fremde Heere Ost* (Foreign Armies East) the military intelligence department of the German General Staff dealing with the Eastern front

FHW   *Fremde Heere West* (Foreign Armies West) dealing with military intelligence in the West

Filbert   a reflecting screen carried inside a barrage balloon for radar deception

Fortitude   the overall deception plan to conceal Neptune

Freak   a double agent in the Yugoslav Ring

Führerhauptquartier   Hitler's headquarters

Funkabwehr   German signal intelligence system

FUSAG   First United States Army Group, a fictitious formation, part of Quicksilver and Fortitude

Garbo   a Spanish double agent working for the XX Committee

Gelatine   an agent in the Yugoslav Ring

Gestapo   German abbreviation for *Geheime Staatspolizei,* Himmler's secret state police, part of the SS

Glimmer   deception operation simulating invasion fleet off Boulogne on the eve of D-Day

Gold   one of the invasion beaches in Normandy

Gooseberry   part of Mulberry, a breakwater of sunken blockships

Götterdämmerung   Twilight of the Gods — extinction

Halcyon   the codename for Y-Day, when all preparations for Neptune had to be completed

HFDF   High Frequency Direction Finding

Hochdruckpumpe   a German name for the London Gun (V-3)

Husky   the invasion of Sicily, July 1943

Hydra   Royal Air Force raid on Peenemünde, 17/18 August 1943

Jael   overall deception plan for the war against Germany, later Bodyguard

Jeff   a double agent working for the XX Committee

JIC   Joint Intelligence Committee

JSC   Joint Security Control (American)

Jubilee   the Dieppe raid in August 1942

Juno   one of the invasion beaches in Normandy

Kriegsmarine   the German navy

Kriegspiel   an indoor exercise, literally, war game

LCS   London Controlling Section, dealing with deception

Lobster   the German Intelligence attack on Britain before Sealion

Luftwaffe   the German air force

Maquis — maquisard   another name for the Resistance, and a member of it

Martians   the intelligence cell in London collating information from France

Mercury   the German operation against Crete in 1941

Messages personnels   coded instructions broadcast to Resistance Groups by the BBC

Meteor   an agent in the Yugoslav Ring

MI5   the British counter-intelligence and security organization

MI6 the British espionage service

Mincemeat the deception operation 'The Man Who Never Was'

Monday codename of British officer operating an escape route through the Pyrenees

Moonshine a radar deception device

Mulberry an aritificial harbour designed and built for Overlord

Mutt a double agent used by the XX Committee

Neptune the assault phase of Overlord

North Pole a German counter-intelligence operation

OB West von Rundstedt's headquarters at St Germain-en-Laye

OKW Oberkommando der Wehrmacht, the German Supreme Command

Omaha one of the invasion beaches in Normandy

OSS Office of Strategic Services, American department of intelligence and secret operations

Overlord the Allied invasion of France

OWI Office of War Information — American political warfare

Pastorius German espionage mission to America

Phoenix part of Mulberry, the inner main breakwater

Plan 303 a fictitious plan mentioned by 'Monty's Double' for the benefit of enemy agents

Pointblank Anglo-American bomber offensive in 1943-4

PWE Political Warfare Executive — British political warfare

PI Photographic Interpretation or Interpreter

Quadrant the Quebec Conference in August 1943

Quicksilver deception scheme to build up a fictitious Order of Battle in south-east England threatening an attack across the Pas de Calais

Rattle Allied conference at Largs, June and July 1943

Reseau a spy network

Résistant a member of the French Resistance

Ripcord codeword used in postponing D-Day

Rosebud part of the Fortitude deception plan

Royal Flush deception plan in Spain

Rutter the original plan for the Dieppe raid, later Jubilee

SACSEA Supreme Allied Commander, South East Asia

Schnorkel a German 'breathing device' for submarines

Schutzstaffel 'Guard Brigade', Himmler's para-military organization founded in 1929 and later expanded into a fourth armed service. Usually abbreviated to SS

Schwarze Kapelle the 'Black Orchestra' the conspirators in the plot to assassinate Hitler

SD *Sicherheitsdienst,* 'Security Service', the intelligence and counter-intelligence arm of the SS

Sealion the German plan for the invasion of England

SHAEF Supreme Headquarters, Allied Expeditionary Force

Skye the deception plan relating to the fictitious British 4th Army forming in Scotland

SLUs   Special Liaison Units formed to disseminate and protect intelligence obtained from Ultra

SOE   Special Operations Executive

Spud Piers   part of Mulberry

SS   see Schutzstaffel

Sword   one of the invasion beaches in Normandy

Tausendfusil   a German name for the London Gun

Taxable   Bomber Command deception operation on the eve of D-Day

Tiger   an invasion exercise on Slapton Sands

Titanic   airborne deception just before the D-Day landings

Todt   the Todt Organization was responsible for building the defences of the Atlantic Wall

Torch   the invasion of north-west Africa in November 1942

Treasure   An agent working for the XX Committee

Ultra   the codeword for intelligence derived from decrypting German signals enciphered by the Enigma machine

Utah   one of the invasion beaches in Normandy

V-1   the Flying Bomb

V-2   the rocket

V-3   the London Gun

Hitler's secret weapons that were going to win the war

Vendetta   deception operation creating a threat to southern France

Wehrmacht   the 'War Machine', the German armed forces

Whale   codename for the Mulberry Spud Piers

Window   British codename for the tinfoil strips for baffling enemy radar

Worm, The   an agent in the Yugoslav Ring

Wurst   German sausage

X2   The American counterpart of the XX Committee

XX Committee   the British organization for turning and exploiting enemy agents

Y-Day   codenamed Halcyon

Zeppelin   deception operations in south-east Europe

Bibliography

Bibliography

BARKAS, G., *The Camouflage Story,* London, 1952

CARELL, Paul, *Invasion – They're Coming!* London, 1962

CAVE BROWN, Anthony, *Bodyguard of Lies,* London, 1976

CHURCHILL, Winston S., *The Second World War,* 6 vols, London, 1948-54

CLAUSEWITZ, Karl von, *Vom Kriege,* Berlin, 1880

EATON, Captain Hamish B., *APIS, Soldiers with Stereo,* Ashford, 1978

EDWARDS, Commander K., *Operation Neptune,* London, 1945

EISENHOWER, Dwight D., *Crusade in Europe,* New York, 1968

FOOT, M. R. D., *SOE in France,* London, 1966

FORD, Corey and McBAIN, Alastair, *Cloak and Dagger: The Secret Story of OSS,* New York, 1946

FURSE, Colonel George Armand, *Information in War,* London, 1895

GEHLEN, General Reinhard, *The Gehlen Memoirs,* trs. David Irving, London, 1972

GISKES, Oberleutnant H. J., *London Calling North Pole,* London, 1953

HASWELL, Jock, *British Military Intelligence, London, 1973*
Spies and Spymasters, London, 1977

HENDERSON, Lieutenant Colonel David, *Field Intelligence, Its Principles and Practice,* London, 1904

HMSO *The Second World War, A Guide to Documents in the Public Record Office,* London, 1972

MASTERMAN, J. C., *The Double-Cross System in the War of 1939-1945,* London, 1972

McNISH, Lieutenant Colonel Robin, *Iron Division, The History of the 3rd Division,* London, 1978

MONTGOMERY, Field Marshal, The Viscount, *Normandy to the Baltic,* London, 1947
Official History of Combined Operations, RUSI Library

OSMAN, W. H., *Pigeons in World War II,* London, 1950

PERRAULT, Gilles, *The Secrets of D-Day,* trs. Len Ortzen, London, 1964

PINTO, Lieutenant Colonel O., *Spycatcher Omnibus,* London, 1962

POPOV, Dusko, *Spy/Counterspy,* London, 1975

RAMSAY, Admiral Sir B. H., *The Assault Phase of the Normandy Landing (London Gazette* Supplement), 1947

SCHELLENBERG, Walther, *The Schellenberg Memoirs,* London, 1956

SPEIDEL, Lieutenant General Dr Hans, *We Defended Normandy,* trs. Ian Colvin, London, 1951

STAGG, Group Captain J. M., *Forecast for Overlord,* London, 1972

Index

Index